Thomas Estler

FAST TRAINS
WORLDWIDE

FAST TRAINS WORLDWIDE

Thomas Estler

4880 Lower Valley Road • Atglen, PA 19310

Published by Schiffer Publishing, Ltd.
4880 Lower Valley Road
Atglen, PA 19310
Phone: (610) 593-1777; Fax: (610) 593-2002
E-mail: Info@schifferbooks.com

For our complete selection of fine books on this and related subjects, please visit our website at **www.schifferbooks.com**. You may also write for a free catalog.

This book may be purchased from the publisher. Please try your bookstore first.

We are always looking for people to write books on new and related subjects. If you have an idea for a book, please contact us at *proposals@schifferbooks.com*.

Schiffer Publishing's titles are available at special discounts for bulk purchases for sales promotions or premiums. Special editions, including personalized covers, corporate imprints, and excerpts can be created in large quantities for special needs. For more information, contact the publisher.

In Europe, Schiffer books are distributed by
Bushwood Books
6 Marksbury Ave.
Kew Gardens
Surrey TW9 4JF England
Phone: 44 (0) 20 8392 8585; Fax: 44 (0) 20 8392 9876
E-mail: info@bushwoodbooks.co.uk
Website: www.bushwoodbooks.co.uk

Copyright © 2013 by Schiffer Publishing, Ltd.

Library of Congress Control Number: 2013937343

Design Adaptation by Mark David Bowyer
Type set in Futura Std / The Mix Bold

ISBN: 978-0-7643-4447-3
Printed in China

Cover photo: *South Korea's KTX-II, on a trial run, altered for front cover publication.*

Picture credits:
Alstom: 21, 26, 27 left, 30 (2x), 31 (2x), 37, back cover; Alstom/KTX: 132, 133; AnsaldoBreda: 43; Arlanda Express: 71; Bombardier: 41, 52, 56, 57, 72, 83, 144; BritRail: 39; CAF: 91 right, 92; CD: 94; Christoph Grimm: 69, 70; DSB/Jens Hasse/Chili foto: 7, 8, 9; Heidi Estler: 93, 137 left; Jernbaneverket/Njäl Svingheim: 59; Karl-Wilhelm Koch 23 left, 46, 50, 510, 53, 58 left, 62, 63, 81; National Express: 36; Otto Blaschke: 23 right (2x); QR: 101; Renfe/Patier: 89; Rick Wong: I08, 110; Siemens 14 right, 67; SJ/Stefan Nilsson: 68, 74; SZ: 77; Talgo: 82; TCDD: 95, 96; Ted Talbot: title below, 25 (2x), 33, 123 (2x), 124 (3x), 125 right, 126 left, 128 right, 129 right; THSRC: 136, 137 right; Trenitalia: 49; Voith: 34, 78, 97, 107, 135; VR: 17, 20; Wikipedia: 111 left, 114 left, 115, 117 (Alancrh), 106 (Alex1991) 111 right (AlexHe34) 54, (Arnold de Vries), 64 below, 65 below, 66 (Black leon), 32 (Duncan Harris), 47 below, 48 right (Federico Cantoni), 129 left (Jet-o), 118 below, 127 (JKT-c) 113 left (kanegen), 113 right (Mark Fischer), 40 (Mattbuck), 55 (Mauritsvink), 51 below (NAC), 35 below, 38 (Phil Sangwell), 126 right (spaceaero2) 128 below left, 130 (Sui-seta), 131 below and 131 right (sukhoi37), 42 (Sunil Prasannan) 125 left, (TC411-507), 86 (Thealx) 114 right (Thyristorchopper), 131 above (Toshinori baba); X -Trafik: 73; the remaining photos were supplied by the author.

Schnelle Züge Weltweit, written by Thomas Estler, was originally published by transpress Verlag. Ein Unternehmen der Paul Pietsch Verlage GmbH & Co. KG, Postfach 103743, 70032 Stuttgart. www.transpress.de. This edition was translated into English by Omicron Language Solutions, LLC.

CONTENTS

FOREWORD

The quest for greater speed is almost as old as the train itself. Already, in the nineteenth and the first half of the twentieth centuries, notable things were being done under the slogan "Speed is essential." One need only recall the famous Rainhill Trials of 1829; the 1903 speed test run, when an electric three-phase express railcar reached a sensational speed of 130.6 mph [210.2 km/h]; the German "Rail Zeppelin" (143 mph [230 km/h]) of 1931; or the DRG (*Deutsche Reichsbahn-Gesellschaft*, German National Railways) high-speed railway network from the mid-1930s. After the Second World War, the hunt for speed went briskly on. In 1955, the French clearly broke through the 186 mph [300 km] limit with two electric locomotives, which ultimately kept their speedometers up at 206 mph [331 km/h]. In commercial high-speed rail transport, it was the Japanese who created a sensation just ten years later: They built an entirely new, dedicated high-speed standard rail track between the capital Tokyo and Osaka, Japan's second largest city. On these rails ran the new "Bullet Trains," also known as *Shinkansen*, at a top speed of 130 mph [210 km/h], in half-hourly intervals, on the super-fast "*Hikari*" line (= light, only two intermediate stops); just five minutes later, the somewhat slower "*Kodama*" line (= echo, eight intermediate stops) followed. The Europeans could not take this lying down, of course: the first new rail lines for new trainsets were built in France (1981), Germany (1991), Italy (1991), and Spain (1992). They also committed themselves to speeding up transport on regular routes, and developed specifically designed trains with tilting technology for this purpose.

This book presents a survey of all high-speed—and sometimes not so very fast—trains. It will quickly become clear that currently a few large companies determine what happens with the trainsets themselves, and, based on modular design principles, are putting trains, adapted to each country, on the tracks. Fortunately, there are still a few "exotics," which create non-standard technologies, such as the railway vehicle maker Talgo. Collecting the data for this work was often close to a Sisyphean task, but the result justifies all the effort.

I give my sincere thanks to everyone who provided images and material, as well as to my wife Heidi and daughter Nina, who, at least sometimes, let me work in peace.

Thomas Estler

A SHORT NOTE ON THE TABLES

The notation (Bo)' or (2)' or (1)' for the "wheel arrangement," indicates a Jacobs truck, or a single axle running gear, in which two car halves are supported on one truck or running gear.

German nomenclature is used for the "unit configuration." Thus:

T = powered end or intermediate car (*Angetriebener End- oder Mittelwagen*),

S = unpowered control car (*Antriebsloser Steuerwagen*),

M = unpowered intermediate car (*Angriebsloser Mittelwagen*)

BIBLIOGRAPHY

Various editions of the magazines *Railway Journal* [*Eisenbahn-Journal*], *Railway Courier* [*EISENBAHN-Kurier*], *Railway Magazine* [*eisenbahnmagazin*], *Railway Revue International* [*EISENBAHN-REVUE International*], *Hobby Train* [*Hobby Tren*], *International Railway Journal*, *Locomotive Report* [*LOK Report*], *Railway Digest*, *Today's Railways Europe*, *TRAINS*, and *Via Libre*. The many company websites were also exceptionally helpful: these provided countless details, and without their information, this book would never have been possible.

DENMARK

For the last three decades, Denmark's railway policy has been marked by two big mistakes. One was making the unfortunate choice of using the 25kV/50 Hz power system to electrify their railroads in the early 1980s—while the Norwegian, Swedish, and German railroads power their electric trainsets with 15 kV/16 2/3 Hz—and the second was ordering 83 diesel, multiple-unit trainsets for valuable passenger railway transport from AnsaldoBreda, instead of expanding and continuing to electrify other important main routes. As to the second point, at least, it had started very well. "Good trains for everyone" (*GodeTog til all*) was the motto of the major modernization program that enabled the Danish State Railways (*DSB*) to spend funds at the level of billions in the late 1990s, with support of almost all political parties represented in Parliament.

This was to improve the quality of rail transport nationwide within a few years. From 2006 on, the plan envisioned an extended range of modern rolling stock, more frequent direct connections between eastern and western Denmark, and shorter travel times. The *DSB* wanted to increase frequency by up to 20% with this program.

The politically decisive measure was to provisionally abandon building new lines and more electrification, in favor of using diesel-powered express railcars, which could run at up to a speed of 124 mph [200 km/h]. This proved to be a serious mistake, in the view of well-known rail transport experts, because using diesel railcars on the Copenhagen-Fredericia route, which has been electrified for years, was not very effective and did not make much economic sense.

DENMARK

Series designation:	IC4 (MG+FH+FG+MG)
Road numbers:	5601-83/6601-83/6801-83/5801-83
Track gauge (ft [mm]):	4' 8.5" [1,435]
Wheel arrangement:	(1A)(A1)'(2)'(1A)'(A1)
Maximum speed (mph [km/h]):	124 [200]
Engine power output (HP):	4 x 762
Engine power output (kW):	4 x 560
Transmission:	mechanical
Empty weight (t):	140
Service weight (t):	163
Maximum axle load (t):	
Entire train length (ft [mm]):	282 [86,000]
Distance between truck centers (mm):	4 x 19,100
Axle distance: powered truck (ft [mm]):	10 [3,000]
Axle distance: trailer truck (ft [mm]):	10 [3,000]
Driver wheel diameter (ft [mm]):	3 [860]
Trailer wheel diameter (ft [mm]):	3 [860]
Seats:	208
Commissioning:	2007–2012

A small locomotive labors as it shunts an IC4 by the workshop in Randers.

THE IC4

In December 2000, the DSB ordered 83 four-car, diesel, multiple-unit trainsets for long-distance travel from AnsaldoBreda, worth around $897 [€670] million. These four-car train sets, designated as IC4 (DSB Series MG) in Pininfarina design, were to be delivered during 2003 to 2005. The proven, Denmark-built IC3, the so-called rubber nose, was then to be shifted to secondary regional rail service. The IC4 car bodies are made of a light aluminum alloy, reducing the weight considerably, and are completely recyclable. The aerodynamically shaped ends of the train have retractable, coverable automatic couplings. Each of the four powered trucks has an "Underfloor PowerPack" (IVECO engine, transmission, cooling system, generator, compressor) as the final drive on

a powered axle, which meets the EURO III emission standards. The four under-floor, eight-cylinder, diesel engines, each with 643 hp [480 kW] power output, give the IC4 a top speed of 124 mph [200 km/h]. Optionally, engine output can be increased to 751 hp [560 kW]. The cars are connected to each other with Jacobs trucks. Up to five units can be combined in multiple-unit operation. Striking features are the spacious mid-carriage entrances, instead of doors at the car ends, a solution used relatively rarely for long-distance transport. The design was done jointly by the famous Italian design company Pininfarina and the DSB, and emphasized Scandinavian design features: maximum comfort, clear functionality, and exclusive use of authentic materials (no imitation wood or leather, etc.). The versatile layout of the passenger area includes a low-floor area accessible to handicapped persons, where baby carriages and bicycles can also ride. Each train provides a total of 187 seats in the 1st and 2nd classes, and 21 folding seats.

THE DISASTER

The trainsets were to be delivered starting in 2003. The DSB initially calculated it would be able to put the first of them into regular service by January 2005. However, by the end of 2006, only a few units had been delivered and tested, and there was no sign of serial delivery and regular service. There were various problems. The DSB criticized AnsaldoBreda for planning and organizational errors in handling the contract. Things were made more complicated by having to coordinate thirty subcontractors from ten different countries. In 2004, the IVECO engines in the first trains had to be replaced due to leaky cylinder heads, and the design had to be reworked. The PowerPacks repeatedly gave cause for complaints. There were also serious shortcomings in the trains' software and system integration. Integrating the Danish train control system ATC also created a few problems. By the end of 2006, damage claims against the manufacturer amounted to some $40 million [€30 million], and meanwhile, the Danish Parliament got involved. Beyond all this, the new trains resulted in unexpected costs, due to the need to adapt many train platforms for both length and boarding height.

The delay in delivering the IC4 trainsets had far-reaching consequences for the DSB fleet, including that the Series MR/MRD and MO, the local transport cars of type Bn, and the leased double-decker cars had to be kept in service longer than planned. To be able to complete the planned operating program in December

2007 at all, the DSB had to rent, long-term, eleven of the total nineteen remaining ICE-TD (DB Series 605) of the German Railways. These tilting trains were given a "Danish package" so they could run on the DSB network, and replaced such trains as the IC3 on the Hamburg-Puttgarden-Rodby-Copenhagen and Hamburg-Aarhus connections. Some trains from Copenhagen/Aarhus also made a through connection from Hamburg on to Berlin. The other drama, in detail: In September 2006, there were only nine IC4 trainsets that had not been removed in Denmark. The first trial service for passengers began in June 2007, in regional service between Aarhus and Alborg. At this time, the significant failings included a lack of approval for use on the Storebaelt crossing and non-functioning multiple unit control. In early 2008, the DSB temporarily ceased trial operations, since the overheated exhaust pipes caused unpleasant odors inside the trains. Finally, DSB gave a twelve-month ultimatum, with these demands:

IC4 units 4, 7, and 6 undergoing various modifications in this hall on the grounds of the Bombardier factory in Randers.

- fourteen multiple units had to pass approval for domestic transport by May 2009;
- fulfillment of all contractual provisions with another train.

Otherwise, the DSB threatened to cancel the entire order. Although AnsaldoBreda was able to deliver the required units by May 2009, it achieved only a limited design approval for coupled trains. In addition, there were still substantial software problems. After tough negotiations, including threatened lawsuits, in the summer of 2009, the DSB reached an agreement with the manufacturer, with the following compromise: AnsaldoBreda must now deliver eighty-three IC3s and twenty-three IC2 trainsets by autumn 2012. The DSB would receive a compensation payment of $400 million [€300 million], nearly half of the original contract value. Important aspects of this agreement were certainly the facts that, in the short term, there was no alternative modern diesel available, and electrifying more DSB routes could only be realized after the new train control system (ETCS) had been introduced, by around 2020.

In November 2010, the Danish Supervisory Authority issued the DSB the long-awaited permission for the IC4 to run while double heading. In May 2011, the DSB once again stopped AnsaldoBreda's delivery of IC4 railcars. The reason was that the trains were still very unreliable. At this time, the DSB used between four and nine train sets daily—from the eighteen trainsets it had already taken over. Just forty-three of the total of eighty-three trainsets ordered had been delivered so far. As of the timetable change in June 2011, the IC4 was to run between Copenhagen, Esbjerg, Aarhus, and Aalborg, instead of the IC3. The Copenhagen-Fredericia route would be traveled in combination, before the two units were separated.

OUTLOOK

It was certainly unexpected that this Italian railcar, very attractive in design, would turn out so badly technically, so that even years of testing and improvements initially brought no success. Despite the additional political scandal about the IC4, the DSB had ordered twenty-three basically structurally identical two car units for regional and inter-city traffic. These railcars will run in the future under the designation IC2 or as DSB Series MP/FP.

The first IC2 made its first test runs in January 2011 on the test ring at Velim in the Czech Republic. The two car version of the new IC4 will, in future, be used not only in regional service on secondary routes, but also in inter-city service between Copenhagen and Jutland. They run in combination between the capital and Fredericia; from there they travel on in different directions.

GERMANY

The first new German high-speed rail line (*Neubaustrecke*/NBS), the 203 mile [327 km] long Hannover-Würzburg rail line, was built beginning in 1973. However, it was not first opened until the 1991 summer schedule, at the same time as the new 62 mile [99 km] long Mannheim-Stuttgart NBS line, which included a link to Karlsruhe. A distinguishing feature of both routes is the large number of tunnels ("the most beautiful subways in Germany"). The rail lines are designed for a top speed of 174 mph [280 km/h], although normally trainsets only run at 155 mph [250 km/h]. Rail transport was to be a mixture of fast passenger and freight traffic, although the latter tends to be rather rare in practice.

These and the new lines that followed were designed so that they were linked to the traditional main lines at major railway stations. Outside of these connection stations, the new high speed lines use their own rail routes. The Hannover-Würzburg new line, for example, connects to the Göttingen, Kassel-Wilhelmshöhe, and Fulda train stations, all on the "traditional" North-South Göttingen-Kassel-Bebra-Fulda route, which lost its long-distance service when the new routes began operating.

All new lines are equipped with LZB (*Linienzugbeeinflussung* [Automatic Train] Linear Train Control) driver's cab signaling systems. LZB was introduced in the 1970s. Its main feature is a cable between the tracks, which provides a signal-independent indication of a train on the line. The LZB was adapted for use on the new high speed routes, and therefore stationary signals are only needed in exceptional circumstances. The new Nuremberg-Munich route is now also equipped with ECTS (European Train Control System) Level 2 signaling. When the rail line was opened, this was still beyond the horizon.

German's existing rail routes have been and will be converted for much higher speeds—the so-called upgraded lines (*Ausbaustrecken*/ABS). These still are used for mixed traffic, and often have parallel freight or local train tracks. The upgraded lines are typically designed for a top speed of 124 mph [200 km/h]. But there is no rule without an exception, since the Hamburg-Berlin line was upgraded for 143 mph [230 km/h], and some sections of the ABS between Cologne and Aachen can carry the Thalys and ICE3M at even 155 mph [250 km/h]. The following table on page 11 provides an overview of the status of new and upgraded lines in Germany.

More highly controversial new lines are in the planning stage: To create additional capacity for the increasing freight traffic to the ports of Hamburg and Bremerhaven, a new line between Hannover and Hamburg/Bremen—the so-called Y-route—is under discussion. One of the major criticisms of this project is the fact that the existing congestion at the junctions (Bremen main station, Hamburg-Harburg station, and Buchholz/Nordheide) will not be eliminated, since no significant increase of capacity is to be expected from the new route. Furthermore, by 2019, the 35 mile [57 km] long new Wendlingen-Ulm route should be built, which allegedly is inseparable connected to the Stuttgart 21 project (rebuilding the underground and restructuring the Stuttgart main station).

Another project will connect the new Cologne-Frankfurt link with the Mannheim-Stuttgart new line.

GH-SPEED LINES	LENGTH	OPENING	TOP SPEED	COST
W LINES (NBS)				
annover-Würzburg	203 mi [327 km]	06/02/1991	174 (155) mph [280 (250) km/h]	$8 billion [€6 billion]
annheim-Stuttgart/Graben-Neudorf	61.5 mi [99 km]	06/02/1991	174 (155) mph [280 (250) km/h]	$3 billion [€2.3 billion]
annover-Berlin	164 mi [264 km]	09/27/1998	155 mph [250 km/h]	$3.5 billion [€2.6 billion]
ologne-Frankfurt-Flughafen (Airport)/ iesbaden	110 mi [177 km]	08/01/2002	186 mph [300 km/h]	$8 billion [€6.0 billion]
uremberg-Ingolstadt	55 mi [89 km]	05/28/2006	186 mph [300 km/h]	$4.8 billion [€3.6 billion]
AJOR UPGRADED ROUTES (ABS)				
ologne-Aachen (only partially ABS)	48 mi [77 km]	11/14/2003	155 mph [250 km/h]	$1.2 billion [€0.9 billion]
amburg-Berlin	178 mi [286 km]	12/12/2004	143 mph [230 km/h]	$4.7 billion [€3.5 billion]
zkonzept (The so-called "mushroom aped] concept") Berlin main station and nnecting lines	53 mi [85.2 km]	05/27/2006	99.4 mph [160 km/h]	$5.2 billion [€3.9 billion]
rlin-Leipzig/Halle	99 mi [187 km]	05/28/2006	124 mph [200 km/h]	$2.4 billion [€1.8 billion]
golstadt-Munich-Obermenzing	51 mi [82 km]	05/28/2006	124 mph [200 km/h]	included in (1)
W AND UPGRADED LINES UNDER CONSTRUCTION				
alle-Erfurt (new)	76 mi [122 km]	2015	186 mph [300 km/h]	$3.6 billion [€2.7 billion]
furt-Ebensfeld (new)	60 mi [96 km]	2017	186 mph [300 km/h]	$3.4 billion [€2.53 billion]
uremberg-Ebensfeld (upgrade)	52 mi [84 km]	2017	143 mph [230 km/h]	$2.8 billion [€2.14 billion]
endlingen-Ulm (new)	92 mi [148 km]	2019?	155 mph [250 km/h]	$3.75 billion [€2.8 billion]
arlsruhe-Basel (ugrade, part new)	118 mi [190 km]	2016?	155 mph [250 km/h]	$6 billion [€4.5 billion]
mmerich-Oberhausen (upgrade)	45 mi [72 km]	2010	up to 124 mph [200 km/h]	$1.3 billion [€1 billion]
aarbrücken-Ludwigshafen (upgrade)	79.5 mi [128 km]	2013	up to 124 mph [200 km/h]	$752 million [€562 million]
openweier-Kehl-Strasbourg (upgrade)	9 mi [14 km]	2013	up to 124 mph [200 km/h]	$166 million [€124 million]
ANNED ROUTES				
ine Main-Rhine Neckar (new)	50 mi [81 km]	2018?	186 mph [300 km/h]	$3.5 billion [€2.6 billion]
oute Hannover-Bremen/Hamburg (new)	57 mi [92 km]	2018?	124 mph [200 km/h]	$1.7 billion [€1.3 billion]
hmarn Belt Tunnel Germany-Denmark	11 mi [17.6 km]	2020?		$7 billion [€5.2 billion]

experiments even up to 217 mph [350 km/h]. In March 1985, the first power unit was ready to be turned over to the DB, and by August, the entire train was complete. It consisted of two all-axles-powered power units (410 001 and 002) and three intermediate cars. Two intermediate cars (810 001 and 002) served as demonstration cars for future design possibilities, while the 810 003 served as a test car. In designing the train, special attention was given to aerodynamics, economical energy consumption, and to hardening the trains to pressure surges caused both when trains pass each other while underway and when trains enter tunnels. The power unit car bodies were manufactured using a welded lightweight design. Aluminum and fiberglass reinforced composite materials are used for non-load-bearing components. Already, proven brushless, asynchronous, three-phase AC induction motors were used to drive all the power unit axles. The power transmission was largely adopted from the Series 120 electric locomotives.

The prototype underwent an extensive trial, testing, and demonstration program. May 1, 1988, was a memorable day. The two power units with two intermediate cars

The proposed new Rhine/Main-Rhine/Neckar link was originally intended to bypass both Darmstadt and Mannheim. After years of discussion, it was provisionally decided to use a route bypassing Darmstadt. However, the state of Baden-Württemberg would not accept bypassing Mannheim. The final direction of the route remains open.

Longer term plans include a 44 mile [71 km] long new link from Minden via Seelze (near Hannover), to reduce travel times from the Rhine-Ruhr region to Berlin (and via the Y-line to Hamburg and Bremen). In addition, a 78 mile [126 km] long new link from Fulda to Hanau, east of Frankfurt, is under discussion, in order to provide better, and above all, faster connections from Frankfurt to the new Hannover-Würzburg line. However, as yet there are not even specific target objectives for either of these projects.

SERIES 410.0

The DB's high-speed era began with the test vehicle Intercity Experimental (ICE, later ICE-V). The development work for this multiple-unit train began in mid-1983 under the direction of the BZA (Federal Railroad central offices [*Bundesbahn-Zentralämter/Bundesbahn*]) in Munich. The requirement was for a planned top speed of 155 mph [250 km/h]. However, demonstration runs were to reach 186 mph [300 km/h], and in

At many functions, the ICE-V has to be involved, such as here at the Reutlingen station in summer 1989.

SERIES DESIGNATION:	410.0 + 3 x 810 + 410.0
Wheel arrangement:	Bo'Bo'+2'2'+2'2'+2'2'+Bo'Bo'
Power system:	16 2/3 Hz/15 kV
Track gauge (ft [mm]):	4' 8.5" [1,435]
Maximum speed (mph [km/h]):	217 [350]
Hourly output (hp [kW]):	11,260 [8,400]
Nominal power (continuous power) (hp [kW]):	9,759 [7,280]
Service weight (t):	299
Maximum axle load (t):	20
Coupling distance (mm):	114,640
Distance between truck centers (mm):	11,460 + 3 x 17,000 + 11,460
Axle distance, powered truck (ft [mm]):	9.8 [3,000]
Axle distance, trailer truck (ft [mm]):	9.2 [2,800]
Driver wheel diameter (ft [mm]):	3.3 [1,000]
Trailer wheel diameter (ft [mm]):	3 [920]
Seats:	87
Commissioning:	1985
Current whereabouts:	410 001 + 810,001 (FTZ Memorial Minden), 410 002 (Deutsches Museum, Munich)

The 401 004 "Mühldorf on the Inn," a re-routed ICE to Munich, travels through the Fellbach station on 04/19/2010.

SERIES DESIGNATION:	401.0 +INTERMEDIATE CAR +401.5
Wheel arrangement (fourteen car):	Bo'Bo'+12 x 2'2'+Bo'Bo'
Power system:	16 2/3 Hz/15 kV
Track gauge (ft [mm]):	4' 8.5" [1,435]
Maximum speed (mph [km/h]):	174 [280]
Nominal power (continuous power) (hp [kW]):	2 x 6434 [2 x 4,800]
Service weight (t), fourteen car:	80 + 625 + 80 (from 401 051/551: 78)
Maximum axle load (t):	20
Coupling distance (ft [mm]), fourteen car:	117,428 [357,920]
Distance between truck centers (mm):	14,460 + 12 x 19,000 +14,460
Axle distance, powered truck (ft [mm]):	9.8 [3,000]
Axle distance, trailer truck (ft [mm]):	9.1 [2,800]
Driver wheel diameter (ft [mm]):	3.4 [1,040]
Trailer wheel diameter (ft [mm]):	3.2 [1,000]
Seats (fourteen car):	645 + 40 (dining car)
Commissioning:	1990–1993

set a new world record for rail vehicles of 252.8 mph [406.9 km/h]. After ICE scheduled service began, using the new ICE-1 multiple-unit trains, the prototype was used for further trials. Starting operation of a second test train in 1996 marked a turning point: The original ICE was only sporadically used, and was finally taken out of service on the mandatory deadline on May 5, 1998; it has been preserved as a museum piece since the summer of 2000.

SERIES 401

The DB put new electric multiple unit trainsets (ICE-1) in service between 1990 and 1992, for high-speed transport (InterCity Express) on their new lines. The 174 mph [280 km/h] trainsets consist of two Series 401 power units and up to fourteen intermediate cars, of Series 801, 802, 803, and 804. The 120 power units are divided between two series. The first forty (401 001–020 and 501–520) are equipped with traction converters in normal thyristor technology; the other sixty (from 401 051 and 551) got converters with gate turn-off thyristors (GTO) with CFC-free hot-water cooling systems. Each power unit is equipped with four proven, three-phase, asynchronous motors. Some were given a second, narrower pantograph (current collector) to run on the SBB (Swiss National Railway) network (the numbers are in the seventies and eighties). Data is transmitted to the train via two fiber optic lines.

The four types of intermediate cars for the ICE-1 were made, as for the pre-series ICE (410.0), of large aluminum extrusion press profiles. Some 198 first class intermediate cars run as Series 801. Second class intermediate cars account for the largest share on the Series 802, with 376 units. Sixty service cars (Series 803) were built. As a single car, the dining cars, with

their distinctive 1.4' [45 cm] high "hump," dominate the ICE train; 60 units were also built (Series 804).

After fifteen years of hard use, the ICE-1 has undergone complete modernization since 2005. Up to 2008, some 118 power units and 708 intermediate cars were completely gutted, all components (toilets, wall paneling, seats, on-board restaurants, etc.) were removed and to a large extent replaced. New, now well-known, seats were installed on the ICE-3 and the interior walls were refinished in shades of brown. Travel comfort was enhanced with outlets at the seats, modern displays for passenger information systems, and electronic seat reservations. The power units got new truck frames. There were further improvements on the brakes, the anti-skid protection, the control software, and the energy supply for the air conditioning. Total costs were about $241 million [€180 million].

SERIES 402, 410.1

After the highly successful introduction of ICE transport, it soon became apparent that smaller units were also needed. High operational outlay would be needed to adapt the ICE-1 to changing demands. To make smaller units available for off-peak hours, as well as to facilitate production of coupled multi-unit trains, in August 1993, a consortium under the overall control of Siemens and AEG (later ADtranz) received a contract to develop the ICE-2 as a short distance train with only one power unit, six intermediate cars, and one control car. The Series 402 power cars are broadly similar to their predecessors. To create double trains, they are equipped, as are the control cars, with an automatic Scharfenberg coupling, which is hidden behind a front hood. The ICE-2 intermediate cars were manufactured with a weight savings of five tons, compared to its predecessors. This was achieved by having fewer under-floor welded parts, vertical-frame free construction, simplified pressure protection, more efficient energy supply, new lightweight seats, using lighter materials, and omitting compartments. Unlike the steel-spring trucks of the ICE-1, air-suspended type SGP 400 trucks were used in the ICE-2. A total of forty-four units were delivered between 1995 and 1997. The cab cars run as Series 808, while the intermediate cars are Series 805 (1st class), 806 (2nd class), and 807 (dining car). Two power units and a control car serve as a reserve.

In autumn 2009, planning began for a redesign of the ICE-2 for another fifteen years of operation, similar to the ICE-1. Modification of a model train began in October of 2010. The rest of the fleet was to be modernized by mid-2012. The changeover of forty-six power cars, forty-five cab cars, and 264 intermediate cars will cost more than $134 million [€100 million]. This amount does not include approximately $54 million [€40 million] for spare parts and equipment. In the future, there will be thirteen more seats available per train. All seats are equipped with an electrical outlet. Two new wheelchair places, with adjustable tables and service call buttons, will be included in each train. LCD monitors in ceiling gondolas will provide passenger information.

Some 56,000 ft2 [17,000 m2] of carpet, 5,100 blinds, 3,200 tables, and 130,000 ft2 [40,000 m2] of paint were also replaced. As part of the redesign, the trains' lateral dampers are to be replaced to reduce strain on the car bodies. Since the experimental ICE (series 410.0) had meanwhile become outmoded, a new test

train was built in 1996 based on the ICE-2. Two other power units were put into service as 410 101 and 102 to make trial runs. Unlike the 402, they are approved for 217 mph [350 km/h] (and higher). The test powered intermediate cars 410 201, 202, and 203, as well as the unpowered intermediate car 410 801, belong to the Siemens/Bombardier (formerly ADtranz) consortium.

SERIES DESIGNATION:	402.0 + 6 x INTERMEDIATE CAR + CONTROL CAR	410.1
Wheel arrangement (eight car):	Bo'Bo' + 7 x 2'2'	Bo'Bo'
Power system:	16 2/3 Hz /15 kV	16 2/3 Hz / 15 kV
Track gauge (ft [mm]):	4' 8.5" [1,435]	4' 8.5" [1,435]
Maximum speed (mph [km/h]):	174 [280]	217 [350]
Nominal power (continuous power) (hp [kW]):	6434 [4,800]	6434 [4,800]
Service weight (t), eight car:	78 + 340	78
Maximum axle load (t):	20	20
Coupling distance (ft [mm]):	674 [205,400] (eight car)	67 [20,560]
Distance between truck centers (mm):	14,460 +7 x 19,000	14,460
Axle distance powered truck (ft [mm]):	9.8 [3,000]	9.8 [3,000]
Axle distance trailer truck (ft [mm]):	9.1 [2,800]	-
Driver wheel diameter (ft [mm]):	3.4 [1,040]	3.4 [1,040]
Trailer wheel diameter (ft [mm]):	3.2 [1,000]	-
Seats (fourteen cars):	645 + 40 (dining car)	-
Commissioning:	1995-1997	1996

SERIES 403, 406

The new line between Frankfurt and Cologne, with gradients of up to 40% and a line speed of 186 mph [300 km/hr], presented new requirements for high-speed trains. The trains also had to be able to operate in neighboring countries, using all possible power systems, and being able to run on the gauge used there. This required departing from the existing power unit concept and returning to a "classic" railcar for the third ICE generation. In 1994, the DB AG ordered from the Siemens/AEG (later ADtranz, now Bombardier) consortium a total of fifty ICE-3s, including thirty-seven Series 403 trains to operate with 15 kV/16 2/3 Hz and thirteen Series 406 four-system trains. The NS (Nederlandse Spoorwegen—Netherlands Railways) put four 406 in service for the Amsterdam-Cologne-Frankfurt link in 1995.

Technically, the eight car ICE-3 trainsets consist of two four-car train halves, which cannot operate separately, and are assembled as mirror images. After the powered end cars with converters (403.0 and 403.5) comes an unpowered transformer car with the DB pantograph

ICE-2 "Luther's City Wittenberg" arrives at the Hannover main station on May 9, 2010, with control car 808 026 driving.

On July 24, 2009, the 403 561 "Celle" and another unit running as the ICE to Munich, rushed through the Stuttgart-Obertürkheim train station.

SERIES DESIGNATION:	403.0+403.1+403.2+ 406.0+406.1+406.2+ 403.6+403.5	403.3+403.8+403.7+ 406.3+406.8+406.7+ 406.6+406.5
Wheel arrangement:	Bo'Bo'+2'2'+ Bo'Bo'+2'2'+	2'2'+ Bo'Bo'+2'2'+ Bo'Bo'
Power system:	16 2/3 Hz /15kV	25 kV/50 Hz; 15 kV/16 2/3 Hz, 1.5 kV DC; 3 kV DC
Track gauge (ft [mm]):	4' 8.5" [1,435]	4' 8.5" [1,435]
Maximum speed (mph [km/h]):	205 [330]	205/137 [330/220] (under DC)
Nominal power (continuous power) (hp [kW]):	10,723 [8,000]	10,723 [8,000] (5,764 [4,300] with 3 kV DC; 4826 [3,600] with 1.5 kV DC)
Service weight (t):	409	435
Maximum axle load (t):	17	17
Coupling distance (ft [mm]):	657.2 [200,320]	657.2 [200,320]
Distance between truck centers (ft [mm])	8 x 17,375	8 x 17,375
Axle distance powered truck (ft [mm]):	8.2 [2,500]	8.2 [2,500]
Axle distance trailer truck (ft [mm]):	8.2 [2,500]	8.2 [2,500]
Driver wheel diameter (ft [mm]):	3 [920]	3 [920]
Trailer wheel diameter (ft [mm]):	3 [920]	3 [920]
Seats:	415	404
Commissioning:	1999-2002	1999-2002

(403.1 and 403.6), a powered intermediate car with converter (403.2 and 403.7), and an unpowered intermediate car (403.3 and 403.8), where battery and charger are housed. The aerodynamically optimized front end was also newly designed for the ICE-3, with an automatic Scharfenberg coupling covered by a front hood. The multi-system trainsets have a corresponding construction. The pantograph for direct current operation is located on intermediate cars 406.2 and 406.7. Pantographs with narrower compensators for the AC networks of Belgium, France, and Switzerland are on the intermediate cars 406.3 and 406.8. The first ICE-3 was introduced on July 9, 1999. From June 2000 on, the ICE-3 ran in scheduled service to Hannover for the EXPO. After the new Frankfurt/Main to Cologne link was completed in autumn 2002, the trains have naturally been primarily running there; they travel from Frankfurt and Cologne in all directions of the compass.

Service between Frankfurt and Paris became a new addition from mid-June 2007.

SERIES 407

In December 2008, DB AG ordered 15 eight-car multiple-system trainsets for international high-speed transport from Siemens, at a cost of 666 million dollars [495 million euro]. This included the Velaro, a further development of the ICE-3, now known as the Velaro D (D for Deutschland [Germany]). After the trains for Spain, China and Russia, these trains are the fourth realized version of the Velaro platform. DB still speaks, however, of a "new" ICE-3.

Compared with its predecessors, the Velaro D roof was raised by 40 cm to improve aerodynamics, and to aerodynamically accommodate the pantograph, high-voltage equipment, parts of the air conditioning and braking resistors. Behind each cab, in place of the previous passenger lounges, there is a utility room especially for the components of the control technology and automatic train control systems. Of course, the current TSI (Technical Specification for Interoperability) guidelines are taken into account. This includes the new aluminum design of the end car heads, which had to be adapted to integrate crash modules (impact protection). The front hood is no longer divided vertically, but rather horizontally, so that the coupling is no longer pushed forward via telescopic rod. The type SF 500 powered and trailer trucks used in the Velaro D were completely reworked. The axles were redesigned, newly dimensioned, and equipped with a powered and coupled axle-monitoring and diagnostics system. In addition to generative brakes, the multiple-unit trainsets have eddy current brakes and pneumatic friction brakes with disc brakes. Traction and traction power were designed for slopes of up to forty percent. With 460 seats (including 111 in first class and 16 in the bistro area), the Velaro D provides more seats with the same seating comfort as the ICE-3. Several equipment cabinets were

Is there something "cute" in the design of the new 407, or is this just a matter of perspective?

SERIES DESIGNATION:	407.0+407.1+407.2+ 407.3+407.8+407.7+407.6+407.5
Wheel arrangement:	Bo'Bo'+2'2'+Bo'Bo'+2'2'+2'2'+Bo'Bo'+2' 2'+Bo'Bo'
Power system:	25 kV 50 Hz, 15 kV/16 Hz%; 1.5 kV DC; 3kV DC
Track gauge (ft [mm]):	4' 8.5" [1,435]
Maximum speed (mph [km/h]):	198/137 [320/220] (with DC)
Nominal power (continuous power) (hp [kW]):	10,723 [8,000] (5,630 [4,200] with 3 kV DC and 1.5 kV DC)
Empty weight (t):	454
Maximum axle load (t):	17
Coupling distance (ft [mm]):	658.5 [200,720]
Distance between truck centers (mm):	8 x 17,375
Axle distance powered truck (ft [mm]):	8.2 [2,500]
Axle distance trailer truck (ft [mm]):	8.2 [2,500]
Driver wheel diameter (ft [mm]):	3 [920]
Trailer wheel diameter (ft [mm]):	3 [920]
Seats:	460 (333 + 111 + 16)
Commissioning:	2009-2012

rearranged and the compartments were eliminated in favor of only open-plan seating, to make this possible.

In mid-January 2011, trial runs of the first full train began at the Wegberg-Wildenrath test center. Velaro D scheduled service was to begin with the train timetable change in December 2011, and all fifteen trains were to be delivered by 2012. During train timetable year 2012, the trains are to take over the connections served up to now by the ICE-3, between Frankfurt and Brussels (via Cologne) and between Frankfurt and Paris (via Saarbrücken). Beyond this, service between Frankfurt/Main and Marseille is planned on a first section of the LGV (*Ligne à grande vitesse*) Rhine-Rhone. It is expected that by late 2013, the Velaro D will run through the Channel Tunnel to London. This will require installing additional fire fighting systems on the traction units and special fire doors.

SERIES 411, 415

In the early 1990s, tilting technology was the magic word for improving speed and comfort on conventional winding rail routes. For service on older electrified tracks, in 1994, DB AG ordered 32 seven car trainsets for Series 411 and 11 five car trainsets for Series 415, from the "IC NeiTech" consortium (DWA Berlin, DUEWAG, Fiat and Siemens). In spring 2002, DB AG awarded Siemens a follow-up contract to supply 28 additional seven car tilting trainsets (411 051–078) with only minor modifications, which were delivered by March 2006.

Multiple-unit trainsets are constructed in a modular system. The two unpowered end or control cars (411.0, 411.5, 415.0, and 415.5) act as transformer cars and carry the pantograph. The transformers are mounted beneath the bottom of the car. Two powered intermediate cars (411.1, 411.6, 415.1, and 415.6) follow, as converter cars. Two other powered intermediate cars (411.2 and 411.7) are connected to 411 without traction technology; on the five car 415, only one runs in the middle as 415.7. In the middle of the seven car 411, an unpowered intermediate car (411.8) is at the end, where a second can be inserted as necessary. Initially, both series were referred to as ICT; today they officially run as ICE-T. Their electrical equipment corresponds largely to that of the ICE-3. The proven integral aluminum construction was also used for the ICE-T car bodies. Both multiple-unit trainsets have a Fiat tilting system similar to the Italian "Pendolino." The electronically controlled and hydraulically operating tilt technology could thus be fully integrated into the trucks. The trains tilt up to 8° to either side when rounding a curve, and trains can drive up to 30% faster around curves. A mechanical tracking drive keeps the pantograph always at the center, relative to the overhead cantenary wire. Using tilting technology, and adjusting the routes accordingly, has yielded travel time gains of up to 20%.

On an out-of-service trip, the 411 051 passes through the Berlin S-Bahn (commuter train) Landsberger Allee station on June 13, 2009.

From May 30, 1999, the 415 ran in scheduled service between Stuttgart and Zurich, alternating with the "Cisalpino." For this, the five multiple-unit trainsets 415 080–084 were given a "Switzerland package" of additional SBB equipment for cross-border traffic. After Cisalpino service was ended, starting in December 2006, the 415 was expanded to seven-car units to meet capacity needs. While retaining their order numbers, they now run as BR 411. The 411 020–024, minus intermediate cars, were correspondingly redesignated as 415. The 411 001–005 and 007–016 got an "Austria package" for service in that country. Subsequently, 411 014–016 were sold to ÖBB and renamed as 411 090–092.

SERIES DESIGNATION:	411.0 + 411.1 + 411.2 + 411.8 + 411.7 + 411.6 + 411.5	415.0 + 415.1 + 415.7 + 415.6 + 415.5
Wheel arrangement:	2'2'+(1A)(A1)+(1A) (A1)+2'2'+(1A)(A1)+(1A) (A1)+2'2'	2'2'+(1A)(A1)+(1A) (A1)+ (1A)(A1)+2'2'
Power system:	16 2/3 Hz/15 kV	16 2/3 Hz/15 kV
Track gauge (ft [mm]):	4' 8.5" [1,435]	4' 8.5" [1,435]
Maximum speed (mph [km/h]):	143 [230]	143 [230]
Nominal power (continuous power) (hp [kW]):	5,362 [4,000 (8 x 500)]	4021 [3,000 (6 x 500)]
Service weight (t):	368	273
Maximum axle load (t):	14.5	14.5
Coupling distance (ft [mm]):	605 [184,400]	435 [132,600]
Distance between truck centers (mm):	7 x 19,000	5 x 19,000
Axle distance powered truck (ft [mm]):	8.8 [2,700]	8.8 [2,700]
Axle distance trailer truck (ft [mm]):	8.8 [2,700]	8.8 [2,700]
Driver wheel diameter (ft [mm]):	3 [890]	3 [890]
Trailer wheel diameter (ft [mm]):	3 [890]	3 [890]
Seats:	357 + 24 (dining car)	250
Commissioning:	1998-2006	1998-2000

SERIES 605

Already in summer 1994, DB AG ordered 37 electric ICE-standard multiple-unit trainsets with tilting technology (ICE-T, Series 411 and 415) from the ICNT consortium (DWA, Düwag, Fiat, and Siemens). However, since not all routes which definitely offered a potential for high-value, long-distance traffic were electrified, DB decided in 1996 also to procure twenty corresponding diesel, multiple-unit trainsets with tilt technology. In partnership with DWA and Düwag, under overall control of Siemens, four car trainsets featuring active tilting systems (in order: 605.0, 605.1, 605.2, and 605.5), a top speed of 124 mph [200 km/h], 195 seats, and a maximum axle load of 14.5 tons were developed. A full dining car menu in the Bistro car provides the necessary travel amenities.

To be able to use the car interiors exclusively for passengers, the entire traction and auxiliary equipment systems had to be installed under the floor. The most powerful diesel engines, which met the Euro-II emissions standards, were ordered for the trains.

Underneath each car, a Cummins diesel engine with 750 hp [560 kW] drives a three-phase AC synchronous generator in the motorized truck, which in turn supplies both three-phase asynchronous traction motors in the powered truck, using well-known GTO

technology. Multiple unit operation of up to three units can be done from one driver's cab. From 2001, the diesel ICE ran on the "*Sachsenmagistrale*" Nuremberg-Hof-Chemnitz-Dresden main route in Saxony, and the Munich-Lindau route, with the traditional connection to Zurich. However, various problems, with the tilt technology and other features, initially prevented any resounding success; the trains made themselves better known by their breakdowns. Whether or not all these growing pains could have been overcome, DB decided to stop further operation after Dec. 14, 2003. By April 2006, all trains had been brought to a halt; by then only a few units were used to expand transport from Hamburg. Thirteen units were converted from mid-December 2007 on for service in Denmark and in part leased long term to the DSB. Since then, they have run from Hamburg to Copenhagen and Aarhus.

SERIES DESIGNATION:	605
Wheel arrangement:	2'Bo'+Bo'2'+2'Bo'+Bo'2'
Track gauge (ft [mm]):	4' 8.5" [1,435]
Maximum speed (mph [km/h]):	124 [200]
Engine power (hp [kW]):	4 x 750 [4 x 560]
Transmission:	electric
Service weight empty (t):	216
Maximum axle load (t):	15
Coupling distance (ft [mm]):	350 [106,700]
Distance between truck centers (mm):	19,000 + 19,000 + 19,000 + 19,000,
Axle distance powered truck (ft [mm]):	8.5 [2,600]
Axle distance trailer truck (ft [mm]):	8.5 [2,600]
Driver wheel diameter (ft [mm]):	2.8 [860]
Trailer wheel diameter (ft [mm]):	2.8 [860]
Seats:	195
Commissioning:	1999-2001

A triple unit ICE-T running as a relief ICE in the Ruhr region, has just departed for its trip to Hamburg-Altona on April 17, 2006.

FINLAND

For historical reasons, Finland laid rail tracks of the Russian broad gauge (5 ft [1,524 mm]) right from the beginning; they are still in use today. The wave of modernization only reached the Finnish railways quite late in time. In the 1960s, Finnish Railways (VR *Valtionrautatiet*) launched a large-scale route modernization program. In 1968, an extensive electrification program was started, using the 25 kV 50 Hz system. A year later, the first electric railway stretch between Helsinki and Kirkkonummi began operating. The last steam locomotives were taken out of service in 1975. New inter-city trains were introduced in the mid-1980s. Restructuring the Finnish State Railways VR began in the 1980s; in 1990, Finnish State Railways ceased to be a public department. It was converted into a state enterprise. Soon afterwards, deliberations on how to further expedite transport among the main centers of the country followed.

On the Road to High-speed Travel

This quickly led to the following findings: speed can be increased either by using newly built high-speed lines, or by upgrading existing lines. The first solution would require considerable financial resources and a long-term implementation period, since environmental impact must be taken into consideration. The only trains on the market were the French TGV or the German ICE. Overall, this possibility was found to be too costly in relation to the benefits, due to Finland's comparatively low population density. The second option offered tilting technology as an alternative; this would minimize the requirements for track improvements and, above all, this technology gives the trains a speed advantage. In 1992, the existing trains with this technology on the market were the Swedish X2000, the Italian Pendolino, and the Spanish Talgo. Ultimately, the VR decided on the Pendolino, since it had a well-developed technology with low axle weight, sufficient capacity, and pressure-tight cars. The Italians' was also a financially attractive offer.

In 1992, Fiat Ferroviaria got the order to develop and manufacture two Finnish Pendolino "S220" (Series S1T13) prototypes, in collaboration with Rautaruukki-Oy Transtech, a Finnish rail carriage company (in the meantime, taken over by the Talgo group). The Italian national railway's ETR.460 served as the basic model, adapted for the specific requirements of the VR and the different climatic conditions.

The Finnish Pendolino

The Pendolino S220 represents the third generation of Italian tilting trains (ETR.460 etc.). Fiat Ferroviaria developed the Pendolino concept. Tilting trains are able to round curves up to 35% faster than conventional trains. Oy Transtech was involved already at the design phase for the Finnish trains and thus ensured that the trains, with their complex tilting and control mechanisms, would also function in the harsh

climatic conditions near the Arctic Circle. The car bodies were assembled and the trains mechanically fitted out in the Fiat factory in Savigliano. Then they were shipped to Finland, where the final assembly was done at the Oy Transtech Oulu factory in the north of the country.

The train design was to a large extent modular, to keep the axle loads low, but also to meet the existing safety standards. Each unit consists of six individual cars; the intermediate cars have no powered axles. Each powered truck has only one axle with a 670 hp [500 kW] three-phase asynchronous motor, driven by a cardan shaft and final drive. To reduce unsprung weight, the drive motors are installed under the car body. The two unpowered intermediate cars each carry the high-voltage electrical equipment for two powered cars. This takes the 25 kV 50 Hz electric current from the overhead catenary wire, which is converted by transformers and GTO thyristors to supply the train's motors and internal systems. The self-supporting car bodies are made of large aluminum extrusion press profiles. The aerodynamically shaped driver's cabs in the end cars are built with an aluminum frame, and the casing is of fiber-reinforced plastic. The entire train is designed to be pressure-tight and has a relatively low axle load. Thanks to the larger Finnish vehicle clearance profile, it was possible to make these railcars 1.3 ft [400 mm] wider and 6" [200 mm] higher than the ETR.460. The S220 is designed to run in temperatures ranging from -104° F to +95° F [-40° C to +35° C].

Helical-type primary and secondary suspension was preferred to pneumatic suspension, because of its superior reliability and ride quality. The trains have special protection features to prevent accumulation of ice and snow in the secondary suspension and the connections between truck and car body. Specially designed trucks provide the tilting system. The S220's active tilt technology functions using a tilting bolster, with four pendulums and two hydraulic cylinders, and allows for a tilt angle of up to 8 degrees. The tilting bolster is on the coil springs and, in turn, connected to the car body cross bar. Since the pantograph must not tilt along with the car, it is supported directly on the tilting bolster of the truck beneath. The tilting delay for the first car is practically zero, while the following cars tilt in actual time. Each unpowered axle has three steel shoe brakes; each powered axle has two disc brakes. Both motor trucks and unpowered trucks can be demounted. Braking energy can be recovered in every speed range.

In the two prototypes, the seating layout for all first and second class cars is 2 + 1, providing a total of 264 seats, including two for disabled passengers with wheelchairs. One of the two unpowered intermediate cars has a specially designated buffet compartment. The Pendolino's interior design provided service standards not available on earlier Finnish trains, including an office compartment with telephones, fax machines, and overhead projectors for business passengers. Screens in each car provide detailed information about the current course and the next connection.

ORDERING THE SERIES

In November 1994, the first Pendolino S220 ran under its own power in Finland, but at first with only three cars. After extensive testing and trial runs, on November 27, 1995, the two prototypes started regular service on the coastal route between Helsinki and the western Finland port city of Turku.

A Pendolino double unit (Sm3 7103 heads the train) near Töölönlahtion on September 23, 2006, just departing on its trip to Joennsu as S7.

In 1997, the first eight series multiple-unit trainsets were ordered, for a total cost of $138.9 million [€103.6 million], but with several changes: "Giugiaro Design," the Italian company responsible for the interior design, changed the S220's entire interior once again. In the second class, the seating arrangement was changed from 1 + 2 to 2 + 2, providing 308 seats. The restaurant car was redesigned and the number of seats doubled to about twenty-two. Alterations in the kitchen made it possible now to serve hot meals. The smoking section, still at the end of the train in the prototype, was moved to the middle, next to the restaurant. Travelers with large pets were given their own places. These alterations increased the axle load to 15.6 tons. The technical equipment was generally kept as is. The only alterations were improved snow protection, adding sanding equipment, and quieter wheels.

Delivery of the Pendolino series began in November 2000. Almost a year later, on October 22, 2001, the Finnish tilting trains started to run on a second line: they now commute between Helsinki and Jyväskylä. As of June 2, 2002, the Pendolino started running beyond Jyväskylä to Kuopio, and, for the first time, from Helsinki via Seinäjoki to Oulu. The two prototypes were altered to match the series trains between 2001 and 2004. They returned to regular service in January 2004 (unit no. 1) and on April 2, 2004 (unit no. 2). However, unit No. 8 did not even survive transport to its new place of work: it was irreparably damaged by a storm in the Bay of Biscay in October 2001, while being shipped to Finland. On March 26, 2002, the VR ordered eight more units for $18 million [€13.5 million] each. Six months later, on October 9, 2002, VR disclosed that they would not redeem their option for seven more trains. The third series also included the replacement of the badly damaged Unit No. 9, so nine trains were delivered between February 2004 and October 2006. Today, the Finnish Pendolino fleet's total stock is eighteen units.

Series designation:	Sm3
Road numbers:	7601 - 7618
Unit configuration:	2T + 2 M + 2T
Wheel arrangement (railcar):	(1A) (A1)
Wheel arrangement (intermediate car):	2'2'
Power system:	25 kV/50 Hz
Track gauge (ft [mm]):	5 [1,524]
Maximum speed (mph [km/h]):	137 [220]
Output powered cars (hp [kW]):	2 x 670 [2 x 500]
Empty weight (t):	328
Maximum axle load (t):	15.6
End car length (ft [mm]):	90.7 [27,650]
Intermediate car length (ft [mm]):	84.9 [25,900]
Entire train length (ft [mm]):	521.3 [158,900]
Distance between truck centers (ft [mm]):	62 [18,900]
Axle distance powered truck (ft [mm]):	8.8 [2,700]
Axle distance trailer truck (ft [mm]):	8.8 [2,700]
Driver wheel diameter (ft [mm]):	2.9 [890]
Trailer wheel diameter (ft [mm]):	2.9 [890]
Seats 1st/2nd class:	308 (47/261)
Commissioning:	1995-2006

PENDOLINO SERVICE IN 2011

Pendolino service was already extended to Joensuu in eastern Finland on November 7, 2005. By the end of 2006, the Iisalmi-Kontiomäki-Oulu and Kontiomäki-Vartius routes had been electrified, and the S220 has been running to Kajaani since January 7, 2007. The speed limit for conventional trainsets is usually a maximum 99 mph [160 km/h]. Exceptions are the Kerava-Tampere route, and, of course, the new Kerava-Hakosilta (near Lahti) route, which was opened on September 3, 2006.

"High Life" in the Helsinki main station rail yard on September 23, 2006: At left a Sm4 running as a commuter train to Kerava; two Pendolino on the sidings (center and far right); a third train is arriving at the station (right).

This new rail lines relieved traffic on the most densely traveled route in Finland, from Helsinki to Riihimäki, which had increasingly become a bottleneck. Previously, all trains from Helsinki to the north and east, to Joensuu, Kuopio, Oulu, Vainikkala, and Russia, had to travel through this bottleneck, which was also burdened with heavy commuter rail traffic. The double-decker Intercity (IC 2) can speed along at 124 mph [200 km/h] through the countryside on the new line; the route is covered by the Sr2, approved for 130 mph [210 km/h]. The Pendolino trains have even more freedom: they can run between Kerava-Hakosilta at their top speed of 137 mph [220 km/h]. The Pendolino is allowed to travel between Tikkurila and Tampere at 124 mph [200 km/h] and at 112-124 mph [180-200 km/h] between Kirkkonummi and Turku. By the end of 2010, Finland had electrified some 1,906 miles [3,067 km] of a 3,678 mile [5,919 km] total rail network. Today, just over 80% of all rail traffic runs on electric traction. Fast Pendolino direct connections were available in the train schedule year 2011 as follows:

Direct Pendolino connection from Helsinki to	Travel time	Average speed	Pendolino per direction
Joensuu (300 mi [482 km])	4:20	69.6 mph [112.1 km/h]	2/2
Jyvaskyla (212.5 mi [342 km])	2:55	73.2 mph [117.9 km/h]	4/5
Kajaani via Lahti (377 mi [607 km])	5:55	63.9 mph [102.9 km/h]	1/1
Kouvola (103 mi [166 km])	1:23	73.6 mph [118.6 km/h]	3/4
Kuopio via Tampere (317.5 mi [511 km])	4:28	71 mph [114.3 km/h]	2/2
Kuopio via Lahti (272.7 mi [439 km])	3:57	69 mph [111.1 km/h]	2/2
Lahti (64.6 mi [104 km])	0:48	80.7 mph [130.0 km/h]	3/4
Lappeenranta (156.5 mi [252 km])	2:08	73.5 mph [118.3 km/h]	2/2
Mikkeli (173 mi [279 km])	2:23	72.2 mph [116.3 km/h]	2/2
Oulu (422.5 mi [680 km])	6:35	64 mph [103.0 km/h]	4/4
Seinäjoki (215 mi [346 km])	2:34	83.6 mph [134.6 km/h]	5/7
Tampere (116 mi [187 km])	1:26	81.2 mph [130.8 km/h]	8/10
Turku (120.5 mi [194 km])	1:43	70.9 mph [114.1 km/h]	3/3

The New "Allegro"

To provide service with the new tilting trains to St. Petersburg, Russia, VR and Russian Railways (RZD) founded a joint company, "Oy Karelian Trains," which ordered four of the new Series Sm6 Pendolino in September 2007. From the outside, the Sm6— apart from its "Allegro" paintwork—is very similar to the Pendolino Sm3. Technically, it is based on Alstom's "New Pendolino" design (ETR.600); the construction differs from the Sm3 in many ways. The Sm3 have the Fiat-designed hydraulic tilting system, but the Sm6 was given the new Alstom trucks with pneumatic tilting devices. The Sm6 are equipped with both Finnish and Russian safety, signaling, and communications systems.

Series designation	Sm6 "Allegro"
Road numbers:	7051 - 7054
Unit configuration:	2T+3M+2T
Wheel arrangement (railcar):	(1A)(A1)
Wheel arrangement (intermediate car):	2'2'
Power system:	25kV/50Hz, 3kV DC
Track gauge (ft [mm]):	5/4.9 [1,524/1,520]
Maximum speed (mph [km/h]):	137 [220]
Power output (hp [kW]):	7,373 [5,500]
Empty weight (t):	480
Maximum axle load (t):	17
End car length (ft [mm]):	89 [27,200]
Intermediate car length (ft [mm]):	82 [25,000]
Entire train length (ft [mm]):	606 [184,800]
Distance between truck centers (ft [mm]):	62 [18,900]
Axle distance powered truck (ft [mm]):	8.8 [2,700]
Axle distance trailer truck (ft [mm]):	8.8 [2,700]
Driver wheel diameter (ft [mm]):	3.2 [980]
Trailer wheel diameter (ft [mm]):	3.2 [980]
Seats 1st/2nd class:	377 (48/329)
Commissioning:	2010

A "dynamic" advertising image of the new Sm6 on a trial run.

Their dual voltage equipment includes the Finnish 25 kV 50 Hz AC and the Russian DC with 3 kV. The axles fit both the Finnish (5 ft [1,524 mm]) and the slightly smaller Russian broad gauge (4.9 ft [1,520 mm]). The doors have a retractable step to allow easy boarding at both Finland's 1.8 ft [550 mm] and Russia's 3.6 ft [1,100 mm] high platforms. The train's maximum speed is again 137 mph [220 km/h]. At this speed, travel time between Helsinki and St. Petersburg should be reduced to three hours in the near future, down from the previous travel time of 5 ½ hours. Two pairs of "Allegro" trains started operating in time for the 2011 schedule; two other paired units were to follow in the summer of 2011. The current travel time is now 3 hours 36 minutes.

FRANCE

The 1973 oil crisis made France recognize it was too dependent on oil, which it had to import for the most part. As a result, the government decided to increase construction of nuclear power plants and to intensify high-speed transport on the rail lines. Although, in the early 1970s, Jean Bertin's Aerotrain seemed a technology of the future, Alsthom and the TGV (= *Train à Grand Vitesse = Great Speed Train*) quickly took center stage. After Alsthom demonstrated that the gas turbine-powered TGV prototype could be configured as readily as an electric multiple-unit train, planning began for the first new high-speed line from Paris to Lyon.

The 1981 start-up of the TGV *Sud-Est* [Southeast] between Paris and Lyons was a milestone for French transportation, of similar importance to the introduction of the *Shinkansen,* or "Bullet Train," in Japan in 1964. Since that first Bullet Train, high-speed rail transport has enjoyed great technical and commercial success in all countries that have adopted the technology. High-speed transport is not only fast, it has proven itself as a safe, convenient, and efficient means of transportation for the whole population. In short, it has brought the railway back to life and is now considered to be a symbol of a modern society.

Between 1981 and today, some 1,180 miles [1,900 km] of high-speed routes have begun operating, enabling the TGV to let itself go on a grand scale. Other routes, with a length of about 1,430 miles [2,300 km], are currently in the planning stage or already under construction, as the following table (on page 22) shows:

Route designation	Section	Length	Maximum speed	Costs	Opening
Completed high-speed lines					
LGV Paris Sud Est	St. Florentin-Sathonay (Lyon)	194 mi [312 km]	186 mph [300 km/h]	$2.4 billion [€1.8 billion]	9/22/1981
LGV Paris Sud Est	(Paris-) Lieusaint-St. Horentin	73 mi [117 km]	186 mph [300 km/h]		9/25/1983
LGV Atlantique	Montparnasse Courtalain-Connerré (-Le Mans)	110 mi [177 km]	186 mph [300 km/h]	$2 billion [€1.5 billion]	9/20/1989
LGV Atlantique	Courtalain-Tours	63 mi [102 km]	186 mph [300 km/h]		9/25/1990
LGV Nord Europe	Paris-Lille-Channel Tunnel	207 mi [333 km]	186 mph [300 km/h]	$2.7 billion [€2.0 billion]	9/26/1993
LGV Jonction	Vémars-Coubert	65 mi [104 km]	168 mph [270 km/h]	$1.6 billion [€1.2 billion]	5/29/1994
LGV Rhône-Alpes	Montanay-St. Marcel-lès-Valence	75 mi [121 km]	199 mph [320 km/]h	$1.2 billion [€945 million]	7/03/1994
LGV Méditerranée	St Marcel-lés-Valence-Marseille	183 mi [295 km]	186 mph [300 km/h]	$5.1 billion [€3.8 billion]	7/06/2001
LGV Est Européenne	Vaires-Baudrecourt	186 mi [300 km]	199 mph [320 km/h]	$4.3 billion [€3.2 billion]	10/07/2007
LGV Languedoc-Roussillon	Perpignan-Figueres (Spain)	28 mi [45 km]	217 mph [350 km/h]	$969 million [€720 million]	12/19/2010
High speed lines under construction					
LGV Rhin-Rhône	Villers-les-Pots-Petit Croix	87 mi [140 km]	199 mph [320 km/h]	$3 billion [€2.3 billion]	2011
Planned high speed lines					
LGV Bretagne-PDL	Connerré-Rennes	113 mi [182 km]	199 mph [320 km/h]	$4.5 billion [€3.4 billion]	2015
LGV Est Européenne	Baudrecourt-Vendenheim	66 mi [106 km]	199 mph [320 km/h]	$2.8 billion [€2.1 billion]	2015
LGV Rhin-Rhône	Petit Croix-Lutterbach	22 mi [36 km]	199 mph [320 km/h]	not specified	not specified
	Lutterbach chord	not specified	not specified	not specified	2012
	Montbard-Oijon-Genlis	43 mi [70 km]	199 mph [320 km/h]	not specified	not specified
LGV PACA	A1x-en-Provence-Nice	112 mi [180 km]	not specified	$21.5 billion [€16 billion]	2023
LGV Languedoc-Roussillon	Manduel-Lattes	50 mi [80 km]	217 mph [350 km/h]	$1.8 billion [€1.4 billion]	2016
	Lattes-Perpignan	124 mi [200 km]	not specified	$8 billion [€6 billion]	2020
LGV SEA	Tours-Bordeaux	188 mi [302 km]	199 mph [320 km/h]	$9.6 billion [€7.2 billion]	2016
	Bordeaux-Toulouse	124 mi [200 km]	224 mph [360 km/h]	$3.9 [€2.9 billion]	2020
	Bordeaux-Spain	155 mi [250 km]	not specified	$5.1 billion [€3.8 billion]	2020
	Poitiers-Limoges	71 mi [115 km]	199 mph [320 km/h]	$1.7 billion [€1.3 billion]	2017
LGV Paris-Clermont-Lyon	Paris-Clermont-Ferrand-Lyon	249 mi [400 km]	not specified	not specified	2025

TGV Paris Sud-Est (TGV PSE)

The TGV *Sud-Est* emerged as the first version of the TGV. They consisted of ten car units with a power car at each end. Since the trains were to travel on inclines of up to thirty-five percent and at a speed of 168 mph [270 km/h], they required some 8,043 hp [6,000 kW] drive power. Due to the engine weight and resulting excess axle load, the drive power could not be accommodated in the two power cars. A powered truck with two motors had to be housed in the cars adjacent to the power unit. Most power units have dual-voltage systems (25 kV 50 Hz and 1,500 V DC). Only eighteen power units (nine units), which were to run in Switzerland, were given additional AC power equipment for 15 kV 16 2/3 Hz. The car bodies are carried on Jacobs trucks; they have a tubular support beam structure, encased in stainless steel, glass, and polyester. Conventional hitches and shock absorbers connect the two power cars with the eight-car articulated train. The automatic Scharfenberg couplings on the power unit fronts make multiple-unit control possible for double heading. Between 1978 and 1986, a total of 101 dual-voltage trainsets (units 01-102, no unit 99) and a spare power car, eight triple-voltage trainsets (units 110–117; units 112 and 114 belong to the SBB), and five half trainsets were manufactured for the French Post Office (units 951–955). These correspond technically to the standard TGV PSE, but have no windows; the cars are used to store carts and containers for mail bags.

Meanwhile, the TGV PSE had to undergo various alterations. All units got new carrier trucks with better suspension, and the interiors were renovated.

A double unit TGV PSE (Unit No. 76 driving), in the old paint style, rushes through the Montelimar station on March 10, 1989.

The TGV Atlantique 312 has just arrived at the Paris-Montparnasse station.

There are two modernized styles. In one version (forty-two units), a First Class carriage was converted to Second Class to increase seating. The original orange paintwork was changed to the TGV's new universal silver/blue color scheme. Meanwhile, almost all trains have received the TVM 430 signaling system, which now makes it possible for the trains to run at a top speed of 186 mph [300 km/h]. There also were some other modifications: Unit 38 was converted in 1995 to a TGV Postal (unit 956/957). Unit 88 was the prototype for the TGV Atlantique and then became the ninth triple-voltage train (No. 118). Unit 101 was experimentally given tilting equipment (prototype P01), but was reconverted to the standard version. Units 46 and 70 were taken out of service after accidents.

TGV ATLANTIQUE (TGV-A)

There were two fundamental innovations in the construction of the second generation TGV, which went on the rails exclusively as dual-voltage trainsets (25W/50 Hz and 1,500 V DC): First, the trains got self-commutated three-phase synchronous motors, because brushless synchronous motors have more power output per weight and volume than conventional DC motors. At the same time, maintenance costs were significantly lower. This meant that eight engines were sufficient, each with 1,475 hp [1,100 kW] ; these could be easily accommodated on the power unit's axles. With the 11,796 hp [8,800 kW] power and lower maximum grades on the Atlantique route, the manufacturers could add two more cars and increase

Several TGV A units have a rendezvous at the Paris-Montparnasse station, including No. 362 (center left) and No. 324 (center right).

maximum speed to 186 mph [300 km/h]. The trains were now fitted with a much more comfortable air suspension, and the TGV PSE even got coil springs as a secondary suspension system. All trains were equipped with new pantographs and a new braking system. Between 1988 and 1992, exactly 105 trainsets (units 301–405) and a reserve power unit were supplied. The new TGV blue/silver paintwork was used for the first time. The first modernization work was done on this series beginning in 2006.

FRANCE

Series designation:	TGV Atlantique (TGV A)
Road numbers:	301–405
Wheel arrangement (12 car):	Bo'Bo'+2'(2)'(2)'(2)'(2)'(2)'(2)'(2)'(2)'2'+Bo'Bo'
Power system:	25 kV/50 Hz; 1.5k V DC
Track gauge (ft [mm]):	4' 8.5" [1,435]
Maximum speed (mph km/h):	186 [300]
Power output (hp [kW]):	8 x 1466 [8 x 1,094 (25 kV/50 Hz)], 8 x 650 [8 x 485 (1.5 kV DC)]
Empty weight (t), 12 car:	444
Service weight/mass (t), 12 car:	485
Maximum axle load (t):	17
Coupling length (ft [mm]), 12 car:	0.7-1.9 [237-590]
End car length (ft [mm]):	72.6 [22,150]
Intermediate car length (mm):	21,845 + 8 x 18,700 + 21.845
Distance between truck centers (mm):	14,000 + 10 x 18,700 + 14,000
Axle interval powered truck (ft [mm]):	9.8 [3,000]
Axle interval trailer truck (ft [mm]):	9.8 [3,000]
Driver wheel diameter (ft [mm]):	3 [920]
Trailer wheel diameter (ft [mm]):	3 [920]
Seats (12 car):	485 (1st class: 116; 2nd class: 369)
Commissioning:	1988-1992

Réseau unit 501 running as TGV service to Luxembourg, on June 19, 2011.

TGV RÉSEAU (TGV R), THALYS PBA

Technically, the TGV R is an eight car version of the TGV Atlantique, with very similar power cars. The cars are now all open-plan; so-called half-compartments, used in the TGV-A First Class, were dispensed with. Another difference is the slightly reduced seat density in Second Class, since the TGV R, as a universal vehicle, was intended to run on the entire network and thus have to serve for longer travel distances. Initially, 50 dual-voltage trainsets (25 kV/ 50 Hz and 1,500 V DC, units 501–550) were delivered, between 1992 and 1994. Another 45 triple-voltage trainsets (25 kV/50 Hz, 1,500 V DC, and 3,000 V DC) were supplied between 1994 and 1996; these had different versions of the reserve power units: units 4501–4506, for service to Italy (Paris-Turin-Milan), have a modified pantograph and the Italian FS driver's cab signaling system. Units 4507–4530 were first made available for service to Belgium. Finally, units 4531–4540 were built with altered pantographs and Dutch ATB equipment, to run as Thalys PBA on the Paris-Brussels-Amsterdam connection. They were given the Thalys red/silver paint design; in 2008, the interiors were renovated and the trains were equipped with ETCS.

Series designation:	TGV Reseau (TGV R), Thalys PBA
Plant numbers:	501–553 (dual voltage with gaps), 4501–4551 (tri-voltage with gaps), 4532–4540 (Thalys PBA)
Wheel arrangement (10 car)	Bo'Bo'+2'(2)'(2)'(2)'(2)'(2)'(2)'2'+Bo'Bo'
Power system:	25 kV/50 Hz, 1.5 kV DC; 3 kV DC
Track gauge (ft [mm]):	4' 8.5" [1,435]
Maximum speed (mph [km/h]):	199 [320] (25 kV/50 Hz), 137 [220] (1.5 kV DC and 3 kV DC)
Power output (hp [kW]):	8 x 1466 [8 x 1,094 (25 kV/50 Hz)], 8 x 650 [8 x 485 (1.5 kV DC and 3 kV DC)]
Empty weight (t), ten car:	386
Service weight (t), ten car:	416
Maximum axle load (t):	17
Coupling length (ft [mm]), ten car:	722 [200,190]
End car length (ft [mm]):	73 [22,150]
Intermediate car length (mm):	21,845 + 6 x 18,700 + 21,845
Distance between truck centers (mm):	14,000 + 8 x 18 700 +14,000
Axle interval powered truck (ft [mm]):	9.8 [3,000]
Axle interval trailer truck (ft [mm]):	9.8 [3,000]
Driver wheel diameter (ft [mm]):	3 [920]
Trailer wheel diameter (ft [mm]):	3 [920]
Seats (ten units):	377 (1st class: 120; 2nd class: 257)
Commissioning:	1992-1996

For the opening of the LGV Est in 2007, all the TGV R train interiors were renovated, and the top speed raised to 199 mph [320 km/h]. There were some modifications: on nineteen units (515–533), the cars had to be able to operate with the new TGV POS power units, while the power units (of the units 515–526, 529–530, 532–533, 4507–4509) were coupled with duplex trains. The power cars of units 527, 528, and 531 were coupled with the car sets of units 4507–4509, and given the new numbers 551–553. The Thalys PBA unit was converted in 2007 into a normal triple-voltage TGV-R, and now runs as number 4551. Already, in 1997, unit 502 was involved in a serious accident, which destroyed its power unit. The second power car has been kept in reserve since then, while some of the cars had to be used to repair the PBKA Thalys unit 4342.

Meanwhile, the past: A Eurostar using the English conductor rail power system underway to the Channel Tunnel.

EUROSTAR

The special new rail line through the Channel Tunnel (Eurotunnel) started operation on November 14, 1994. This tunnel runs under the English Channel at its narrowest point, connecting the mainland at Cocquelles, in Belgium (near Calais), with Folkestone in Great Britain. For the high-value passenger, traveling through the Channel Tunnel, the French National Railways (SNCF), Belgian National Railways (SNCB/NMBS), and British Railways founded the Eurostar Group Ltd. joint marketing company. Because the longest stretches of the Paris-London and Brussels-London connections ran on French high-speed rail lines, the decision was made to develop high-speed trains based on the TGV for this service, under the overall control of Alstom.

A Eurostar unit passing the conductor rail at London's Wandsworth Road station on September 9, 1998.

The so-called Eurostar trains are set up as double TGV, with two identically designed, ten-car half-trains coupled together to make a Eurostar. At the end of the "end-intermediate car" of the two half-trains, normal trucks were installed instead of Jacobs trucks. Here, the two half-trains are connected with an automatic close coupler. This design was necessary to meet safety requirements for the Channel Tunnel, which then required accessibility throughout the train. To provide enough drive power, while still using just two power units, drive motors were installed in each intermediate car truck adjacent to the power unit (as for the TGV PSE). Thus, a Eurostar unit can be separated at three places.

A normal Eurostar train consists of two power cars and eighteen intermediate cars. It is almost 1,312 feet [400 meters] long and seats 750 passengers, 206 in First Class and 544 in Second Class. The Eurostar front car shape had to be newly designed, due to the specific conditions (air resistance, flicker effect in the tunnel), and differs significantly from the "usual" TGV. For the first time, the driver's console was installed in the center of the cab. The Eurostar trains were first manufactured as triple-voltage vehicles (25 kV/50 Hz, 3 kV DC, and in Great Britain for 750 V DC via conductor rail). The twelve three-phase asynchronous motors operate using 25 kV AC at 1,020 kW, using 3 kV DC at 475 kW, and with 750 V DC at 283 kW. A total of thirty-one Eurostar trainsets (= sixty-two half trains) were supplied to the "Eurostar Group Ltd."; these were assigned to the participating railroad operators as follows: eleven units to Eurostar U.K. Ltd., (3001–3002 to 3021–3022); four units to SNCB (3101–3102 to 3107–3108); and sixteen units to SNCF (3201–3202 to 3231–3232).

FRANCE

SERIES DESIGNATION	EUROSTAR, REGIONAL EUROSTAR
Road numbers:	3001–3022 (EU), 3101–3108 (SNCB), 3201–3232 (SNCF), 3301–3314 (EU, Regional Eurostar)
Wheel arrangement (20 car, 16 car):	Bo'Bo'+Bo'(2)'(2)'(2)'(2)'(2)'(2)'(2)'2'+2'(2)' (2)'(2)'(2)'(2)'(2)'(2)'Bo'+Bo'Bo'; Bo'Bo'+Bo'(2)'(2)'(2)'(2)'(2)'2'+2'(2)'(2)'(2)' (2)'(2)'Bo'+Bo'Bo' (Regional Eurostar)
Power system:	25 kV/50 Hz, 750 V DC (decommissioned); 3 kV DC; in part also 1.5 kV DC
Track gauge (ft [mm]):	4' 8.5" [1,435]
Maximum speed (mph [km/h]):	186 [300] (25 kV/50 Hz), 137 [220] (1,5 kV DC and 3 kV DC)
Power output (hp [kW]):	12 × 1363 [12 × 1,017 (25 kV/50 Hz)], 12 × 637 [12 × 475 (1.5 kV DC and 3-D DC)], 12 × 379 [12 × 283(750 V DC)]
Empty weight (t), 20 car 16 car:	752.4; 665 (Regional Eurostar)
Service weight (t), 20 car, 16 car:	816; 680 (Regional Eurostar)
Maximum axle load (t):	17
Coupling length (ft [mm]), 20 car, 16 car:	1292 [393,720], 1046 [318,920] (Regional Eurostar)
End car length (ft [mm]):	73 [22,150]
Intermediate car length, half train (mm):	21,845 + 7 × 18,700 + 21,845, 21,845 + 5 × 18,700 + 21,845 (Regional Eurostar)
Distance between truck centers (mm):	14,000 + 18 × 18,700 +14,000, 14,000 + 14 × 18,700 + 14,000 (Regional Eurostar)
Axle interval powered truck (ft [mm]):	9.8 [3,000]
Axle interval trailer truck (ft [mm]):	9.8 [3,000]
Driver wheel diameter (ft [mm]):	3 [920]
Trailer wheel diameter (ft [mm]):	3 [920]
Seats (20 car):	794 (1st class: 210, 2nd class: 584); 604 (Regional Eurostar 1st class: 132, 2nd class: 472)
Commissioning:	1992-1996

After a short time, it became a reasonable idea to extend the Eurostar train service via Paris on to the Alps/southern France. This, however, required installing 1.5 kV DC equipment, which was done on nine Eurostar trainsets (3201–3202, 3203–3204, 3207–3208, 3209–3210, 3215–3216, 3223–3224, 3225–3226, 3227–3228, 3229–3230). At first, in Great Britain, the trains ran on conventional tracks using conductor rail 750 V DC power. Since November 14, 2007, however, the English began operation of a complete, newly electrified line (HSL 1) with 25 kV/50 Hz, from the Channel Tunnel to London's St. Pancras station. This meant that the power system used for conductor rail operation could be shut down.

Another seven so-called "regional Eurostar" (fourteen half-trains) were also manufactured, which were originally intended to extend Eurostar service beyond London. Since the length of British station platforms could not accommodate 1,312 foot [400 meter] long trains, two First Class and two Second Class cars had to be removed. This reduced the number of seats to 128 in First Class and 432 in Second Class.

These "short" Eurostar trainsets run under the numbers 3301–3302 to 3313–3314. The service north of London did not materialize, however. As a result, some short Eurostar trainsets were loaned to GNER (Great North Eastern Railway) for use on the London-Leeds/York routes. As of 2007, the SNCF took over six trains for service between Paris Nord to Lille and Valenciennes. Another half-train (3307) is used by SNCF as a relief train, while half-train 3308 has never moved a meter; it is used for static tests at the Temple Mills depot in London.

TGV DUPLEX, TGV R DUPLEX

New ways had to be developed to cope with the extremely rapid increase in traffic on the Paris-Lyons route. Station platforms could not accommodate two coupled TGV trains, and shortening the intervals between trains eventually reached its limit. Passenger demand for increased space between seats, especially in Second Class, had to be taken into account. Thus, the idea was born to develop a double-decker TGV, which could carry 40% more passengers more comfortably than a TGV Réseau, put the same weight on the scale, and actually cost only 24% more.

As usual, the TGV Duplex consisted of two power cars and eight intermediate cars, connected by Jacobs trucks. The drive technology is designed like the TGV R; the most obvious alterations on the new version of the train, are the more round-shaped power cars, with one-piece windshield and centrally set driver's console. To remain within the 17.5 ton allowable axle load, the intermediate cars were largely built with aluminum extrusion-press profiles. Many other details, such as weight-reduced seats, cables with

Fresh from the factory, the first Duplex 201 unit is presented to in-house photographers.

26

A canal, a rail line, and a new TGV Duplex on a trial run: What more could a photographer want?

Still in the old design, the Thalys 4342 (owned by SNCF) leaves the Aachen main station on October 29, 2005, enroute to Cologne.

thinner covers, hollow axle shafts, and altered brake discs contributed significantly to complying with the total weight allowable. Between 1995 and 2007, a total of eighty-nine trainsets were delivered in several installments; these were numbered 201–289.

The double-decker TGV population also increased, by the introduction of the TGV POS. Cunningly, SNCF had ordered nineteen TGV Duplex trainsets with triple-voltage power cars, for service to southern Germany and Switzerland. These power cars then operated with TGV R intermediate cars, while the TGV R power cars (units 515–526, 529–530, 532–533, 4507–4509) were coupled with the double-decker intermediate cars. Thus, SNCF created sixteen dual-voltage TGV R Duplex (units 601 to 612, 616 to 619) and three triple-voltage TGV R Duplex (units 613–615 from the former power cars of units 4507–4509).

THALYS PBKA

For high-speed service connecting Paris, Brussels, Cologne, and Amsterdam (PBKA), the participating railroad companies SNCF, SNCB, DB, and NS agreed in June 1992 to use a common train. These four-voltage PBKA high-speed trains, with their distinctive burgundy and gray metallic finish, are a further development of the TGV, marketed under the brand name "THALYS." The four railways involved initially ordered seventeen trains from GEC Alsthom. Of these, SNBC got seven units (4301–4307), SNCF six (4341–4346), the NS two (4331–4332), and the DB two (4321–4322), which are run internally

by DB as Series 409. Since December 14, 1997, the Thalys PBKA has been running from Paris to Brussels, then on to Amsterdam and Cologne.

With its rounded nose, the Thalys PBKA is similar in appearance to the TGV Duplex, but technically it is a relative of the TGV Reseau, the third generation TGV. The Thalys PBKA was about 50% more expensive than the TGV Reseau, because it must accommodate four different power and seven different signaling systems, which its on-board computer automatically recognizes. The Thalys is designed both for both left-hand and right-hand traffic, so the driver's console is set centrally. The main controls are available

The Hohenzollern bridge in Cologne on June 20, 2010, creates the setting for the Thalys unit 4304 (owned by SNCB), already in the new style.

on both sides. The pantograph contact force is adjusted automatically, depending on speed, direction, and network. It can be adapted to any different design of the overhead catenary wire. Power output and operating speed depend on the electric current system. The trains' continuous power is only 4,933 hp [3,680 kW], using 1.5 kV DC (conventional Dutch network) and 15 kV/16 kV Hz AC (on the German network). Using 3 kV DC (conventional Belgian network), it is at least 6,984 hp [5,210 kW]. All this is just enough to achieve a top speed of 137 mph [220 km/h]. The Thalys reaches its maximum 186 mph [300 km/h] using only 25 kV/50 Hz (parts of the French network, as well as French, Belgian, and Dutch high-speed lines) at a power output of 11,796 hp [8,800 kW].

A complete train consists of two power cars and eight intermediate cars. The intermediate cars are connected with Jacobs trucks and form an operational unit. Five intermediate cars (with a bar) are for Second Class passengers and there are three First Class intermediate cars. There is space for 377 passengers in the roughly 656 foot [200 meter] long Thalys. Meanwhile, the trains got an intensive "fresh cell" therapy with the following innovations: a new interior design and a new face in flaming red and silver—based on the previous Thalys colors, but with new graphic elements. The crew members shine in attractive new uniforms. A new service concept was introduced, and of course there is now broadband Internet access via satellite technology. The trains are serviced in Brussels, so the DB trains were not given DB numbers. Currently, they run for about two hours in Germany, on the Paris-Cologne route.

TGV POS

For the high-speed service between Paris, eastern France (Strasbourg), and southern Germany, the French railway company SNCF acquired the "*Train à Grande Vitesse* Paris-Eastern France—Southwest Germany" (TGV POS). The core of the TGV POS is first and foremost the newly built high-speed line, to provide a better connection between Strasbourg and Paris. A four-hour trip was just no longer acceptable, if you wanted to compete with private transport. The new route, with a top speed of 217 mph [350 km/h], is a good 267 miles [430 km] long, and makes connections to Nancy, Reims, Luxembourg, and Basle. The TGV Est trainsets were designed to run at 217 mph [350 km/h]. On May 9, 2000, DB AG and SNCF agreed to the standardization of cross-border vehicles, routes, and signals.

The POS-world record unit 4402 can be seen frequently in Germany, on the TGV to Stuttgart, (April 9, 2011 Ettlingen.)

Because of the tight schedule, and some discrepancies, there was no joint high-speed train. Instead, there is a mixed operation of ICE and TGV. Both trains had to undergo a number of trial runs in the neighboring country to obtain an operating license. The TGV POS is not really a completely newly developed train generation. Rather, the TGV POS is a mixture of new power cars and TGV Reseau intermediate cars. The new power cars generally correspond mechanically to those of TGV Thalys PBKA (Paris-Brussels-Cologne/Amsterdam). The electrical equipment, for three power systems (25 kV/50 Hz and 1.5 kV DC in France, 15 kV/16 2/3 Hz in Germany and Switzerland) runs using asynchronous technology with IGBT-controlled three-phase asynchronous motors. There are two pantographs on the roof. The one with a 5.4 ft [1,650 mm] wide compensator is used for 25 kV/50 Hz in France and Switzerland; the second, with 6.3 ft [1,950 mm] wide compensator and metallized carbon slip piece, is used in Germany. In France, with 1,500 V DC voltage, the 6.3 ft [1,950 mm] pantographs of both power cars must be set on both power units. The intermediate cars come from the TGV Reseau. However, they have been extensively modernized in the Bischheim factory, brought up to date technically, and, as a result, are distinctly different from the other TGV generations. A train consists of two power cars and eight intermediate cars. The intermediate cars are connected with Jacobs trucks and form an operational unit. Five intermediate cars (with a bar) are available for Second Class passengers and there are three First Class intermediate cars. A TGV POS, about 656 feet [200 meters] long, can accommodate 360 passengers. Up to now, the rail operators have acquired nineteen units, numbered 4401 to 4419; unit 4406 was meanwhile sold to SBB. In France, the trains are allowed to run at their top speed of 199 mph [320 km/h] on the high-speed routes; in Germany, the maximum speed allowed on the high-speed lines is 155 mph [250 km/h]. TGV 4402 is an exceptional train. Its power cars and three modified intermediate cars, the V150 "world record train," set an incredible new world railway speed record at noon on April 3, 2007, on the LGV Est. In thirteen minutes, the unit accelerated to 357.1 mph [574.8 km/h]. The two power cars have kept their striking world record bond, making everyone aware of their high speed accomplishment, and from time to time are even seen in Swabia.

Due to construction sites, the TGV POS (unit 4410) was diverted to Munich on April 23, 2010, and has just rushed through the Stuttgart-Sommerrain S-Bahn station.

TGV DASYE

With the start of the new millennium, SNCF and Alstom established that they would only acquire future TGVs with IGBT-controlled, three-phase asynchronous propulsion technology. The SNCF also went on only to order double-decker TGVs. First on the agenda, however, was to procure triple-voltage TGV POS trainsets for service to Germany and Switzerland; these were supplied by 2007. Then came two series of "normal" double-decker dual voltage TGVs, which were also to receive the new "ERTMS" European Train Traffic Control System. In 2011, forty-nine trains, named the "TGV DASYE" (duplex asynchronous [traction] ERTMS) were put into service. Of these, units 725–734, with minor modifications, operate on the new Paris-Figueras (Spain) connection, in service since December 2010.

MORE TGV ORDERS

Meanwhile, the SNCF has ordered fifty-five second-generation double-decker TGV trains. The intermediate cars will undergo comprehensive renovation, to provide greater comfort, including passenger information systems, facilities for disabled persons, and wider aisles. Thirty units (4701–4730) will get triple-voltage power cars (like the TGV POS). These are to run on the LGV Rhin-Rhone and in the connections Paris-Dijon-Basel-Switzerland, Zurich-Basel-Lyon-Mediterranean, and Germany-Strasbourg-Lyon-southeastern France. For this, the trains are equipped with the ERTMS-2, LZB-PZB, and Signum signaling systems. There are also plans to adapt some trains for service in Spain, to Barcelona and Madrid, where appropriate. Two trains are to be sold to the SBB after they start operation.

The power units on twenty-five other double-decker TGVs (801–825) will receive only dual-voltage equipment. They are planned primarily to replace the old PSE trains on increasingly busy routes. The power cars, however, are already designed to allow the installation of additional AC power equipment using 15 kV/16 2/3 Hz in Germany and Switzerland, as the need arises.

THE AGV

Alstom and SNCF began the "AGV" project " (*Automotrice à Grande Vitesse* = high speed railcars). After initial studies, Alstrom designed a test power unit and the Spanish company CAF contributed a trial intermediate car. In 2001, the two trains were coupled with the remains of the heavily damaged TGV Reseau 502 (power car and four intermediate cars), and the "AGV Demonstrateur 502" was born. After completing the test runs in 2003, SNCF withdrew from the project. Alstom, in contrast, now determined the technical specifications of the AGV. In October 2006, they began constructing a seven car prototype, which got its official launch on February 5, 2008, at Alstom's La Rochelle factory. Alstom had not waived the AGV operating as an articulated train with Jacobs trucks, as already is the case with the TGV. However, the power cars were eliminated, and the trucks were, for the first time, equipped with an under-floor traction system. This increased the train's capacity by about twenty percent. The electrical traction equipment is divided into several components, so that the three vehicle cars form a unit. The transformer is under the end car; the converters are suspended under the two following intermediate cars, and the auxiliary equipment is housed under the middle car. The 433-foot [132-meter] long trainsets have four

Demonstration AGV 502 getting ready for the next trial run.

Series designation:	AGV prototype
Road numbers:	Pegase
Wheel arrangement (seven car)	Bo'(2)'(2)'(Bo)'(Bo)'(2)'(2)'Bo'
Power system:	25 kV/50 Hz; 15 kV/16⅔ Hz; 1.5 kV DC; 3 kV DC
Track gauge (ft [mm]):	4' 8.5" [1,435]
Maximum speed (mph [km/h]):	223.6 [360] (25 kV/50 Hz), 199 [320] (15 kV/16⅔ Hz), 155 [250] (3 kV DC), and 124 [200] (1,5 kV DC)
Power output (hp [kW]):	8 x 1,019 [8 x 760 (25 kV/50 Hz)]
Empty weight (t), seven car:	
Service weight (t), seven car:	272
Maximum axle load (t):	
Coupling length (ft [mm]), ten car:	433.3 [132,100]
End car length (mm):	
Intermediate car length (mm):	
Distance between truck centers (mm):	
Axle interval powered truck (mm):	
Axle interval trailer truck (mm):	
Driver wheel diameter (mm):	
Trailer wheel diameter (mm):	
Seats (seven car):	
Commissioning:	2008

The "nose" of the AGV prototype is not everyone's cup of tea.

powered trucks, which are propelled by three-phase synchronous permanent magnet motors and a power output of 1,019 hp [760 kW]. The electrical equipment is four-system technology (25 kV/50 Hz, 15 kV/16⅔ Hz, 1.5 kV DC and 3 kV DC). Since the traction motors only generate their full power using 25 kV/50 Hz, the train can only reach its designed speed of 224 mph [360 km/h] with this system. Using 15 kV/16⅔ Hz, the highest speed is still 199 mph [320 km/h]; using 3 kV DC, it is 155 mph [250 km/h] and with 1.5 kV DC, 124 mph [200 km/h]. The future AGV can be produced with seven, eight, eleven, or fourteen cars. Train length varies accordingly, between 433.3 ft [132.1 m] and 830.7 ft [253.2 m]. The AGV has a striking, unique design, especially characterized by the new front. It is no coincidence that the prospectus calls the design reminiscent of a "fighter aircraft cockpit." While the SNCF still prefers the TGV, and continues to give the

AGV the cold shoulder, Alstom was still able to achieve a moderate success. As early as mid-January 2008, the private Italian company *"Nuovo Trasporto Viaggiatori"* (NTV) (= New Passenger Transport) signed a contract for them to supply twenty-five eleven-car AGV trainsets and took an option for ten more units. Due to customer demand, the trains are equipped with five instead of six power trucks, and are only designed for 186 mph [300 km/h]. They can carry about 500 passengers and, from 2011, are to run from Milan to Turin and Naples, as well as from Rome to Venice and Bari. The trainsets cost $876 million [€650 million]; the contract value, including maintenance over thirty years, amounts to $2 billion [€1.5 billion].

RECORDS

One of the great peculiarities of the French is that they always want to be better than everyone else, *even at any price.* This attitude applies to winning the "blue ribbon" on the rail tracks as well. The French first came on the scene on March 28 and 29, 1955, with their two electric locomotives BB 9004 and CC 7107. CC 7107 first reached 203 mph [326 km/h]; a day later, BB 9004 raised the mark to 206 mph [331 km/h]. Almost twenty-

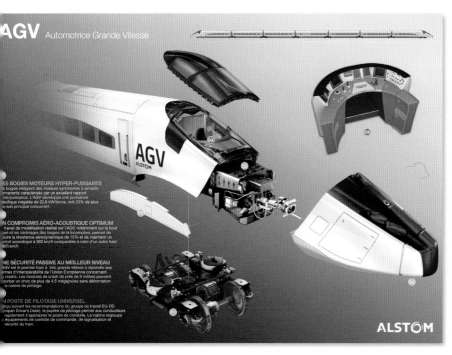

AGV — Automotrice Grande Vitesse

ES BOGIES MOTEURS HYPER-PUISSANTS

N COMPROMIS AÉRO-ACOUSTIQUE OPTIMUM

NE SÉCURITÉ PASSIVE AU MEILLEUR NIVEAU

J POSTE DE PILOTAGE UNIVERSEL

ALSTOM

Alstom even allowed a glance under the "hood" in this factory image.

The AGV prototype, ready to be photographed at its first public presentation on February 5, 2008.

six years later, on February 26, 1981, the specially crafted Series TGV (unit 16) flew along a 39 mile [63 km] section of rail line between Paris and Lyon, which was not yet released for public use, and reached a speed of 236 mph [380 km/h]. To achieve this record, they shortened the TGV to two power cars and five intermediate cars, changed the gear ratio, and increased the driver wheel diameter from 3 ft to 3.4 ft [920 to 1,050 mm].

Unfortunately for France, in Germany on May 1, 1988, the prototype ICE broke through the magical limit of 250 mph [400 km/h] and, by reaching 252.8 mph [406.9 km/h], brought the world speed record back to Germany. The French, of course, could not put up with this, and renewed the attack in the same year. A TGV Atlantique, shortened to three intermediate cars (unit 325), with modified gear ratio, larger wheels, and the power of each three-phase synchronous motor increased by 536 hp [400 kW], finally set a new record of 320 mph [515.3 km/h] on May 18, 1990. Of course, major modifications had to be made on the test track, the southern section of the LGV Atlantique. Then, seventeen years later, the French wanted to do it again. On March 26, 2007, SNCF and Alstom presented the future record-breaking train, named "V 150" (= 150 m/s = 540 km/h [336 mph]), to the public. It was composed of TGV POS unit 4402's two power cars and three latest-model, double-decker intermediate cars. This time, the modifications included additional powered trucks under the intermediate cars to increase power to 26,273 hp [19,600 kW], and again revised gear ratios and wheel diameter. A reinforced structure was built on the track curves, and the catenary wire voltage was increased from 25 kV to 31 kV. Finally, on April 3, 2007, at 13:14 o'clock, the "V 150" reached an absolute top speed of 357 mph [574.8 km/h]. A very different, but very special, record was set on May 26, 2001, by the TGV Reseau 531. This train took just a few seconds less than three hours and twelve minutes to make a non-stop trip on the 663.2 mile [1,067.4 km] long route from Calais-Fréthen to Marseilles. This represents an average speed of almost 190 mph [305 km/h].

GREAT BRITAIN

In the mid-1960s, British railway engineers were engaged in work to rapidly accelerate high-speed long-distance travel, since British Rail (BR) did not want to be left behind by Japan's Shinkansen and the French TGV. Experience with express trains on the East Coast Main Line (ECML), between London and Edinburgh, had already shown that shorter travel times could bring a significant increase in passenger numbers. However, this route was mostly straight, and therefore suitable for high speeds. Other routes, such as the West Coast Main Line (WCML), from London to Glasgow, were not straight enough to make high speed possible using conventional trains. Projects to upgrade the lines, by elevating or straightening them, had only made it possible to achieve speeds up to 124 mph [200 km/h]. In order to reach 155 mph [250 km/h] and shorten travel time accordingly, engineers at the British Rail research center began to develop a train with expanded active tilting technology, the "Advanced Passenger Train" (APT). The system was to tilt the car bodies using sensor-controlled hydraulic cylinders, so that passengers would not be affected by centrifugal force. Several of the engineers involved in the project had experience in the aerospace industry. However, the train was not only to be able to tilt, but was also to be equipped as an articulated train with Jacobs trucks and hydrokinetic brakes. The latter were just as important as the tilt technology, since they would be able to stop the train within existing signal intervals. The fact that the brakes did not function as intended under operating conditions later on was one of the main reasons that this new train was abandoned relatively quickly.

The APT project was intended to design a "TGV" for Great Britain, which was to open the conventional rail infrastructure to entirely new worlds of speed. Three phases were planned: the experimental APT-E, the APT-P prototype, and the series train APT-S. Due to numerous technical problems, and both lack of funding and the necessary political support, the APT project ended prematurely in the second phase, so that the APT never went into series production.

ADVANCED PASSENGER TRAIN (APT)

The APT-E was a four car motor coach with an active tilting system, which was powered by gas turbines via generators and traction motors. Each leading truck of both end cars was powered. There were five 330 hp (246 kW) gas turbines in each end car, four used for traction and one for auxiliary power supply. The two non-powered intermediate cars rested entirely on Jacobs trucks, resulting in the wheel arrangement Bo'(2)'(2)'(2)'Bo'. The APT-E made its maiden voyage on July 25, 1972, and on August 10, 1975, set a new British rail speed record, at 152.2 mph [245 km/h]. The APT-E was followed by three prototype trainsets, named the APT-P, also known as British Rail Series 370 or InterCity APT. Traction now came from a type of electric locomotive in the trainset, instead of gas turbines. Two locomotives, without driver's cabs, were set at the center of each unit, and put about 8,043 hp [6,000 kW] on the rails. On each side of these "locomotives" came five intermediate cars and a control car. Since the "locomotives" in the middle of the train cut off access, passengers could not move from one part of the train to another during the trip. Interestingly, the central "locomotives" also got tilting technology, which was done, above all, to balance the pantograph when the train was tilting. This unusual configuration was necessary primarily due to the relatively simply designed catenary wire, which would allow contact for only one pantograph. One power unit was insufficient, because of the high travel speed, steep route, and the twelve cars.

SERIES DESIGNATION:	370 (APT-P)
Road numbers:	001-006
Wheel arrangement (14 car)	2'(2)'(2)'(2)'(2)'(2)'2'+Bo'Bo'+ Bo'Bo'+2'(2)'(2)'(2)'(2)'(2)'2'
Power system:	25 kV/50 Hz
Track gauge:	4' 8.5" [1,435 mm]
Maximum speed (mph [km/h]):	155 [250]
Hourly output (kW)	
Nominal power (continuous output) (hp [kW]):	8043 [6,000]
Empty weight (t), 14 car:	464.6
Service weight (t), 14 car:	
Maximum axle load (t):	16.8
Coupling length (ft [mm]), 14 car:	964 [293,880]
End car length (ft [mm]):	70.3 [21,440]
Intermediate car length (ft [mm]):	68.8 [21,000] (brake intermediate car: 21,100)
Intermediate railcar length (ft [mm]):	69.2 [20,400]
Distance between truck centers (mm):	17.400 + 4 x 21,000 + 17,400 + 13,000 + 13,000 + 17,400 + 4 x 21,000 + 17,400
Axle interval powered truck (ft [mm]):	10.9 [3,350]
Axle interval end trailer truck (ft [mm]):	8.6 [2,650]
Axle interval Jacobs trailer truck (ft [mm]):	9.8 [3,000]
Driver wheel diameter (mm):	
Trailer wheel diameter (mm):	
Seats 1st/2nd class (14 car):	390 +144
Commissioning:	1979-80

After a relatively long planning and construction period—interrupted by a few strikes—the first "locomotive" left the Derby Locomotive Works in June 1977. The first intermediate and control cars only followed from the Derby Carriage and Wagon Works a year later. Again almost a year later, after another labor dispute, the first test runs with the first complete train began in May 1979. In December 1979, this unit achieved a new British speed record at 162.2 mph [261 km/h]. The second trainset was delivered only in late 1979, and the third followed in spring 1980. Scheduled service was to actually begin in May 1980, but various technical problems led to repeated postponements. The big day finally came on December 7, 1981: At a top speed of 138 mph [222 km/h], the APT-P ran from Glasgow to London Euston in four hours fourteen minutes. But there were problems already on the return trip, when six cars suddenly straightened up on a curve, because a tilting control device had measured lateral acceleration too high. Now, even the weather went crazy, as the next few days brought extreme winter conditions. On December 8th, ice put the APT-P's friction brake out of commission and, a day later, heavy snowfall forced the trip to stop at Crewe. That was the beginning. However, the engineers worked vigorously over the next six months to carefully adjust the tilting technology and solve additional problems. In summer 1982, the APT

The electric ATP-P was in scheduled service for only for a short period (1982–1984) between London and Glasgow, like unit 370 006 here shown tilting on the curve in October 1982.

restarted regular service, without much media hype. At first, the trains ran on a normal schedule, but after a few months of largely trouble-free operation, they again began higher-speed service between London and Glasgow by the end of 1984. But even though, at the end, the train had proved itself to be technically successful, British Rail management had lost interest in this technology. The APT-P was taken out of service in 1985–86. The Crewe Heritage Centre has kept one motor coach, three intermediate, and two control cars. Another motor coach enhances the National Railway Museum at Shildon. The rest of the trains ended up a short time later in the junkyard.

Although the APT project was prematurely terminated early in 1985, it lives on in many ways. The APT tilting technology was sold to Fiat (now Alstom) to improve the second-generation Pendolino tilting trains. Later, this technology returned to the British Isles in the British Pendolino series 390. The APT also strongly influenced the design of newer generations of British trains: the Series 91 electric locomotive, was just one example to be noted here.

THE HST - SERIES 43

With foresight, those responsible at British Rail (BR) not only looked to the APT technology, but in the early 1970s, initiated a parallel project to develop a fast train using conventional technology. The result was the "High Speed Train" (HST), which was also marketed as the "Intercity 125." This was to be one of British Rail's most successful innovations, and is still operating today. A first prototype was available for trial runs in 1972: between two light, 124 mph [200 km/h] fast, four-axle, diesel-electric locomotives (initially Series 41), came a line of new 75-foot [23-meter] long Mark 3 cars. The locomotives, or better, light construction

Freshly decked out, the rail company First's HST power unit 43 023 is ready to start.

power units, had a real, aerodynamically shaped driver's cab at one end. The other end is connected flush with the car, and had only an auxiliary cab for shunting. The drive unit was a Paxman Valenta Type 12RP200L diesel engine with 2,499 hp [1,864 kW] output. The electrical equipment was supplied by Brush. A short time later, the power units were renumbered 43 000 and 001. After the prototype completed successful test runs, some 197 power units (43 002–198) and a corresponding number of intermediate cars were ordered between 1973 and 1977. After the HST Series started operation, the BR test center in Derby took over both prototype power cars, where they provided good service until the early 1980s. The prototype power car 43 001 was sent to the National Railway Museum in York after it was restored, while the other power car was unfortunately scrapped in 1990.

The BREL factory in Crewe had been awarded the contract to build the power cars, and began production at the end of 1974. By late 1975, the first series power units were ready, beginning regular service in February 1976. Number 43 198 was the last power unit to leave the factory, in August 1982. At the same time the power cars were being manufactured, production of the intermediate cars began at BREL in Derby. The external appearance of the series power cars was slightly different from the prototypes. The most striking changes were removing the front buffer, and eliminating the two-part split windscreen and the rear auxiliary driver's cab. The power source remained a Paxman 12RP200L diesel engine, but was now decreased to 2,249 hp [1,678 kW], but this was sufficient for the four Brush electric motors, each with 442 hp [330 kW] output.

The multiple-unit trains were ordered in different batches: The first were twenty-seven units for the Western Region, followed by thirty-two for the East Coast Main Line (ECML), fourteen for western England, eighteen for cross-country service, and finally four additional units for service on the ECML. In general, the HST ran and still runs today with seven or eight intermediate cars.

Even after the privatization of British Rail, the new operators could not do without the HST and so (as of April 2011) 194 of the 197 units built are still operating, distributed as follows among the current rail companies:

OPERATOR	NUMBER OF POWER UNITS
First Great Western	119
East Coast Main Line	30
East Midlands Trains	26
CrossCountry	10
Great Central	6
Network Rail	3

After nearly twenty years of hard service, it became urgent to modernize the HST fleet: on a pilot basis in 2005, First Great Western fitted the two power cars 004 and 43 009 with new Type 16V 4000, [2,010 kW] 2,694 hp MTU engines. The engine proved to be excellent, with its obvious benefits of reducing noise and exhaust emissions, improving reliability, and reducing fuel consumption. As a result, all the operators—First Great Western, East Coast, CrossCountry, Great Central, and Network Rail—equipped their power units with the new engines. Only East Midlands Trains preferred the Paxman 12VP185, also with [2,010 kW] 2,694 hp, as an engine replacement. In the meantime, a large number of the intermediate cars also had to be modernized.

Still during "British Rail" times, 89 001 and its Intercity rushes through the countryside near Eaton Crossing, on the London-Leeds route.

SERIES DESIGNATION:	43 (HST)
Road numbers (power car):	000–198 (after modernization: 202–398 with gaps)
Unit configuration:	T+7M+T or T+8M+T
Wheel arrangement (power car):	Bo'Bo'
Wheel arrangement (intermediate cars):	2'2'
Track gauge (ft [mm]):	4' 8.5" [1,435]
Maximum speed (mph [km/h]):	125 [201]
Power output (hp [kW]):	2,249 [1,678] (after modernization: 2,694 [2,010])
Service weight power unit (t):	70.25
Maximum axle load (t):	18
Power car length (ft [mm]):	58.3 [17,790]
Intermediate car length (ft [mm]):	75.3 [22,960]
Distance between truck centers, power car (ft [mm]):	33.7 [10,290]
Distance between truck centers, intermediate car (ft [mm]):	52.4 [16,000]
Axle interval powered truck (ft [mm]):	8.5 [2,600]
Axle interval trailer truck (ft [mm]):	8.5 [2,600]
Driver wheel diameter (ft [mm]):	3.3 [1,020]
Trailer wheel diameter (ft [mm]):	3.3 [1,020]
Commissioning:	1972-1982

SERIES 89

In a shift away from the style of the electric locomotive series built in the 1960s, the prototype 89 001 made its appearance in the 1980s in a totally different basic construction. The locomotive was built between 1985-87 at BREL in Crewe, a subcontractor for Brush Traction. The locomotive's design was a complete break from earlier types. The locomotive body, with its streamlined ends, was reminiscent of the HST power cars and rested on two three-axle trucks. When it began operation, this machine, with a capacity of 7,856 hp [5861 kW], was the most powerful electric locomotive in Great Britain. The machine was propelled by six DC motors using a thyristor control, with all components made by Brush in Loughborough. While the design would appeal to the high-speed transport market, the locomotive, with its good running capacity, could also score for freight transport. The two three-axle trucks provided fifty percent more traction power than a locomotive with two Bo'Bo' trucks. This tractive power could have eliminated a lot of double heading on freight trains on the steep routes, but BR engineers still favored the Bo'Bo' configuration, mainly due to better track dynamics.

By October 1987, the 89 001 had travelled some 10,000 miles on trial runs, often on the West Coast Main Line (WCML). In late 1987, the locomotive began service on the East Coast Main Line (ECML). Because of its solo status, a number of smaller defects, and a serious failure, the machine had to be taken out of service in late 1990. In mid-1992, British Rail sold the 89 001 to a group of Brush engineers, who saw the engine's potential and did not consider it ready for the junkyard. At first, it remained parked for several years at the Midland Railway Centre at Butterley. In early 1996, the locomotive was transferred to Brush in Loughborough, where some employees attempted to put the 89 001 back in working order during their leisure time. After the privatization of British Rail, the new operator of the ECML, the Great North Eastern Railway (GNER), urgently needed more rail power to cover for the insufficient numbers of Series 91 available, and to be able to offer more train service. The existence of a nearly new, 124 mph [200 km/h] electric locomotive in private ownership could not be hidden, and so GNER bought the 89 001 at the end of 1996. After refurbishment in 1997, it went back into operation. However, just a year later, more and bigger problems emerged; the locomotive was under repair at Brush for almost a year, until the end of 1999. Unfortunately, its service was short-lived, as another technical problem emerged. Thereafter, the 89 001 remained parked at Doncaster until the end of 2004, when the area was to be cleared out. The "AC Locomotive Group" offered GNER a place to store the locomotive at their home in Barrow Hill, where it went on December 17, 2004. GNER finally offered the machine for sale in October 2006, and the "AC Locomotive Group" was able to buy it in December 2006 after very successful fundraising. More rebuilding work, to make it operational, is being considered at this time.

SERIES DESIGNATION:	89 "AVOCET"
Road numbers:	001
Wheel arrangement:	Co'Co'
Power system:	25 kV/50 Hz
Track gauge (ft [mm]):	4' 8.5" [1,435]
Maximum speed (mph [km/h]):	125 [201]
Hourly output (hp [kW]):	7,856 [5,861]
Nominal power (continuous output) (hp [kW]):	5,847 [4,362]
Service weight (t):	105
Maximum axle load (t):	17.5
Length (ft [mm])	64.9 [19,798]
Distance between truck centers (ft [mm]):	35.7 [10,900]
Axle interval powered truck (ft [mm]):	6.8+7.5 [2,100+2,300]
Driver wheel diameter (ft [mm]):	3.5 [1,070]
Commissioning:	1987

SERIES 91

The APT project was dead after 1984, and design and construction of new locomotives and carriages for the West Coast Main Line (WCML) got top priority. The InterCity 225 project was quickly born, which included power cars with driver's cab (similar to the APT-P) at one end, a new generation of passenger coaches, and a control car at the other end of the train. Strict requirements that the locomotives had to be designed to haul fast passenger trains by day and slower sleeper cars and freight trains at night had to be taken into account. In autumn 1984, further electrification of the East Coast Main Line (ECML) was approved. Although originally, the Series 89 electric locomotive, already under development, was planned for use on the ECML, British Rail decided now to provide the IC225 primarily for the ECML. In February 1986, GEC received a contract to initially supply ten units.

Mechanical engineering was done by BREL in Crewe, as a subcontractor. Just two months after signing the contract, on February 14, 1988, the first locomotive of the new Series 91 rolled out of the factory. This asymmetrically constructed machine displayed many new design features.

A gleaming 91 111, freshly painted in new "National Express" colors.

They had a streamlined driver's cab for high-speed service, and at the same time, a straight, box-shaped cab for slower speeds (up to 110 mph [177 km/h]). The engines were mounted on a frame and propelled the axle drive in the powered trucks via articulated shafts. This reduced the unsprung weight and thus the strain on the track at high speeds. The transformer was suspended under the frame, so that the locomotive body appears relatively empty, compared to the other types. A computer-based thyristor control regulates drive power and braking. Much of the technology was based on the experience with the APT trains.

After extensive trial runs, the locomotives began regular service in October 1989. Meanwhile, British Rail was convinced that the engine would be reliable, so nothing stood in the way of delivery of another twenty-one locomotives, which was completed in February 1991. The Series 91, with its push-pull trains, now quickly became the backbone of the service on the—meanwhile electrified—ECML between King's Cross in London and Leeds, Newcastle, Edinburgh, and Glasgow. The push-pull trains consist of Mark4 rail coaches and a control car, which has a similar external appearance to the electric locomotive. In the second half of the 1990s, failures piled up for the quickly and "cheaply" produced locomotives. As a result, between 2000 and 2003, all of the engines were thoroughly overhauled and modernized, with new driver's cab facilities, to make them more reliable. They were then renamed Series 91/1, and the Road numbers—with the exception of 91 023—were raised by 100; the latter mutated to 91 132.

After British Rail was privatized, the entire IC225 fleet went to the Great North Eastern Railway (GNER) franchise, and from 2007, to National Express East Coast. National Express, however, had substantially miscalculated and had to return the franchise to the government in autumn 2009. Since November 14, 2009, the trains have run under government control and the flag of East Coast Main Line.

SERIES DESIGNATION:	91 "ELECTRA"
Road numbers:	001-031, after remodeling: 101-122, 124-132
Wheel arrangement:	Bo'Bo'
Power system:	25 kV/50 Hz
Track gauge (ft [mm]):	4' 8.5" [1,435]
Maximum speed (mph [km/h]):	140 [225]
Hourly output (hp [kW]):	6,300 [4,700]
Nominal power (continuous output) (hp [kW]):	6,086 [4,540]
Service weight (t):	84
Maximum axle load (t):	21
Length (ft [mm])	63.6 [19,400]
Distance between truck centers (ft [mm]):	34.4 [10,500]
Axle interval powered truck (ft [mm]):	10.9 [3,350]
Driver wheel diameter (ft [mm]):	3.2 [1,000]
Commissioning:	1988-91, Reconstruction: 2000-02

SERIES 390 "PENDOLINO BRITANICO"

In 1997, "Virgin Trains," a network rail company, won the InterCity West Coast franchise. Virgin Trains quickly decided to replace the fleet of trains it had inherited (Series 86, 87, and 90 electric locomotives, with push-pull trains made up of Mark 2 and Mark 3 carriages) with newly ordered ones. Virgin Trains gave Alstom and Fiat a contract to produce 53 eight and nine car "Pendolino Britanico" type tilting trains (Series 390). Tilting trains were nothing new on the 25 kV AC electrified West Coast Main Line (WCML) London-Manchester/Liverpool/Glasgow route; fifteen years ago, the revolutionary, but ultimately failed Series 370 Advanced Passenger Train (APT) had run on those tracks.

The Series 390 railcars are actually a "true" European design: FIAT provided the car bodies and trucks. SIG Switzerland (later FIAT-SIG, now Alstom) developed the tilt technology, which gave a tilt angle of up to eight degrees. The tilting bolster is guided on rollers on the truck frame; it includes an integrated electromechanical tilting actuator, with passive car body centering in case the tilting system fails. On the

two end cars and four of the seven intermediate cars, on both trucks, each of the inner axles is powered. The IGBT-controlled Alstom AC asynchronous motor is suspended from the car body and drives the axles by an articulated shaft. A safety clutch protects the motor from shock and torque overload.

Final assembly was done in Alstom's Washwood Heath factory near Birmingham.

The new trains are designed for a speed of 140 mph [225 km/h], but may not travel faster than 124 mph [200 km/h]. It was originally planned that the WCML would be upgraded for travel at 140 mph [225 km/h], but modernization costs ran out of control, and the maximum speed was subsequently limited to the lower speed of 124 mph [200 km/h]. The first operating unit was introduced on February 14, 2001, at the new Alstom test center in Asfordby, Leicestershire. Scheduled service, initially running twenty-nine trainsets from London Euston to Manchester Piccadilly, began on July 23, 2002.

In 2004, the British Pendolino's working radius was extended, when they began to travel up to Glasgow Central. The WCML began a new timetable on September 25, 2004, which would put all train service north of Preston in the hands of Series 390. Actually, all locomotive-hauled trains were to have been replaced by the end of 2004, but the Pendolino made itself conspicuous with some technical problems. As a result, the last locomotive-hauled trains could only be dispensed with at the end of 2006.

A series 390 Pendolino is made ready for its next trip at the Edge Hill Depot (Liverpool).

As passenger numbers rose significantly, due to the modernized rail lines, the Transport Ministry, in cooperation with Virgin Trains, decided to increase capacity. In September 2008, four eleven-car trains were ordered from Alstom, and the thirty-one existing trainsets were each enlarged with two more cars. They also agreed on an option to expand the remaining twenty-one trains. Since the Alstom plant in Washwood Heath had closed in 2005, the new cars were built in Italy's Alstom plant in Savigliano. The first eleven-car Pendolino reached England on December 6, 2010, and has undergone a six-month testing and service start-up program. The three other eleven-car trainsets were to have been delivered in January, August, and December 2011. Integrating more cars into the existing trains was to start in April 2012 and be completed by the end of 2012.

SERIES DESIGNATION:	390 "PENDOLINO BRITANICO"
Road numbers:	001-057
Wheel arrangement (nine car):	(1A)(A1)+(1A)(A1)+2'2'+(1A)
(A1)+2'2'+(1A)(A1)+2'2'+(1A)(A1)+(1A)	
(A1)	
Power system:	25 kV/50 Hz
Track gauge (ft [mm]):	4' 8.5" [1,435]
Maximum speed (mph [km/h]):	140 [225]
Hourly output (kW):	
Nominal power (continuous output) (hp [kW]):	6,836 [5,100 (12 x 425)]
Empty weight (t), nine car:	
Service weight (t), nine unit:	466
Maximum axle load (t):	15
Coupling length (ft [mm])	nine car: 713 [217,400], eleven car: 869 [265,000]
End car length (ft [mm]):	75.6 [23,050]
Intermediate car length (ft [mm]):	78.4 [23,900]
Distance between truck centers (mm):	9 x 17,290
Axle interval powered truck (ft [mm]):	8.8 [2,700]
Axle interval trailer truck (ft [mm]):	8.8 [2,700]
Driver wheel diameter (ft [mm]):	2.9 [890]
Trailer wheel diameter (ft [mm]):	2.9 [890]
Seats 1st/2nd class:	nine car: 439 (145/294) 11 unit: 589 (145/444)
Commissioning:	2001-2011, renovation 2011-2012

SERIES 180 "ADELANTE"

The First Great Western (FGW) network rail company initiated the work to develop the Series 180 five-car diesel railcar, which Alstom manufactured between 2000 and 2001. In the late 1990s, FGW was eager to increase the frequency of its train service from London Paddington to South Wales, to every half hour. This required more high-speed trains, but these were not available. FGW decided therefore to acquire fourteen new, 124 mph [200 km/h] fast diesel, multiple-unit trains from Alston, in a contract worth $115.5 million [£74.5 million]; these trains were comparable to the Series 175 made for its sister company First North Western, only faster. Like the Series 175, the faster 180s belong to the Coradia 1000 family.

A First Hull Trains Adelante (180 113), photographed on May 10, 2010, at Cromwell Moor on the ECML.

All cars in a trainset are equipped with a proven type QSK19 (749 hp [559 kW]) Cummins diesel engine, which works on a truck. Unusual, at least for British conditions, is that the vehicles were made with diesel-hydraulic rather than diesel-electric drive. A three-gear turbo transmission is an essential component, with integrated torque converter, two fluid couplings, a hydrodynamic retarder, and a mechanical reversing unit. Power transmission is via an articulated shaft to the axle drive. With the high power reserve of their under-floor engines, the trains can accelerate to 124 mph [200 km/h], even when running at faster than 99 mph [160 km/h]. The retarder makes it possible to use wear-free, hydrodynamic brakes and delivers a short-time braking power of 1,005 hp [750 kW] (continuous output 563 hp [420 kW]). Unit 180 101 was the first presented to the public, on April 18, 2000. New trains tend to have their pitfalls; at first, there were a lot of problems to solve before the unit could finally start extensive test runs under operating conditions in December 2000. It was almost a year until the new trains were declared ready; therefore they only began regular service under the brand name of "Adelante," in time for the timetable change in December 2001. The railcars ran under the direction of FGW, on the main routes in southwest England, such as London Paddington to Exeter and Penzance. The Adelante proved to be unreliable, prompting First Great Western to return most of its trains to the owner Angel Trains, in spring 2008. The last Series 180 unit was taken out of service by FGW on March 30, 2009. The trainsets were transferred to other operators and are currently operated by First Hull Trains, Northern Rail and Grand Central. First Hull Trains has four units running between London King's Cross and Hull. At least until mid-2011, three Northern Rail motor coaches (borrowed from East Coast) ran from Hazel Grove and Manchester Victoria to Preston and Blackpool North. Grand Central has five units in service from London to Sunderland and Bradford International, with the new name "Zephyr." East Coast has two units hanging around, unemployed.

A Series 220 Voyager makes its way through the idyllic English countryside.

SERIES DESIGNATION:	180 "ADELANTE"
Road numbers:	180 101-114
Unit configuration:	5T
Wheel arrangement:	2'B'+2'B'+2'B'+B'2'+B'2'
Track gauge (ft [mm]):	4' 8.5" [1,435]
Maximum speed (mph [km/h])	125 [201]
Engine power (hp [kW]):	3,747 [2,795 (5 x 559)]
Transmission:	hydraulic
Empty weight (t):	252.5
Service weight (t):	278
Maximum axle load (t):	
End car length (ft [mm]):	77.7 [23,710]
Intermediate car length (ft [mm]):	75.5 [23,030]
Coupling length (ft [mm]):	382.2 [116,500]
Distance between truck centers (mm):	5 x 16,000
Axle interval powered truck (ft [mm]):	8.5 [2,600]
Axle interval trailer truck (ft [mm]):	8.5 [2,600]
Driver wheel diameter (mm):	
Trailer wheel diameter (mm):	
Seats (1st/2nd class + folding seats):	284 (42/226 +16)
Commissioning:	2000-2002

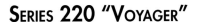

SERIES 220 "VOYAGER"

- In contrast to the noise and vibration levels on non-powered passenger cars, the under-floor diesel engines caused increased noise and vibration.
- The car bodies were designed for tilting technology that was never installed.
- This decreased space, compared to conventional carriages.
- The new four-car trains were usually shorter than the previous trains. As a result, despite increased trips, there was often not enough capacity. There is not enough space for large pieces of luggage or bicycles.
- Most seats are arranged as in an airplane, and have only fold-down tables that are too small for laptops. The Voyager isn't really suitable for business travelers, since there are only six tables that can be used for work. Virgin Trains was the sole operator when Series 220 Voyager trains began service. They were used for Virgin West Coast franchises and Virgin Cross Country.

The rail operator Virgin Trains ordered 34 four-car Series 220 diesel-electric railcars (Virgin Voyager) from Bombardier in the late 1990s. They were to replace both locomotive-hauled trains and the HST units on non-electrified lines. Each car is equipped with a Cummins diesel engine (749 hp [559 kW]), which powers two electric motors via a generator. These are suspended under the car body and propel the truck's inner axle via a cardan shaft and final drive. The truck design is interesting (similar to the Series 222), with an inner frame; which supports the axles behind the wheels. The outside of wheel face is fully visible. A unit's four coaches weigh between 45 and 48 tons. They are all air conditioned and have power outlets for laptops, etc. There are also restrooms for people with restricted mobility and space for bicycles. There are twenty-six First Class seats (seat layout 2+1) and 174 Second Class seats (seat layout 2+2). But the trains have a number of deficiencies, which have come under criticism:

SERIES DESIGNATION:	220 VOYAGER
Road numbers:	220 001-034
Unit configuration:	4T
Wheel arrangement:	(1A)(A1)+(1A)(A1)+(1A)(A1)+(1A)(A1)
Maximum speed (mph [km/h]):	125 [201]
Engine power (hp [kW]):	2,997 [2,236 (4 x 559)]
Transmission:	electric
Empty weight (t):	182.7
Service weight (t):	204.6
Maximum axle load (t):	15
End car length (ft [mm]):	78.2 [23,850]
Intermediate car length (ft [mm]):	74.8 [22,820]
Coupling length (ft [mm]):	312.9 [95,400]
Distance between truck centers (mm):	
Axle interval powered truck (ft [mm]):	7.3 [2,250]
Driver wheel diameter (ft [mm]):	2.5 [780]
Trailer wheel diameter (ft [mm]):	2.5 [780]
Seats (1st/2nd class + folding seats):	200 (26/174)
Commissioning:	2000-2001

When the Cross Country franchise went to Arriva in November 2007, the new owner took over the entire Voyager fleet. Some of them run for Arriva in double heading with Series 221 railcars, which have no tilt technology.

SERIES 221 SUPER VOYAGER

The Series 221 diesel-electric "Super Voyager" was built by Bombardier Transportation between 2001 and 2002 for Virgin Trains, as forty five-car and four four-car units. They are essentially the same railcar as the Series 220, but are equipped with a hydraulic tilting system, which allows a tilt angle of up to six degrees. Each car is powered by the proven Cummins diesel engine (749 hp [559 kW]). This drives an electrical generator, connected to two electric motors, which propel, via cardan shaft and final drive, the truck's inner axle. The railcars were made with larger, conventional-type trucks with an outer frame, because of the tilting technology. Pneumatic and electric resistance brakes complete the technical equipment.

The Super Voyager's biggest problem was that it was conceptualized as a non-tilting train, and then had to be adapted accordingly. The result was a train clearly susceptible to problems, with each car weighing about five tons more than a normal Voyager. The drive power was kept the same, despite the greater weight. Beyond this, the six-degree tilt angle is more limited than the Pendolino Series 390's eight degrees, resulting in some restrictions on speed when rounding corners. One good decision, however, was to launch nearly the entire fleet as five-car trains, to be prepared for the expected increase in passenger numbers.

When Virgin Trains put the Super Voyager in service in 2002, it ran on the CrossCountry routes, the West Coast Main Line (WCML), and to coastal towns in North Wales.

CrossCountry Trains (CCT) took over the franchise on November 11, 2007, and got a part of the Super Voyager fleet, including units 221 119 to 141. CCT has a comparatively large operating area, serving the connections Penzance/Paignton-Manchester/Edinburgh/Aberdeen, Bournemouth-Manchester/Edinburgh/Aberdeen, Birmingham, Stansted and Nottingham-Cardiff. On this network, the Voyager, originally purchased by Virgin Trains, and the Super Voyager, equipped with a tilt system, are the showpieces of the fleet. However, Super Voyager's tilting system has currently been taken out of operation.

After the loss of the CrossCountry network, Virgin Trains continued to run long-distance traffic on the West Coast Main Line (WCML) from London Euston to Birmingham, Holyhead, Manchester, Liverpool, Glasgow, and Edinburgh. In November 2010, Virgin Trains created two five-car trains (221 142 and 143) from its three remaining four-car trains. Unit 221 144's two end cars were put in reserve. This change was made to ensure more flexibility and continuity for the service between Birmingham and Scotland, and between London and North Wales.

SERIES DESIGNATION:	221 SUPER VOYAGER
Road numbers:	221 141-221 144 (four car) 221 101-221 140 (five car)
Unit configuration:	4T, 5T
Wheel arrangement:	(1A)(A1)+(1A)(A1)+(1A)(A1)+(1A)(A1), (1A)(A1)+(1A)(A1)+(1A)(A1)+(1A)(A1)+ (1A)(A1)
Maximum speed (mph [km/h]):	125 [201]
Engine power (hp [kW]):	2,997 hp [2,236 (4 x 559)], 3,747 [2,795 (5 x 559)]
Transmission:	electric
Empty weight (t):	223 (four car), 278.3 (five car)
Service weight (t):	250 (four car), 311.7 (five car)
Maximum axle load (t):	17
End car length (ft [mm]):	78.2 [23,850]
Intermediate car length (ft [mm]):	74.8 [22,820]
Coupling length (ft [mm]):	312.9 [95,400 (four car)] 382.8 [116,700 (five car)]
Distance between truck centers (mm):	
Axle interval powered truck (ft [mm]):	8.8 [2,700]
Driver wheel diameter (ft [mm]):	2.5 [780]
Trailer wheel diameter (ft [mm]):	2.5 [780]
Seats (1st/2nd class + folding seats):	200 (26/176), 250 (26/224)
Commissioning:	2001-2003

CrossCountry's Super Voyager 221 130 departs Bristol Temple Meads for Edinburgh, on July 6, 2010.

SERIES 222 "MERIDIAN"

Between 2004 and 2006, Bombardier supplied twenty-seven Series 222 diesel railcars, similar in design to the Voyager Series 220 railcars. In the Series 222 units, however, more components were housed under the floor to create more space inside the cars, allowing a more generous interior design than possible in the Voyager. Each carriage has a Cummins diesel engine with 749 hp [559 kW of power], supplying two motors through a generator. The inside axles of the trucks are propelled via cardan shaft and final drive. The brakes are supplemented by an electric rheostatic braking system, and the resultant heat is dissipated through roof-mounted resistors. Like Series 220, it also has FLEXX Eco trucks with inner axle bearings, notable for their extremely compact and lightweight design. They weigh thirty percent less than conventional trucks, allowing a significant reduction in energy consumption and noise emission.

Midland Mainline rail network operator started operating the first of their twenty-three Series 222 units on May 31, 2004, giving them the brand name "Meridian." Midland Mainline got seven nine-car and sixteen four-car trainsets. The nine-car multiple unit trains run between London and Nottingham, and London and Sheffield. When the trains were ordered, Midland Mainline had overestimated the number of First Class passengers, so that soon there were not enough seats for Second Class passengers in the four-car. By the end of 2006, Midland Mainline removed an intermediate car from each nine-car trainset and expanded seven four-car trains to five cars. After East Midlands Trains was formed as a new franchise in November 2007, it took over the entire Series 222 fleet from Midland Mainline.

The trainsets were rearranged again between March and October 2008. Six seven-car trains were kept. The remaining intermediate cars were made into more five-car trains, so that there are now seventeen five-car trains available. The domain of the seven-car motor coaches is almost exclusively the fast hourly connections between London St. Pancras and Sheffield. The five-car trains operate primarily between St. Pancras and Sheffield, Nottingham, or Corby, with more intermediate stops. By February 2011, Meridian began a comprehensive renovation of its entire fleet. Renovation included new upholstery and carpets in the Second Class. The First Class got new leather seats, new carpets, and fresh new interior colors. The entire process should have been completed by spring 2012.

SERIES DESIGNATION	222 M, 222/1
Road numbers	222 001–222 006 (seven car), 222 001–222 023 (five car), 222 101–222 104 (four car)
Unit configuration:	4T, 5T, 7T
Wheel arrangement, railcar:	(1A)(A1)
Maximum speed (mph [km/h]):	125 [201]
Engine power (hp [kW]):	2,997 [2,236 (4 x 559)], 3,747 [2,795 (5 x 559)], 5,245 [3,913 (7 x 559)]
Transmission:	electric
Service weight (t):	
Maximum axle load (t):	15
End car length (ft [mm]):	78.2 [23,850]
Intermediate car length (ft [mm]):	74.8 [22,820]
Coupling length (ft [mm]):	530.8 [161,800] (seven car), 381 [116,160] (five car), 306.2 [93,340] (four car)
Distance between truck centers (mm):	
Axle interval powered truck (ft [mm]):	7.3 [2,250]
Driver wheel diameter (ft [mm]):	2.5 [780]
Trailer wheel diameter (ft [mm]):	2.5 [780]
Seats (1st/2nd class + folding seats):	seven car: 342 (106/236), five car: 242 (50/192), four car: 181 (33/148)
Commissioning:	2004-2006

A four-car Series 222 Meridian belonging to Midland Mainline awaiting passengers.

SERIES 395 "JAVELIN"

The Southeastern rail network operator runs these Series 395 dual-voltage electric railcars, from London on the new HS1 rail line, and beyond on older lines to the coastal towns in the county of Kent. Hitachi Europe in 2004 was awarded a contract worth $388 million [£250 million] to supply twenty-eight type "A" high speed trains. A twenty-ninth train was later added to the order, to increase capacity. All the trainsets were built by Hitachi in Japan. The first unit arrived on English soil at Southampton on August 23, 2007.

Javelin 395 008 in Ebbsfleet International train station, awaiting its next trip on 09/01/2009.

Three more trains followed in the same year. The first trainset just had to be there, when the first British high-speed rail track, High Speed 1 (HS1), and the specifically renovated St. Pancras station opened in London on November 6, 2007.

The HS1 was the first major new railway in Britain for over one hundred years, and connects London to the Channel Tunnel under the English Channel, by a 67 mile [108 km] long, 25 kV AC-electrified high-speed line. It replaces the old route through Kent, where Eurostar trains could only creep along at a maximum of 99 mph [160 km/h], in conductor rail operation. On September 28, 2003, the first section of the route, from the Channel Tunnel to Fawkham Junction, started operations. The second section, to the revamped St Pancras station in London, opened on November 6, 2007. The new Hitachi railcars served internal traffic on the HS1, and more units were delivered in rapid succession. When the last unit was unloaded in Southampton on August 17, 2009, the invasion by the last "Japanese" was temporarily over. Some elements of Hitachi's A-Train family flowed into the design of the Series 395, including the welded aluminum body shells. In contrast, the truck's godfather was the mini-Shinkansen 400 Series. The cabs are similar to those of the Series 885 Cape gauge electric railcars, which are used in Japanese high-speed train service. As dual-voltage trains, they can run both on the conductor rail (750 V DC) electrified older tracks, and on the AC 25 kV/50 Hz high-speed lines. On the latter, they can travel at maximum speed of 140 mph [225 km/h], making them the fastest trains in Britain's national service. They are powered by IGBT-controlled, three-phase asynchronous motors, rather than conventional models.

As a novelty for the British railway scene, the coaches have sliding doors running along the inner

walls, which create an extremely smooth, streamlined exterior. This type of sliding door had proven its worth on the Japanese Shinkansen for over forty years. There are some unusual features on this high-speed train: doors and entry areas are not at the car ends over the trucks. To reduce any delay at stations, doors are positioned at about 1/4 and 3/4 of the way along the car length in all six cars.

Beginning on June 29, 2009, a few railcars started a so-called preliminary scheduled service between London St Pancras and Ebbsfleet International, with a few further connections during rush hour to Ashford International. Continued service to Ramsgate via Canterbury West or Dover was added by September 7. Full scheduled service began at the timetable change on December 13, 2009. From London St Pancras, the trains run every half hour to Faversham, with some connections on to Margate. The Javelin runs every hour from London via Ashford to Ramsgate and on to Margate. There are also hourly connections between London and Dover. Since May 23, 2011, the motor coaches have also run at peak times from London St. Pancras via Strood to Maidstone West.

During the Olympic Summer Games in 2012, these units took over the so-called "Javelin shuttle service" for visitors to the main venue in Stratford. The name "Javelin" somehow quickly caught on, and so these railcars got their nickname.

SERIES DESIGNATION:	395
Road numbers:	001-029
Unit configuration	S+4T+S
Wheel arrangement (six car):	2'2'+Bo'Bo'+Bo'Bo'+Bo'Bo'+ Bo'Bo'+2'2'
Power system:	25 kV/50 Hz, 750V DC
Track gauge (ft [mm]):	4' 8.5" [1,435 mm]
Maximum speed (mph [km/h]):	140 [225] (25 kV/50 Hz), 99 [160] (750V DC)
Hourly output (kW):	
Power output (hp [kW]):	4,504 [3,360 (16 x 210)]
Empty weight (t), six car:	270.9
Service weight (t), six car:	303.4
Coupling length (ft [mm]), six car:	399.4 [121,760]
End car length (ft [mm]):	68.5 [20,880]
Intermediate car length (ft [mm]):	65.6 [20,000]
Distance between truck centers (mm):	6 x 14,070
Axle interval motor truck (ft [mm]):	7.3 [2,250]
Axle interval trailer truck (ft [mm]):	7.3 [2,250]
Driver wheel diameter (ft [mm]):	2.8 [870]
Trailer wheel diameter (ft [mm]):	2.8 [870]
Seats 2nd class only (six car):	340 + 12 folding seats
Commissioning:	2007-2009

ITALY

In December 2009, Italy celebrated the completion of the last section of the so-called "North-South Route" high speed line, from Milan via Bologna, Florence and Rome to Naples, covering a total of 447.3 miles [720 km]. The Turin-Milan (77.6 mile [125 km]) and Naples-Salerno (23.8 mile [38.4 km]) high-speed lines also opened in December 2009 and were connected to this route, creating a network totaling almost 560 miles [900 km]. This meant significant reductions in travel time: the 445 mile-long [716 km-long] Turin-Rome connection could now be made in 4 hr 22 min (still 6 hr 5 min in 2005), while Milan and Salerno (528 miles [850 km]) were now just 5 hours and 44 minutes apart.

Early on, Italy's railways had taken on development of a high-speed network. Mussolini did not only ensure that the trains ran on time, but also increased train speed during the 1930s. At that time, some railcars already ran at up to 112 mph [180 km/h], and record trips during that decade included making the Florence-Milan connection (196 miles [315 km]) at an average

speed of 102 mph [164 km/h]. Today, a 186-mph [300-km/h] high-speed link runs on this route, but the high speed trains, at 1 hour 45 minutes, do not travel much faster, although they do make a stop in Bologna.

In any case, construction of more direct, faster train routes began very early on in Italy, because many lines ran on very tortuous, single-track lines through the Apennine Mountains, which divide the country in two. The first "Direttissima" (direct route) was begun nearly a century ago in 1913 (completed 1934) and ran from Bologna to Prato, just before Florence. In 1927, the Rome-Naples Direttissima was completed, which reduced travel time between the two cities from 4 hr and 25 min to 2 hours 50 minutes (on the new high-speed link today, it is 1 hr 10 min).

The 560 mile [900 km] long North-South high-speed corridor was built in stages; this began about forty years ago with the construction of the Florence-Rome Direttissima. This 158 mile [254 km] long route was 33 miles [53 km] shorter than the old winding rail track that served all the larger cities between Florence and Rome. The new route was designed for 155 mph [250 km/h], with both high-speed trains and (in some areas) slower locomotive-pulled trains running on it. As a result, there were many connections to the conventional route. The opening of Italy's first true high-speed line, planned for 1974, was delayed for a number of reasons. Start up of the route began in sections, and could not be completed until May 31, 1992. At that time, the TGV had been running in France for over ten years, and Germany had meanwhile launched its ICE service. Today, ETR.500 trainsets run between Florence and Rome; these are designed to travel at 186 mph [300 km/h], but are not allowed to travel at this speed: as before, the maximum allowed is 155 mph [250 km/h]. Several Pendolino trains also travel on this route, which use their tilting capacity to make further connections on conventional tracks. The track is also used for a variety of locomotive-hauled trains, ranging from the 124 mph [200 km/h] fast InterCity to the only 99 mph [160 km/h] regional trains, to a small number of freight trains.

Unfortunately, this first high speed line was electrified with 3,000-volt direct current, like the rest of the Italian power network. This turned out to be a mistake, because the relatively low DC voltage now prevents trains from reaching higher speeds on the *Direttissima*. All other European high-speed lines are electrified with 15 or 25 kV AC, for this reason. Conversion to 25 kV/50 Hz has indeed been debated for many years, but there are still no concrete plans to do this. As the first true high-speed line was being completed, the government began considering plans for a high-speed network, to shorten travel time, while also creating additional capacity for commuter and freight trains. The latter was especially needed in the north of the country, since, before the parallel-running high speed line was opened in December 2008, capacity on the conventional route between Milan and Bologna had been stretched to the limit. It was finally decided to build a T-shaped high-speed network, with the "cross beam" made by the Turin-Milan-Verona-Venice railway line, while the upright was made by the Milan-Bologna-Florence-Rome-Naples-Salerno line, with, if necessary, a possible extension to Battipaglia. The latter lies in the commuter belt where 40% of the Italian population—over 20 million people—live and work. The new routes (see accompanying table) were to be designed for 186 mph [300 km/h] and—as much as possible—electrified with the cheaper and more efficient 25 kV/50 Hz AC system. The new European Train Control System (ETCS) was used for signaling technology.

Construction of the 150 mile [240 km] high-speed Milan-Venice link at the time of this writing was going on at a very leisurely pace. While the access routes to the end points (Milan-Treviglio and Venice-Padua) were already operational in 2007, planning was completed for the Treviglio-Brescia section (35 miles [56 km]). The construction contract for the first lot of this section was issued on March 7, 2011. It was expected to be completed in 2015 and cost $2.74 [€2.05] billion. However, the rest of the route from Brescia via Verona to Padua, is still in the middle of the planning phase, and financing must still be secured. The high-speed Milan-Genoa link was officially approved in 2005, but the start of construction work, when this book was written, has still to be set.

In addition to the high-speed lines, Italy invested heavily in expanding conventional routes, initially, for the most part, by double-tracking many of the original single-track lines. Substantial construction work is required where the main routes are wedged into extensive urbanized areas. It will take enormous work to upgrade the links between Ventimiglia-Genoa and Rimini-Foggia, for example, and require many new tunnels, since the old line here is wedged very tightly between the sea and mountains. In some cases, the conventional lines could

ITALIAN HIGH SPEED LINES						
SECTION	LENGTH	TUNNEL	VIADUCTS AND BRIDGES	MAXIMUM SPEED	COSTS	OPENING
North-South corridor						
Milan-Bologna	113 mi [182.0 km]	2.1 mi [3.5 km]	20 mi [32.0 km]	186 mph [300 km/h]	$8.5 [€6.4] billion	12/14/2008
Bologna-Florence	48.7 mi [78.5 km]	45.9 mi [73.9 km]	0.6 mi [1.1 km]	155 mph [250 km/h]	$6.9 [€5.2] billion	12/13/2009
Florence-Rome	157.5 mi [253.6 km]	47 mi [75.0 km]		186 mph [300 km/h]	not specified	05/26/1992
Rome-Naples	127.1 mi [204.6 km]	24.2 mi [39.0 km]	24.2 mi [39.0 km]	186 mph [300 km/h]	$6.9 [€5.2] billion	12/19/2005
Naples-Salerno	26.7 mi [43.0 km]			155 mph [250 km/h]	$467 [€350] million	06/2008
East-West corridor						
Turin-Milan	77.4 mi [124.7 km]	2.7 mi [4.4 km]	13.3 mi [21.5 km]	186 mph [300 km/h]	$9.8 [€7.4] billion	12/13/2009
Milan-Treviglio	14.2 mi [23.0 km]			186 mph [300 km/h]		02/07/2007
Treviglio-Padua	119.3 mi [192.0 km]			186 mph [300 km/h]	$9.7 [€7.3] billion	2012/13
Padua-Venice	15.5 mi [25.0 km]			186 mph [300 km/h]		03/01/2007
Milan-Genoa	78.2 mi [126.0 km]			186 mph [300 km/h]	$6.2 [€4.7] billion	not specified

also be upgraded for travel at 112 or 124 mph [180 or 200 km/h], such as Milan-Piacenza, Bologna-Verona, Pisa-Rome, and Salerno-Reggio Calabria. The double tracked expansion of the Messina-Palermo link in Sicily includes plans for some new sections for travel at up to 137 mph [220 km/h]; the existing rail routes only allow 43 to 62 mph [70 to 100 km/h].

The new Italian high speed lines have a distinctive feature, while they run over many viaducts and through tunnels, they only go on or through a few embankments or cuts. The tunnels are necessary in the mountainous regions, because there is no other reasonable routing. Large sections of the Milan-Bologna link are elevated, since it passes through the broad Po Valley, which is known for flooding. The Italians also think that an (ugly) elevated route is cheaper than one built on embankments and less of a barrier to roads and to livestock roaming below them. Additional notable aspects of Italian high-speed lines (as well as many other projects) are overruns in both the cost and schedule. A 1991 agreement provided for building the 543 mile [874 km] high speed network, including the Turin-Milan-Venice, Milan-Rome-Naples, and Milan-Genoa connections, for $12 [€9] billion. By 2005, the costs for Milan-Naples alone had risen to $40 [€30] billion. For the other routes, costs are now estimated at $16.9 [€12.7] billion, a total five-fold increase from the initial expenditure. Most startling is the fact that in Italy, this is generally accepted as normal. Deadlines have been pushed back, partly due to the discovery of historic artifacts, which certainly causes problems in a country rich in antiquities. Another, even weightier, reason appears to be the abnormally high number of bankruptcies among construction companies that had just started work on the lines. While in Germany or France, such work is generally undertaken by the "usual suspects"—a small group of multinational construction companies. In Italy, the projects are often given to small companies with little experience in building high-speed lines. This seems to be a major cause of the low level of economic activity in the new route construction.

THE HIGH-SPEED TRAINS

Even before "real" high-speed lines were built, the Italian State Railways FS had a number of railcars in service that could reach a top speed of 112 mph [180 km/h] on conventional lines. These included the Series ETR.200 trains (ETR = *Elettro Treno Rapido* [Rapid Electric Train]) made by Breda beginning in the 1930s, followed by the famous Settebello (ETR.300) in the 1950s, and finally the air-conditioned ALE.601 as TEE-trains in the 1960s.

ETR.401

From the early 1970s, Fiat engineers started to experiment with tilting technology both for use on older, winding routes as well as high-speed lines. Successful tests in 1974 led to producing the prototype four-unit Pendolino ETR.401, which completed its first trial runs in April 1976, and after three months, was already making its first trips with paying passengers. Its tilt technology used car bodies just 9 ft [2.75 m] wide, swinging freely and suspended on pendulum pivots. The vertical hydraulic cylinders on both sides of the car body guarantee the train tilting up to 10°; these are attached above the truck bolster beams. The two pantographs are not affected by the tilt technology, since they are supported directly on the middle car truck frame. The 347.4 ft [105.9 m] long ETR.401, with 171 First Class seats, had an empty weight of only 136 tons, due to the lightweight aluminum construction and lightweight DC motors. Service weight, when fully loaded, was no more than 173 tons, corresponding to a maximum axle load of just 11 tons.

In 1989, the ETR.401 was sent to Germany for trial runs. It demonstrated its tilting capacity to journalists in the Stuttgart main station.

After completing many test runs and some temporary scheduled service on the Rome-Ancona (-Rimini) route, in the late 1970s, the ETR.401 was shunted to the sidelines. However, in 1984, the FS had a better idea, taking it off the sidings and started more tests, at up to 155 mph [250 km/h]. In May 1985, on a trip for the press, FS finally announced that they recently had signed a contract with Fiat to supply an initial four advanced Pendolino trains.

ETR.450 unit 06 stands ready to depart at the Roma Termini train station on July 18, 2010.

SERIES DESIGNATION:	ETR.401
Road number:	01
Wheel arrangement (four car):	(1A)(A1)+(1A)(A1)+(1A)(A1)+(1A)(A1)
Power system:	3kV DC
Track gauge (ft [mm]):	4' 8.5" [1,435]
Maximum speed (mph [km/h]):	155 [250]
Hourly output (hp [kW]):	2,949 [2,200 (8 x 275)]
Power output (hp [kW]):	2,413 [1,800 (8 x 225)]
Empty weight (t), four car:	136
Service weight (t), four car:	173
Maximum axle load (t):	10.8
Coupling length (ft [mm]), four car:	347.4 [105,900]
End car length (ft [mm]):	90 [27,450]
Intermediate car length (ft [mm]):	83.1 [25,350]
Distance between truck centers (mm):	4 x 18,900
Axle interval motor truck (ft [mm]):	8 [2,450]
Driver wheel diameter (ft [mm]):	2.9 [890]
Trailer wheel diameter (ft [mm]):	2.9 [890]
Seats (four car):	171 (1st class only)
Commissioning:	1975

ETR.450

Delivery of the ETR.450 series trains began in 1987. The five- to eleven-car (431.4 to 935.3 ft [131.5 to 285.1 m] long) trainsets were modeled closely, both technically and physically, on the ETR.401. The rounded design from 1950 was a crucial feature of their front shape, and did not really conform to modern Italian design. The optimized tilting technology allowed a tilt angle of only 8° and newly developed electronics controlled the hydraulic systems. The ETR.450's DC motors now each generated 409 hp [305 kW], and, as on the ETR.401, each propelled the truck's inner axles. The intermediate cars, arranged in a nine car basic unit, remained unpowered. The first ETR.450 began scheduled service in May 1988 on the 393 mile [632 km] long Rome-Milan route, where it traveled at 155 mph [250 km/h] on the completed sections of the Rome-Florence *Direttissima*. A 3 hour 58 minute non-stop travel time, corresponds to a cruising speed of 98.7 mph [159 km/h]. Until 1990, the 15 ETR.450 units

that had been produced ran a purely first-class service on the Rome-Venice, Rome-Genoa, Rome-Naples, and Rome-Bari connections. Later, the trains were adapted to changing requirements, and have included Second Class carriages since 1993. Between 2005 and 2007, some units (01, 07–10, and 12), without First Class service, travelled as the so-called "TrenOK" (cheap long distance trains), decorated in special colors. Since the timetable change in December 2010, no ETR.450 trainsets run on the Italian Eurostar network any longer, with one exception, the Rome-Ancona link. The trains, however, were given a new mission: They now run as InterCity service on the Rome-Formia-Reggio di Calabria and Rome-Potenza/Brindisi routes. ETR.450's previous service on the Italian high-speed network was taken over by ETR.600 units in December 2010.

SERIES DESIGNATION:	ETR.450
Road numbers:	01-15
Wheel arrangement (nine car):	(1A)(A1)+(1A)(A1)+(1A)(A1)+(1A)
(A1)+2'2'+(1A)(A1)+(1A)(A1)+(1A)	
(A1)+(1A)(A1)	
Power system:	3kV DC
Track gauge (ft [mm]):	4' 8.5" [1,435]
Maximum speed (mph [km/h]):	155 [250]
Power output (hp [kW]):	6713 [5,008 (16 x 313)]
Empty weight (t), nine car:	403
Service weight (t), nine car:	435
Maximum axle load (t):	12.89
Coupling length (ft [mm]), nine car:	767.3 [233,900]
End car length (ft [mm]):	89.7 [27,350]
Intermediate car length (ft [mm]):	83.9 [25,600]
Distance between truck centers (mm):	9 x 18,900
Axle interval motor truck (ft [mm]):	8 [2,450]
Axle interval trailer truck (ft [mm]):	8 [2,450]
Driver wheel diameter (ft [mm]):	2.8 [880]
Trailer wheel diameter (ft [mm]):	2.8 [880]
Seats (nine car):	386 (1st class: 168, 2nd class: 218)
Commissioning:	1987-1992

ETR.460, ETR.463

In 1995-96, Fiat produced an improved version of the Pendolino, in nine-car ETR.460 units, which were based on the ETR.450 concept. Three of the ten trains were designed for cross-border traffic on the Milan-Turin-Lyon connection, as dual-voltage versions, using both 3 kV and 1.5 kV DC power. All ETR.460 were pressure-tight and given a new, contemporary slanted front design. The star designer Giugiaro was responsible not only for this, but also for the whole exterior design of the car bodies, manufactured from aluminum extrusions, as well as for the interior design. The trains got an improved, space-saving hydraulic tilting system with a new adjustment mechanism. The active tilting system works on tilting bolster with four pendulums and two hydraulic cylinders. The tilting bolster lies on the coil springs and is in turn connected to the car body cross-bar. Since the pantographs must not also tilt along with the car, they are set directly on the truck tilting bolster. The hydraulic cylinders no longer restrict the width of the passenger compartments, because the entire tilting system was housed under the floor. Although the traction equipment was again distributed along the train, on the ETR.460, only six of the nine cars are motorized. This was made possible thanks to more powerful three-phase asynchronous motors (657 hp [490 kW]), controlled by an inverter and GTO thyristors. From the outset, the trains had First and Second Class cars, the seat layout in the latter now 2+2. ETR.463 unit 29 was severely damaged in a serious accident near Piacenza on January 12, 2006, and never rebuilt.

As already noted, the three ETR.460 units 21, 27, and 28, were equipped with 1.5 kV DC power, for service to Lyon, France. To be able to travel through the Alps, they were designed for better traction, with a lower gear transmission ratio for a reduced speed of 124 mph [200 km/h]. In 2003, service to France was changed to locomotive-pulled trains. The ETR trains were then reconverted to normal gear transmission and running at 155 mph [250 km/h]. The equipment to operate using 1.5 kV DC was retained; these trains were given a new series designation ETR.463 in early 2006.

SERIES DESIGNATION:	ETR.460, ETR.463
Road numbers:	ETR.460: 22-26, 29, 30; ETR.463: 21, 27, 28
Wheel arrangement (nine car):	(1A)(A1)+(1A)(A1)+2'2'+2'2'+(1A) (A1)+(1A)(A1)+2'2'+(1A)(A1)+(1A)(A1)
Power system:	ETR.460 only 3 kV DC, ETR.463 also 1.5 kV DC
Track gauge (ft [mm]):	4' 8.5" [1,435]
Maximum speed (mph [km/h]):	155 [250]
Hourly output (hp [kW]):	8,847 [6,600 (12 x 550)]
Power output (kW):	ETR.460: 7882 [5,880 (12 x 490)], ETR.463 using 1.5 kV DC: 5,255 [3,920 (12 x 327)]
Empty weight (t), nine car:	406.5
Service weight (t), nine car:	452
Maximum axle load (t):	14.5
Coupling length (ft [mm]), nine car:	776.2 [236,600]
End car length (ft [mm]):	90.7 [27,650]
Intermediate car length (ft [mm]):	84.9 [25,900]
Distance between truck centers (mm):	9 x 19,000
Axle interval motor truck (ft [mm]):	8.8 [2,700]
Axle interval trailer truck (ft [mm]):	8.8 [2,700]
Driver wheel diameter (ft [mm]):	2.9 [890]
Trailer wheel diameter (ft [mm]):	2.9 [890]
Seats (nine car):	503 (1st class: 137, 2nd class: 343, restaurant: 23)
Commissioning:	1995–1996

ETR.460 unit 23, photographed on June 2, 2006 in the Rome Termini railway station.

ETR.470

Another Pendolino, the ETR.470, was developed, so that the Italian high speed rail network could be connected to that of central Europe. The Italian State Railways, the Bern-Lötschberg-Simplon (BLS), and SBB Swiss railways founded a new operating company, called "Cisalpino" for this train, which was also called "Cisalpino." For cross-border service from Italy via Switzerland to Germany, the ETR.470 is equipped for both 3 kV DC and 15 kV/16.7 Hz AC power systems, as well as with the train control and safety systems for Italy, Switzerland, and Germany. After construction and tests of a pre-series "Treno zero" train, in 1996–97, nine nine-car series trains were immediately built.

An ETR.470 "Cisalpino" underway in the steep Neckar valley near Talausen, on 08/04/1998.

from Milan to Geneva. Beginning in July 1997, there were twenty daily connections across the Alps, through the Gotthard, Lötschberg, and Simplon passes. From March 1998 to December 2006, two "Cisalpino" train pairs made a direct connection between Stuttgart and Milan. The start of "Cisalpino" service meant travel time between Zurich and Milan could be shortened by almost an hour (thirty-two minutes due to faster cornering, twenty-one minutes by eliminating the border halt (with locomotive change in Chiasso)). However, as operation expanded, the ETR.470 also demonstrated a growing tendency to break down. This ultimately led to Cisalpino AG closing down the service. On December 13, 2009, five of the nine ETR.470 trainsets were taken over by the Italian State Railways (FS Trenitalia); the other four by the SBB. Since then, the trains run in direct cooperation between FS and SBB, and service is now limited to the Gotthard route.

Similar to the ETR.460, its self-supporting car bodies are made of light metal. The driver's cab in the end car is built with an aluminum frame and casing of fiber-reinforced plastic. The entire dual-voltage train is designed pressure-tight. The active tilting system corresponds to that of the ETR.460. To travel on the cross-Alp routes north of Milan in their service area, these trains got additional regenerative brakes and magnetic brakes, and are only allowed to run at 124 mph [200 km/h]. As of June 2, 1996, ETR.470 began regular train service. At first, only three trains traveled

ETR.480, ETR.485

A short time after the ETR.460 was commissioned, in 1997–98, a second series, the ETR.480, followed, also with fifteen nine-car trainsets. It is almost identical to the ETR.460, but the electrical equipment was designed so that it would be easy to include the new 25 kV/50 Hz power system for the high speed lines still under construction. In 2004, the AC equipment of unit 32 was activated; the trainset is now known as ETR.480 P (*politensione* = multi-voltage). Between 2005 and 2009, the remaining trainsets started service. They were given a new pantograph and the transformers were repositioned. The trains are also equipped with the ERTMS-2 and associated ETCS train safety systems, which are generally used on the new lines. The trains then got a new series designation, ETR.485.

Series designation:	ETR.470
Road numbers:	FS: Units 01, 04, 06-08; SBB: Units 02, 03, 05, 09
Wheel arrangement (nine car):	(1A)(A1)+(1A)(A1)+2'2'+(1A)(A1)+(1A)(A1)+2'2'+2'2'+(1A)(A1)+(1A)(A1)
Power system:	15kV/16.7 Hz, 3 kV DC
Track gauge (ft [mm]):	4' 8.5" [1,435]
Maximum speed (mph [km/h]):	124 [200]
Power output (hp [kW]):	12 x 657 [12 x 490]
Empty weight (t), nine car:	419
Service weight (t), nine car:	455.5
Maximum axle load (t):	14.2
Coupling length (ft [mm]), nine car:	776.2 [236,600]
End car length (ft [mm]):	89.2 [27,200]
Intermediate car length (ft [mm]):	82 [25,000]
Distance between truck centers (mm):	9 x 19,000
Axle interval motor truck (ft [mm]):	8.8 [2,700]
Axle interval trailer truck (ft [mm]):	8.8 [2,700]
Driver wheel diameter (ft [mm]):	2.9 [890]
Trailer wheel diameter (mm):	2.9 [890]
Seats (nine car):	456 (1st class: 135, 2nd class: 321)
Commissioning:	1996–1997

On 04/29/06, ETR.480 unit 33 is about to depart from Milan's main train station.

Series designation:	ETR.480, ETR.485
Road numbers:	31-45
Wheel arrangement (nine car):	(1A)(A1)+(1A)(A1)+2'2'+2'2'+(1A) (A1)+(1A) (A1)+2'2'+(1A)(A1)+(1A)(A1)
Power system:	ETR.480 only 3 kV DC, ETR.485 also 25 kV/50 Hz
Track gauge (ft [mm]):	4' 8.5" [1,435]
Top speed (mph [km/h]):	155 [250]
Hourly output (hp [kW]):	8,847 [6,600 (12 x 550)]
Power output (hp [kW]):	7,882 [5,880 (12 x 490)]
Empty weight (t), nine car:	409
Service weight (t), nine car:	ETR.480: 433, ETR.485: 454
Maximum axle load (t):	14-5
Coupling length (ft [mm]), nine car:	776.2 [236,600]
End car length (ft [mm]):	90.7 [27,650]
Intermediate car length (ft [mm]):	84.9 [25,900]
Distance between truck centers (mm):	9 x 19,000
Axle interval motor truck (ft [mm]):	8.8 [2,700]
Axle interval trailer truck (ft [mm]):	8.8 [2,700]
Driver wheel diameter (ft [mm]):	2.9 [890]
Trailer wheel diameter (ft [mm]):	2.9 [890]
Seats (nine car):	503 (1st class: 137, 2nd class: 343, Restaurant: 23)
Commissioning:	1997–1998

ETR.500 unit 46, showing its full-body "Trenitalia" advertisement, in the Rome Termini train station.

ETR.500

In 1996, the FS acquired the first of thirty ETR.500 trains, which were designed for a theoretical top speed of 186 mph [300 km/h]. The trainsets consisted of two DC power units using 3 kV, each with 5,898 hp [4,400 kW] output and eleven, later twelve, intermediate cars. The trains, over 1140 ft [350 meters] long, can seat 180 in First Class and 476 in Second Class. Up to 1999, this train made it possible to gradually introduce hourly up-market service between Milan and Rome, as well as separate connections from Milan to Turin, Venice, Trieste, and Lecce. They ran on the Milan-Florence-Rome-Naples route as so-called Eurostar Italia trains, but could never reach the theoretical maximum speed, given the 155 mph [250 km/h] allowed on the *Direttissima* between Florence and Rome. The decision to procure only DC power cars proved to be short-sighted, since the FS meanwhile had decided that all future high-speed lines (starting with Rome-Naples) would be electrified with 25 kV/50 Hz. The State Railways ordered another thirty ETR.500 trains, this time with dual voltage power cars, the Series E.404.500 P (*politensione*). These were completely redesigned to meet the new, more sophisticated functional requirements of the FS. The front impact protection was significantly improved. Furthermore, the entire

front had to undergo a "facelift" in Pininfarina design, to distinguish the new vehicles from the old DC-power cars. The power units have new power electronics to convert the current to appropriately supply the three-phase asynchronous motors. The power units, delivered between 1999 and 2001, are designed for both 25 kV/50 Hz and 3 kV DC (5,898 hp [4,400 kW] each) current. Some power cars were also equipped to use 1.5 kV DC; here, power output is limited to 3,217 hp [2,400 kW]. ETR.500 trainsets numbered 31 to 60 were made with these power cars and corresponding intermediate cars. In 2003, all ETR.500 units got a twelfth Second Class intermediate car, bringing the total capacity up to 669 passengers.

In 2002, FS decided to replace the Series E.404 100 DC power units with 60 dual-voltage power units, of the newly available Series E.404.600 P. The power cars put into service between 2004 and 2006, first got an ERTMS cab signaling system. At the same time, the E.404.500 power cars were brought to the new standard with single-bar pantographs, improved converters, and ERTMS. The intermediate cars in the first series also enjoyed a refreshing cure, before they were combined with the newly delivered E404.600 power units.

The E.404 660–663 power units were a reorder from 2007–08. They served as replacements for the four power cars sold to the RFI (*Rete Ferroviaria Italiana* = Italian Railway Network, the FS subsidiary responsible for the rail network and rail infrastructure). The two RFI test trains, Y1 and Y2, are used to start service on new lines and to test the European Rail Traffic Management System (ERTMS). Test train Y1 includes power cars E.404 649 and 652 and eight intermediate cars. Power cars E.404 648 and 621 and three intermediate cars made up test train Y2.

E414.113 and its InterCity train at the Bologna railway station on Aug. 20, 2010, ready for its next trip.

SERIES DESIGNATION:	ETR.500 (WITH POWER CARS E.404.500 AND E.404.600)
Road numbers:	01-60
Wheel arrangement (13 car):	Bo'Bo'+11 x 2'2'+Bo'Bo'
Power system:	25 kV/50 Hz; 3 kV DC; Units 54, 57 and 60, also 1.5 kV DC
Track gauge (ft [mm]):	4' 8.5" [1,435]
Maximum speed (mph [km/h]):	186 [300 km/h]
Power output (hp [kW]):	8 x 1,474 [8 x 1,100]
Empty weight (t), 13 car:	598
Service weight (t), 13 car:	645.2
Maximum axle load (t):	17
Coupling length (ft [mm]), 13 car:	1,076.8 [328,230]
Power car length (ft [mm]):	67.4 [20,565]
Intermediate car length (mm):	11 x 26,100
Distance between truck centers (mm):	11,450 + 11 x 19,000 11,450
Axle interval motor truck (ft [mm]):	9.8 [3,000]
Axle interval trailer truck (ft [mm]):	9.8 [3,000]
Driver wheel diameter (ft [mm]):	3.6 [1,100]
Trailer wheel diameter (ft [mm]):	2.9 [890]
Seats (ten unit):	604 (1st class: 128, 2nd class: 476)
Commissioning:	1996–2008

Between 2006 and 2008, Bombardier fundamentally rebuilt the 60 DC E.404.100 power cars from the first 1992 series. They now pull regular passenger cars, as the new Series E.414. They are usually run as an Intercity at 124 mph [200 km/h], in the sequence "power car/IC car/power car" or "power car/IC car/IC control car."

SERIES DESIGNATION:	E.414
Road numbers:	100-159
Wheel arrangement:	Bo'Bo'
Power system:	3kV DC
Track gauge (ft [mm]):	4' 8.5" [1,435]
Maximum speed (mph [km/h]):	155 [250 km/h]
Power output (hp [kW]):	4 x 1,474 [4 x 1,100]
Service weight (t):	68
Maximum axle load (t):	17
Power car length (ft [mm]):	66.4 [20,250]
Distance between truck centers (ft [mm]):	37.5 [11,450]
Axle interval motor truck (ft [mm]):	9.8 [3,000]
Driver wheel diameter (ft [mm]):	3.6 [1,100]
Commissioning/Renovation:	1996-1999/2006-2008

Beginning in 2008, FS Trenitalia introduced new brand names related to their speed, for its high speed trains. Trains with maximum speeds of 186 to 217 mph [300 to 350 km/h] were now known as *Frecciarossa* (= red arrow), so that the ETR.500 units were the only series in this category. The trainsets were given a new color scheme with red stripes and the words FRECCIAROSSA painted on the power cars. In December 2009, FS determined that ETR.500 trainsets with twelve intermediate cars could not sustain the now reduced travel time on the finished high-speed Milan-Rome route, and another intermediate car had to be removed.

ETR.600, ETR.610

In March 2004, FS Trenitalia and Cisalpino AG gave Alstom a contract to make twelve and fourteen seven-car Pendolino trains, since Fiat Ferroviaria had been acquired by Alstom in 2000. This fourth generation Pendolino ("New Pendolino")—in Series ETR.600, a dual-voltage train (3 kV DC and 25 kV/50 Hz) and in Series ETR.610 a triple-voltage version (3 kV DC, 25 kV/50 Hz and 15 kV/16 2/3 Hz)—is a further development of earlier designs. The series trains were built to better meet market demand and customer requirements. Special features include the new interior and exterior design by Italian industrial design house Giugiaro Design. The car bodies were manufactured from aluminum extrusions. Giugiaro based the interior design on four key factors: ergonomics, comfort, communications, and well-being. Both series are equipped with modern passenger information and security systems. Some important technical properties were improved, including drive unit output and redundant components and equipment, to ensure higher reliability. The train front and end meet TSI (Interoperability) standards. They are equipped with an override protection device and compatible energy absorption system. The front and intermediate couplings were given regenerative energy absorption systems. The "new Pendolino" got the appropriate train control systems for the areas they were to operate.

ETR.600 unit 11 has just arrived at the Bologna train station on Aug. 20, 2010.

The Onix drive system ensures optimum performance and also meets TSI standard requirements.

The ETR.600/610 reach top speeds of 155 mph [250 km/h], using only 75% of the available drive power. The drive system is based on tested standard components, such as IGBT technology and the most advanced water-cooled 6.5 kV drive modules. The trains has an additional eight, more powerful, three-phase asynchronous motors, with a capacity of some 938 hp [700 kW]. The Fiat-developed active Tiltronix tilt technology was further improved and provides reactive or proactive train tilting. In reactive mode, sensors measure curves using more accurate angle measurements and accelerometers on the first truck of the front car. The on-board computer calculates the required tilt angle, which is then carried out by the car truck cylinders, as a function of position and train speed. In proactive mode, the tilt system is connected to a track parameter database. By comparing the data with that from the on-board sensors, the system always has the precise position of the train on the track, and

can select the corresponding tilt. Trucks with hydraulic tilting technology and proven standard components activate the tilt of the cars. A side air suspension system ensures centered alignment of the car, improving both the train's dynamics and passenger comfort. By reducing the unsprung and easily suspended weight, the train's action is optimized and wheel force reduced to a minimum. The pantographs are mounted on slide platforms, firmly attached to the railcar roof. When the railcar tilts, a compensating hydraulic system slides the platform to the side to compensate, so that the pantograph is always in its basic central position.

The first ETR.600 was delivered to the Italian State Railways beginning in mid-2008, and this train has run on the Italian high-speed lines without major problems ever since. Significantly more problems were created by the ETR.610, especially when travelling in Switzerland. While the first unit had already taken its first steps in mid-2007, there was a delay before regular service could begin. The Swiss Federal Office of Transport first gave the ETR.610 temporary conditional approval for "commercial pre-operation" with passengers, under close observation, in March 2009. Since July 20, 2009, the first "new Pendolino" have been running between Geneva and Milan, and since November 2009, some trains have even been on the Lötschberg route (Basel-Milan). After Cisalpino AG was dissolved on December 13, 2009, the existing ETR.600 fleet was divided equally between the SBB and FS Trenitalia.

SERIES DESIGNATION:	ETR.600
Road numbers:	001-012
Wheel arrangement (seven car):	(1A)(A1)+(1A) (A1)+2'2'+2'2'+(1A)(A1)+(1A) (A1)
Power system:	3kV DC, 25 kV/50 Hz
Track gauge (ft [mm]):	4' 8.5" [1,435]
Maximum speed (mph [km/h]):	155 [250]
Hourly output (kW):	
Nominal power (continuous output) (hp [kW]):	7,373 [5,500 (8 x 688)]
Empty weight (t), seven car:	387
Service weight (t), seven car:	443
Maximum axle load (t):	16.5
Coupling length (ft [mm]), seven car:	614.8 [187,400]
End car length (ft [mm]):	92.5 [28,200]
Intermediate car length (ft [mm]):	85.9 [26,200]
Distance between truck centers (mm):	7 x 19,000
Axle distance powered truck (ft [mm]):	8.8 [2,700]
Axle distance trailer truck (ft [mm]):	8.8 [2,700]
Driver wheel diameter (ft [mm]):	2.9 [890]
Trailer wheel diameter (ft [mm]):	2.9 [890]
Seats (seven car):	432 (104 + 308 + 20)
Commissioning:	2007–2008

On 06/10/2010, the FS ETR.610 005 with EC 34 (Milan-Geneva), passed the village of St. Saphorin on Lake Geneva.

SERIES DESIGNATION:	ETR.610
Road numbers:	FS: 610.001, 002, 003, 004, 008, 011, 012; SBB: 610.005, 006, 007, 009, 010, 013, 014
Wheel arrangement (seven car):	(1A)(A1)+(1A)(A1)+2'2'+2'2'+2'2'+(1A)(A1)+(1A)(A1)
Power system:	3 kV DC, 25 kV/50 Hz, 15 kV/16 2/3 Hz
Track gauge (ft [mm]):	4' 8.5" [1,435]
Maximum speed (mph [km/h]):	155 [250]
Hourly output (kW):	
Nominal power (continuous output) (hp [kW]):	7,373 [5,500 (8 x 688)]
Empty weight (t), seven car:	394
Service weight (t), seven car:	450
Maximum axle load (t):	16.5
Coupling length (ft [mm]), seven car:	614.8 [187,400]
End car length (ft [mm]):	92.5 [28,200]
Intermediate car length (ft [mm]):	85.9 [26,200]
Distance between truck centers (mm):	7 x 19,000
Axle distance powered truck (ft [mm]):	8.8 [2,700]
Axle distance trailer truck (ft [mm]):	8.8 [2,700]
Driver wheel diameter (ft [mm]):	2.9 [890]
Trailer wheel diameter (ft [mm]):	2.9 [890]
Seats (seven car):	431 (103 + 308 + 20)
Commissioning:	2008–2010

ETR.1000

On Sept. 30, 2010, FS Trenitalia signed a contract to supply fifty eight-car high-speed trains based on the Zefiro platform, with a consortium of Bombardier Transportation and AnsaldoBreda. The contract was worth $2 [€1.54] billion. At the time of this writing, the V300ZEFIRO type multi-system-capable, 656 ft [200 m] long, 600-seat train is expected to fully meet European standards (TSI standard). The units—referred to in Italy as ETR.1000—are to have an operational high speed of 224 mph [360 km/h]. Its unusually high acceleration will let the train ensure outstanding travel times, including on winding routes. The train is also to be fully equipped for

This—or something similar—is how the new ETR.1000 (Zefiro) of FS Trenitalia will look.

cross-border service. A first prototype will be available in spring 2012; commercial operation is planned beginning in 2013 for the series trains.

SERIES DESIGNATION:	ETR.1000
Road numbers:	
Wheel arrangement (eight car):	Bo'Bo'+2'2'+2'2'+ Bo'Bo'+ Bo'Bo'+2'2'+2'2'+Bo'Bo'
Power system:	3kV DC, 25kV/50Hz
Track gauge (ft [mm]):	4' 8.5" [1,435]
Maximum speed (mph [km/h]):	224 [360]
Hourly output (kW):	
Nominal power (continuous output) (hp [kW]):	10,992 [8,200 (8 x 1.025)]
Empty weight (t), eight car:	
Service weight (t), eight car:	
Maximum axle load (t):	
Coupling length (ft [mm]), eight car:	656 [200,000]
End car length (ft [mm]):	86.5 [26,390]
Intermediate car length (ft [mm]):	81.2 [24,775]
Distance between truck centers (mm):	8 x 17,375
Axle distance powered truck (ft [mm]):	8.2 [2,500]
Axle distance trailer truck (ft [mm]):	8.2 [2,500]
Driver wheel diameter (ft [mm]):	3 [915]
Trailer wheel diameter (ft [mm]):	3 [915]
Seats (eight car):	
Commissioning:	from 2013

COMPETITION ON THE RAILS

By 2011, Italy was, as yet, the first country in Europe where there was competition for high-speed lines. Already, in late 2006, there was a nationwide sensation when the NTV (Nuovo Trasporto Viaggiatori) company, founded in December, received the required permit to run commercial passenger service, and, in early 2008, ordered 25 AGV trains (*Automotrice à Grande Vitesse*) from Alstom. The 656 ft [200 m] long, 11-car trainsets have 460 seats, can run at 186 mph [300 km/h] and cost approximately $837 [€650] million. Alstom is also responsible for maintenance and upkeep of the units over 30 years. However, this is billed separately. With four pairs of trains running between Milan and Naples with stops in Bologna, Florence and Rome, service was to begin in September 2011, under the brand name "italo." After delivery of the 25 railcars, NTV now operates 51 trains daily, including 41 on the Turin-Milan-Rome-Naples-Salerna route and 10 on the Venice-Rome-Naples connection. The Ferrari-red painted AGV will compete with the state-run FS Trenitalia and the airlines, especially for business travelers. The service will provide a higher service standard, compared to the competition, and the trains will be slightly faster than the FS Trenitalia.

CROATIA

To expand and modernize their outdated and sometimes rundown fleet, Croatian National Railways HZ (= *Hrvatske Zeljeznice* [Croatian Railways]) began, in 2003, to look for suitable trains that could speed up rail transport on their non-electrified tracks. HZ considered DB's Series 612 ("Regio-Swinger") tilting railcars a good selection; these trains were already being produced. The manufacturer Bombardier, however, was fully occupied with DB's 200 train order. HZ then negotiated with DB to determine if DB would turn over part of their quota to HZ. This was no problem; DB passed the last eight trains of their allocation (planned road numbers: 612 193/693 to 612 200/700) on to HZ. The railcars were painted in HZ's corporate colors at the factory, and were delivered directly to Croatia between late May and early August 2004. There they were added to HZ's rolling stock as Series 7123, although the trains conform completely to the German 612; even the interior design and paint color scheme are the same.

The Series 7123 and 612 technology and fundamental construction principles were taken over from the DB Series 611. The car bodies can tilt up to 8°, using the "*neicontrol-E*" system, via an under-floor mounted electric servomotor, spur wheel gear, and linear spindle drive. Sensors in the trucks record reactive forces from rounding curves, and pass the data on to the power electronics of the tilt technology. There were significant alterations in the 611, including the now-available, more powerful Cummins 749 hp [559 kW] engines, the smoother vehicle front, made of fiberglass-reinforced plastic, and placing the outer entrance doors behind the first truck (third entry).

As early as 2003, HZ had begun the costly adaptation of the non-electrified Ogulin-Knin-Split rail track section, which formed a part of the new tilting train route between Zagreb-Split. When this work was finished in July 2004, nothing stood in the way of a punctual launch of the new tilting train service, on July 26. Three pairs of these trains—the new type ICN (IC *Nagibni* = tilting IC)—were now underway between Zagreb and Split. The railcars required about six hours to make the 260 mile [420 km] trip, while conventional trains up to this point took 7 hours 30 minutes.

However, operating these railcars did not occur under a lucky star; two serious accidents have overshadowed its career so far. On November 24,

2006, a truck blocked unit 7123 003/004, running as ICN 521, on a level crossing on the way to Split, near the Kosovo train station. Then, on July 24, 2009, unit 7123 009/010, running as ICN 521 (Zagreb-Split), had a serious accident about 12 miles [20 kilometers] from Split. Neither train has yet been repaired since the accidents. Unit 007/008 has already been under repair for several years, so that currently only five tilting trains are in operation. The service plan in the 2011 annual timetable is for two pairs of trains between Zagreb and Split (ICN 520–523) and a pair of trains between Zagreb and Osijek (IC 550 and 551).

Series designation:	7123
Road numbers:	7123 001/002 – 015/016
Unit configuration:	T+T
Wheel arrangement:	2'B'+B'2'
Track gauge (ft [mm]):	4' 8.5" [1,435]
Engine power (hp [kW]):	1499 [1,118 (2 x 559)]
Transmission:	hydraulic
Service weight (t):	116
Maximum axle load (t):	15
Coupling length(ft [mm]):	169.7 [51,750]
Distance between truck centers (mm):	17,500 + 17,500
Axle distance powered truck (ft [mm]):	8 [2,450]
Axle distance trailer truck (ft [mm]):	8 [2,450]
Driver wheel diameter (ft [mm]):	2.9 [890]
Trailer wheel diameter (ft [mm]):	2.9 [890]
Seats 1st/2nd class:	134 (24 + 110)
Commissioning:	2004

7123 011 is ready for departure from Zagreb Main Station on June 1, 2006.

THE NETHERLANDS AND BELGIUM

On December 8, 2009, Belgian railways celebrated the full start-up of service on its border-to-border high-speed rail network. After sixteen years of work and an investment of some $6.6 [€5] billion, Belgium is the first European country that has completed its high-speed network, and thus made Brussels the high-speed rail hub of Europe. In connection with upgraded existing lines, three routes link Brussels with the rest of Europe. The first link (LGV 1) is 44 miles [71 km] long, has been operating since 1997, and connects Brussels to the French border. On this route, Paris is only 1 hour and 22 minutes away, and London 1 hour 51 minutes. Both the LGV 2 (parallel to the expressway between Leuven and Liège) and the LGV 3 (from Liège to the German border) run towards Germany. The latter opened in June 2009 and now ensures a travel time of 1 hour and 57 minutes between Brussels and Cologne. The Netherlands connection is via the LGV 4 (from Antwerp to the Dutch border); this was inaugurated on December 8, 2009, and regular train service began on December 13. All high speed lines are designed for an operating speed of 186 mph [300 km/h].

In contrast, the Dutch-continued development of the Belgian HSL 4 was a tragedy in several acts. The HSL Zuid, also designed for a speed of 186 mph [300 km/h], runs from the Belgian border to Rotterdam and on to Amsterdam. The exclusive use of the ETCS Level 2 for the signaling system on this stretch represented the first big problem; this posed considerable trouble and significantly curtailed the number of trains which could travel on it. Currently, the Thalys is the only high-speed train that can utilize this new line. Since December

Route	Connection	Maximum speed	Length	Launch	Train type	Power system	Train safety system
HSL 1 (Belgium)	Brussels-Lille (connection to LGV Nord)	186 mph [300 km/h]	55 mi [88 km]	12/14/97	TGV, Eurostar, Thalys	25 kV/50 Hz	TVM 430
HSL 2 (Belgium)	Leuven-Ans (Brussels-Liège link)	186 mph [300 km/h]	39 mi [62 km]	12/15/02	Thalys, ICE 3M, IC	25 kV/50 Hz	TBL2
HSL 3 (Belgium)	Chênée-Walhorn (Liège-Aachen line)	162 mph [260 km/h]	26 mi [42 km]	12/06/09	Thalys, ICE 3M	25 kV/50 Hz	ETCS Level 2
HSL 4 (Belgium)	Antwerp-Netherlands (connection to HSL Zuid to Rotterdam)	186 mph [300 km/h]	25 mi [40 km]	12/08/09	Thalys, V250, IC	25 kV/50 Hz	ETCS Level 2
HSL Zuid (NL)	Amsterdam-Rotterdam-Antwerp (connection to HSL 4)	186 mph [300 km/h]	78 mi [125 km]	09/06/09	Thalys, V2 50	25 kV/50 Hz	ETCS Level 2
HSL East (NL)	Amsterdam-Utrecht	124 mph [200 km/h]		2015 (planned)	ICE	25 kV/50 Hz	ATB, ETCS Level 2

2010, the Amsterdam-Paris route now takes just over three hours. The Type V250 "Fyra" trains, to be supplied by AnsaldoBreda and intended for the Amsterdam-Brussels connection, were four years overdue when this was written, and once delivered, service was suspended. The AnsaldoBreda trains were intended to travel in every-hour service between Amsterdam and Brussels, as well as on the existing routes to The Hague, Breda, and Eindhoven.

SERIES DESIGNATION:	V250 "FYRA"
Road numbers:	NS: 4801-4816, SNCB: 4881-4884
Unit configuration	T+M+T+M+M+T+M+T
Wheel arrangement (eight car):	Bo'Bo'+2'2'+Bo'Bo'+2'2'+2'2'+Bo'Bo' +2'2'+Bo'Bo'
Power system:	25 kV/50 Hz, 1.5 V DC, 3 kV DC
Track gauge (ft [mm]):	4' 8.5" [1,435]
Maximum speed (mph [km/h]):	155 [250]
Hourly output (kW):	
Nominal power (continuous output) (hp [kW]):	7,373 [5,500 kW (8 x 688 kW)]
Empty weight eight car (t):	423
Service weight eight car (t):	485
Maximum axle load (t):	*17*
Coupling length eight car (ft [mm]):	659 [200,900]
End car length (ft [mm]):	88.4 [26,950]
Intermediate car length (ft [mm]):	80.3 [24,500]
Distance between truck centers (mm):	8 x 17,500
Axle distance powered truck (ft [mm]):	9.1 [2,800]
Axle distance trailer truck (ft [mm]):	9.1 [2,800]
Driver wheel diameter (ft [mm]):	3 [920]
Trailer wheel diameter (ft [mm]):	3 [920]
Seats 1st/2nd class (eight car):	546 (127 +419)
Commissioning:	2008-2011

V250 "Fyra"

The Dutch (NS Hispeed) and Belgian (SNCB) railway operators ordered the first 19 Type V250 trains from AnsaldoBreda in 2004, for high speed service between Amsterdam and Brussels; they got the brand name "Fyra." The NS was to get sixteen units (Series 4800) and SNCB three units (Series 4880). In the meantime, the SNCB has ordered another set; twenty trains are to be manufactured.

After several postponed deliveries, by 2008 it was expected that the first trains would be available in early 2009, and in service by mid-2009. The first train—still without finished interior—was finally ready in March 2009, and took trial runs on the Czech test ring at Velim. In April 2009, the first unit reached Dutch territory in Arnhem, and was sent on to Amsterdam. The train now was thoroughly put through its paces on the HSL Zuid and the Belgian HSL 4 connections.

The eight-car trains can operate using three different train current systems and are designed to use 25 kV/50 Hz AC as well as 1.5 kV or 3 kV DC. In addition to the ETCS Level 2 train control system used on the HSL Zuid, the trainsets are also equipped with the Dutch ATB and the Belgian TBL. Four of the eight cars are powered by three-phase asynchronous motors, controlled by water-cooled IGBT inverters. The car bodies are made of aluminum; the cabs themselves are made of steel. There are 546 seats in the eight cars, 127 in the three First Class cars. There are outlets at the seats. The Italian design firm Pininfarina was also involved in the design of these trains.

Both the NS and SNCB, however, have had their own high-speed trains for years. These were either recruited from the train pool or trains assigned as add-ons from other railroads. The SNCB owns four units (3101–3102 to 3107–3108) from the "Eurostar pool;"

it has seven TGV PBKA (4301–4307) from the "Thalys pool." The NS has two TGV PBKA (4331–4332) trains of its own. They have also ordered four ICE3 (DB series 406) units (NS 4651–4654) to run on the Amsterdam-Cologne-Frankfurt connection.

On a trial run, Fyra unit 4806 whooshes through the Vught station on 8/18/2009.

NORWAY

The completion of the Nordland rail line between Trondheim and Bodo in 1962 brought a temporary end to railway construction in Norway. But in 1992, a new railway age began: on October 8, the Norwegian Parliament approved building a new airport for the capital, Oslo, and all of eastern Norway, at Gardermoen, about 31 miles [50 km] north of Oslo; it would be some distance from the region's more densely populated areas. Constructing the new airport was an extremely controversial decision, preceded by thirty years of discussion about a suitable location. At the same time, the Parliament also made the decision to build a high-speed connection from Oslo to Gardermoen Airport.

The 41 mile [66 km] long "Gardermoen line" is designed for an operating speed of 130 mph [210 km/h] (top speed 143 mph [230 km/h]). Train service started on August 1, 1998. Expanding the new line from Gardermoen on to Eidsvoll, and also connecting it to the existing railway, would create a synergy effect for both local and regional train services. Although the Airport Express Train (*Flytoget*) service itself ends at the airport and returns to Oslo, trains running to or from Lillehammer and Trondheim can, using this extension of the new tracks, add a stop at the airport. The Lillestrom,

Airport Gardermoen, and Eidsvoll Verk train stations were newly designed. Building the Gardermoen line, including the trainsets, cost $1.81 billion [ten billion Norwegian kroner], and took five years, from 1994 to 1999.

Norway has 4.3 million inhabitants, a relatively small population, a population density of just 13 people per km2, and a very rugged landscape. Therefore, constructing high-speed lines would be very expensive, while demand for very fast connections is limited overall. Meanwhile, Norway continued to modernize its existing lines, although slowly. This included an expansion of curve radii to allow greater speed. A short link between Oslo and Drammen was upgraded to let trains run at 124 mph [200 km/h]. The 15.5 mile [25 km] Oslo-Ski route will be upgraded by 2013 to accommodate the same speed. The first modernization work had already begun on the stretch between Drammen and Tonsberg by 1995. Work on this section should be completed by 2016, when it will be possible for trains to run here at 124 mph [200 km/h]. Only the BM 71 (*Flytoget*), BM 73, and BM 73B rail cars can travel this fast. Although the Series El 18 electric locomotives are designed for a speed of 124 mph [200 km/h], there are no passenger coaches for them that can go faster than 99 mph [160 km/h]. However, by 2011, the new FLIRT railcars from Stadler (BM 74 and BM 75) are to be used for the fast regional and local transport, and these are designed for the 124 mph [200 km/h] pace.

THE TRAINS

In autumn 1996, the Norwegian State Railways (NSB) borrowed an X2 trainset from the Swedish State Railways (SJ), at a cost of almost $181,000 [one million Norwegian kroner]. The train ran on the Oslo-Kristiansand route until December 21, 1996, making the 219 miles [353 km] in a travel time of 3 hours 48 minutes. Until then, the shortest travel time had been 4 hours 24 minutes. At the time, the NSB's plans envisaged putting six or seven tilting trains in regular service on this route by 1999. Things developed a bit differently, however; first came the launching of the Oslo airport train.

BM71

ADtranz in Strommen (now Bombardier) developed a new high-speed train for the Airport Express (*Flytoget*) between Oslo Airport Gardermoen and the main railway station. The three-car railcar used the concept of the Swedish X2 as a model, but also incorporated current findings in its construction. While the car bodies are made of light welded stainless steel structures, new methods were used for the basic design features. One power car was omitted and the drive power distributed along the whole train, which means each car has a powered and a trailer truck. Tilting technology was also omitted, as it was not necessary for the airport express. However, the trains were basically conceptualized to incorporate tilt technology. The car body inner configuration was very different from the X2; the doors were in a different place, between the two trucks instead of at the end of the car. The trains are pressure sealed for better passenger comfort when running through tunnels. Unfortunately, the train's weight increased during construction from 149 to 170 tons. To keep to the 158 ton guideline, the original idea of barrier-free passage had to be given up. Although the train can still be boarded at platform level, inside passengers had to climb a few steps to reach the seating area. The hydraulic couplings for multiple unit operation are behind covers on the vehicle front. In designing the

Just in front of the Gardermoen airport train station opening, a BM 71 poses for in-house photographers.

train's nose, ADtranz also trod an idiosyncratic path; it reminds the author, at least, of a dog's head.

Each unit was given a capacity of 3,547 hp [2,646 kW], more than enough to reach the required speed. Up to four units can travel in multiple unit operation. The BM 71 has a top speed of 130 mph [210 km/h], which was chosen to cut the trip from Oslo Central Station to Gardermoen Airport to less than 20 minutes. The first BM 71 railcar saw the light of day in the railway world on September 19, 1997; the last unit was delivered more than four months later on January 30, 1998. For experimental purposes, the last trainset (BM 71 016) had built-in tilt technology, so that it could be fully tested on NSB rail lines—especially the demanding routes to Bergen and Trondheim (Dovre Railway). Before it got the BM 71, NSB had previously ordered similar trains, but with tilting technology and four cars. A few years later, BM 71 016's tilt mechanism was removed from the train.

In 2007, *Flytoget* ordered an additional intermediate car from Bombardier for its three car trainsets. This was to increase capacity in the individual sets by 40%, to 244 seats, and enable the company to better accommodate the 10% annual increase in passenger numbers. The extra intermediate cars were delivered beginning in 2008, and their addition to the railcars was used as an opportunity for an extensive renovation of all the trainsets. All this posed several challenges for Bombardier, since most of the components used in constructing the trains were no longer available. Key parts, such as car bodies and rectifiers, had to be manufactured by Bombardier, based on a discontinued product lines. Many manufacturers of the original interior design were no longer in business.

SERIES DESIGNATION:	BM 71
Road numbers:	71.001-016
Unit configuration:	T+M+2T
Wheel arrangement (four car):	Bo'2'+2'2'+ Bo'2'+ 2'Bo'
Wheel arrangement (railcar):	Bo'2'
Wheel arrangement (intermediate car):	2'2'
Power system:	15 kV/16.7 Hz
Track gauge (ft [mm]):	4' 8.5" [1,435]
Maximum speed (mph [km/h]):	130 [210]
Nominal power (continuous output) (hp [kW]):	3,547 [2,646 (6 x 441)]
Empty weight (t):	210
Maximum axle load (t):	16.5
Length (end car) (ft [mm]):	90.8 [27,700]
Length (intermediate car) (ft [mm]):	84 [25,600]
Length of entire train (four unit) (ft [mm]):	350 [106,600]
Distance between truck centers (mm):	3 x 19,000
Axle distance powered truck (ft [mm]):	8.8 [2,700]
Axle distance trailer truck (ft [mm]):	8.8 [2,700]
Driver wheel diameter (ft [mm]):	2.8 [870]
Trailer wheel diameter (ft [mm]):	2.8 [870]
Seats 2nd class (four unit):	224
Commissioning:	1997–98; renovation in 2008–09

BM 73 AND BM 73B

After successful trials with the Swedish X2, the NSB ordered sixteen four-car railcars with tilting devices, on March 5, 1997. The first train was delivered on October 22, 1999. The age of tilting trains then opened in Norway on November 1, 1999, as the Series BM 73 "*Krengetogs*" (= tilting trains), made by ADtranz, started regular service on the 219 mile [353 km] long Sörlandsbanen Oslo-Kristiansand rail connection. The new railcars, with the brand name "Signature," took forty minutes less on this link than the previously offered fast trains. After 1999, the "*Krengetogs*" travelled on

The BM 73 B 146 has just arrived from Oslo at the Göteborg/ Gothenbur Central Station in September 2008.

BM 73 115, as train no. 73/773, just passes the Stavanger-Paradis station, and, in two minutes, will reach the end of its nearly eight-hour trip.

via Kristiansand to Stavanger. From January 9, 2000, the new tilting trains ran between Oslo and Trondheim, and in the same year, the signature connection from Oslo to Bergen was added. The NSB acquired a total of sixteen Series 73 BM four-car units. On December 15, 1999, NSB ordered six more Series BM 73B trainsets for shorter distances. They began operating in 2001, with the brand name "Agenda," with a modified interior design. They run on the Oslo-Halden route, with separate connections to Gothenburg in Sweden.

Like the BM 71, three cars have a powered truck, with two three-phase asynchronous traction motors; another intermediate car is unpowered. The trains, with 3,547 hp [2,646 kW] output, can again reach a top speed of 130 mph [210 km/h]. Final assembly was done in the factory ADtranz Strömmen near Oslo. The traction equipment and the trucks come from the Swedish ADtranz Västerås factory, as does the tilt technology, adapted from the Swedish X2. The BM 73 has 54 First Class seats and 151 seats in Second Class. There are also a bistro, a wheelchair accessible compartment, and a play area for children. The six BM-73B trainsets were made with just 30 First Class seats and 213 seats in Second Class. Until recently, the two series had different paint designs (BM 73 blue/silver and BM 73B red/silver); in the future, likely all trainsets will get the new red/silver NSB colors.

The BM 73 was not spared its growing pains. The worst was a broken axle from a derailment on June 17, 2000. All the NSB "*Krengetogs*" were taken out of service, so that temporarily, the largely identical, BM 71, which does not have tilt technology, ran on the Oslo-Gardermoen airport line. After mid-July, the BM 73 was back in service, with its tilting technology turned off and again limited to 75 mph [120 km/h]. After protracted negotiations with the manufacturer, the tilting trains got new, stronger axles in 2002–03.

Since then, the two versions of the BM 73 have been running generally without problems; however, their product names of "Signature" and "Agenda," have disappeared into the void, without a trace.

SERIES DESIGNATION:	BM73	BM73B
Road numbers:	73.001-016	73.041-046
Unit configuration:	T+M+2T	
Wheel arrangement (four car):	Bo'2'+2'2'+ Bo'2'+ 2'Bo'	
Wheel arrangement (railcar):	Bo'2'	
Wheel arrangement (intermediate car):	2'2'	
Power system:	15 kV/16.7 Hz	
Track gauge (ft [mm]):	4' 8.5" [1,435]	
Maximum speed (mph [km/h]):	130 [210]	
Nominal power (continuous output) (hp [kW]):	3,547 [2,646 (6 x 441)]	
Empty weight (t):	215.1	215.1
Service weight (t):	227.2	226.5
Maximum axle load (t):	16.5	16.5
Length (end car) (ft [mm]):	90.8 [27,700]	
Length (intermediate car) (ft [mm]):	83.9 [25,600]	
Length of entire train (four unit) (ft [mm]):	350 [106,600]	
Distance between truck centers (mm):	4 x 19,000	
Axle distance powered truck (ft [mm]):	8.8 [2,700]	
Axle distance trailer truck (ft [mm]):	8.8 [2,700]	
Driver wheel diameter (ft [mm]):	2.8 [870]	
Trailer wheel diameter (ft [mm]):	2.8 [870]	
Seats 1st/2nd class:	54/151	30/213
Commissioning:	1999-2001	2001

The just-delivered Flirt railcar BM 74 501 ("Short Regional") undergoing extensive test runs on the Bergen railway, as here on March 28, 2010.

FLIRT. The train thus, in principle, consists of a three-car and a two-car unit. Each powered truck has a converter, which feeds the two three-phase asynchronous motors. The Norwegian carriage profile—broader than that in continental Europe—allows a width of 10.4 ft [3,200 mm], so that the Second Class cars can be comfortably fitted with a 3 + 2 seat layout. The GfK fronts have been redesigned with standardized crash boxes and the driver's area is set relatively far back behind a flat windshield. Since collisions with moose still cause heavy damage in Norway, the front panels and lights can be replaced individually. The train front thus has more joints than normally necessary.

BM 74 AND BM 75 FOR FAST LOCAL AND REGIONAL TRANSPORT

On August 19, 2008, the NSB gave the Swiss manufacturer Stadler a contract to supply fifty five-car, 124 mph [200 km/h] FLIRT multiple-unit trains, plus an option for 100 additional units. Of these, twenty-six sets (BM 75) were fitted out as "Long Local" trains for commuter service in the greater Oslo area, with travel times up to ninety minutes; they got only Second Class seats. The other twenty-four units (BM 74) were designed as an Intercity version with high-end interiors for "Short Regional" service throughout southeastern Norway and on to Bergen. The fifty NSB trains feature high quality winter performance features, that can handle temperatures down to -104° F [-40° C], and are based on the FLIRT for the Helsinki commuter train service. The modular-designed railcars were modified in some aspects to meet the special needs of the NSB. All units are made with five cars, but have three power trucks instead of the usual two in the four- and five-car

SERIES DESIGNATION:	BM 74	BM 75
Road numbers:	74.001-024	75.001-026
Wheel arrangement:	Bo'(2)'(2)'Bo'+2'(2)'Bo'	
Power system:	15kV/16 2/3 Hz	
Track gauge (ft [mm]):	4' 8.5" [1,435]	
Maximum speed (mph [km/h]):	124 [200]	
Hourly output (hp [kW]):	6,032 [4,500 (6 x 750)]	
Nominal power (continuous output) (hp [kW]):	4,021 [3,000 (6 x 500)]	
Service weight (t):	206.2	206.0
Maximum axle load (t):	16	
Coupling length (ft [mm]):	346 [105,500]	
Distance between truck centers (mm):	16,800 +18,000 +18,300 +18,300 +16,800	
Axle distance powered truck (ft [mm]):	8.2 [2,500]	
Axle distance trailer truck (ft [mm]):	9 [2,750 (Jacobs truck)]/8.2 [2,500]	
Driver wheel diameter (ft [mm]):	3 [920]	
Trailer wheel diameter (ft [mm]):	3 [920]	
Seats 1st /2nd class + folding seats:	44/172 + 48	-/235 + 60
Commissioning:	2011–2012	2012–2013

AUSTRIA

Austria's geography does not encourage construction of high-speed rail lines. The distribution of the cities and the population structure (the greater Vienna area has 1.8 million inhabitants, but cities such as Graz have just 255,000 and Linz just 190,000 inhabitants) do not create enough travel demand for high-speed transport on specially built tracks. This led to the decision, made in 1990, to only upgrade existing main lines and only augment these lines with new sections on partial stretches. Expansion plans included the main routes Vienna-Linz-Wels-Salzburg, Vienna-Bruck/Mur-Graz-Klagenfurt-Villach-Tarvis and Kufstein-Innsbruck-Brenner. The new and upgraded projects are currently underway or already partially completed on these main lines. In the future, trains will be able to travel at speeds of up to 143 mph [230 km/h], which is the maximum speed of the "Taurus" fleet (Series 1016, 1116, 1216).

THE "RAILJET"

Railcars or locomotive-hauled train: that was the key question the Austrian Federal Railways ÖBB management posed itself, before acquiring its own high-speed trains. ÖBB finally decided on a budget version: in 2006, they initially ordered twenty-three so-called "railjet" units, each consisting of one end car, five intermediate, and a control car, pulled by a Series 1116 "Taurus" electric locomotive. Like the German Metropolitan Express Train, on the railjet trainsets, the individual cars are connected with shell muff couplings (rod couplings). There are normal screw couplings only at the two train ends. Due to the rigid intermediate couplings, the railcars were given wide airtight inter-car passageways. Fire doors are installed there, but are usually kept open. In theory, the railjets can be shortened or lengthened by one car in the factory, to better adapt the train for the traffic on any connection. This has yet to be done in practice; ÖBB runs double trainsets where there is very high passenger volume. The front of the control car was modeled on that of the Taurus electric locomotive. The Siemens SF 400 family trucks with air suspension ensure the needed ride comfort; these were developed for locomotive-hauled push-pull passenger trains running at up to a maximum speed of 174 mph [280 km/h].

The first railjets in the Austrian long-distance fleet had three different classes—Economy Class, Business Class, and a Premium Class. The Premium Class is in the control car, with a corridor galley and some Business Class seats. The second car has only Business Class seats. Next comes the Cafe car, where the Infopoint, the open-plan area for people with restricted mobility, some Business Class seats, and the cafe are all located. The other four cars are reserved for Economy Class, and the end car also has a family area with a children's movie theater. The Viennese strategic design company Spirit Design did the entire interior and exterior design of the train and the railjet signature features.

SERIES DESIGNATION:	RAILJET TRAINSET
Unit configuration:	S+6M
Wheel arrangement (seven car):	7 X 2'2'
Track gauge (ft [mm]):	4' 8.5" [1,435]
Maximum speed (mph [km/h]):	143 [230]
Empty weight (t):	330
Maximum axle load (t):	17
Length (end car) (ft [mm]):	86.7 [26,450]
Length (intermediate car) (ft [mm]):	86.9 [26,500]
Length of entire train (seven car) (ft [mm]):	608.5 [185,500]
Distance between truck centers (mm):	7 x 19,000
Axle distance trailer truck (ft [mm]):	8.2 [2,500]
Trailer wheel diameter (ft [mm]):	3 [920]
Seats Premium/Business/Economy (seven unit):	408 (16/76/316)
Commissioning:	2008–2014

Manufacture of the cars began in November 2006, at Siemens TS factories in Vienna and Graz. The first car body shell was ready by August 2007, and on April 21, 2008, the first, still short, trainset celebrated its rollout from the Vienna plant. The first twenty-three units were operating by the beginning of 2010. ÖBB took an option to purchase additional units in October 2007, and ordered forty-four more trainsets. But ÖBB had probably taken too much on here, because in December 2010, the Czech Railways CD took over the last sixteen units in this order. They were to be used in the Czech Republic with Series 380 electric locomotives. As of this writing, in 2014, ÖBB's railjet fleet is expected only to include fifty-one units.

The first scheduled service began on December 14, 2008. At first, a pair of railjet trains ran from Budapest via Vienna to Munich, and another pair of trains between Vienna West and Budapest. This service was gradually expanded during the timetable year, to an every-two-hours Budapest-Vienna-Munich connection. In the 2010 timetable, an every-two-hours service to Vienna-Innsbruck-Bregenz-Zurich was added. Passengers from the Rhine-Main region, Stuttgart, Ulm, and Augsburg, were able to benefit from a new railjet special weekend connection to and from Vienna and Budapest, in the 2011 schedule. The railjet departs on Fridays and Saturdays from Budapest via Vienna, Munich, and Stuttgart, to Frankfurt (Main). It runs in the opposite direction early on Saturday morning, from Wiesbaden via Mainz, and on early Sunday morning from Frankfurt/Main via Stuttgart, Munich, and Vienna to Budapest.

Opinions on the railjet are definitely divided. One side loves the comfortable Premium and Business Classes, while the other complains about the uncomfortable seats in Economy and the uninviting, cold-food bistro. Economy passengers tend more often to conclude that the railjet is a "soulless technocrat of a train."

THE RAILJET LOCOMOTIVE

The railjet is pulled or pushed by Series 1116 (Taurus 2) dual-voltage electric locomotives; the locomotive almost always stays on one trainset and is changed only for periodic maintenance. In July 1997, Austrian Federal Railways (ÖBB) ordered a total of 382 "bulls" from Siemens Transportation Technology, fifty of the single-voltage version 1016; 282 of the dual-voltage version 1116 (16 2/3 Hz/15 kV and 50 Hz/25 kV), and another 50 triple-voltage 1216 locomotives, which could also run using 3 kV DC. The ÖBB Series 1016, 1116, and 1216 locomotives are derived from the DB Series 152. The main electrical components, the single wheel control with four pulse-width modulated (PWM) inverters, the three parallel-connected four-quadrant choppers for both DC link circuits, as well as control and operation, correspond broadly to the Series 152. There are significant differences in the front design and the construction of the trucks. The distinctive rounded shape of the train front, with its fiberglass-reinforced plastic hood, creates an aerodynamic image. The new truck, designed for high speed, was first used in the Spanish EuroSprinter. The core element is the so-called high-performance drive with separate brake shaft (HAB), which, in principle, corresponds to a hollow shaft drive

with rubber universal joints. Based on the altered drive power, the "bulls" got smaller wheels, just 1,150 mm in diameter, instead of the 3.7 ft [1,250 mm] wheels on the Series 152. The machines are about 11" [300 mm] shorter than the 152, to take account of the testing facilities in the ÖBB main repair shop in Linz.

SERIES DESIGNATION:	1116
Wheel arrangement:	Bo'Bo'
Power system:	15 kV/16 2/3 Hz; 25 kV/50 Hz
Track gauge (ft [mm]):	4' 8.5" [1,435]
Maximum speed (mph [km/h]):	143 [230]
Hourly output (kW):	
Nominal power (continuous power)(hp [kW]):	8,579 [6,400]
Service weight (t):	85
Maximum axle load (t):	21.25
Distance between buffers (ft [mm]):	63.2 [19,280]
Distance between truck centers (ft [mm]):	32.4 [9,900]
Axle distance powered truck (ft [mm]):	9.8 [3,000]
Driver wheel diameter (ft [mm]):	3.7 [1,150]
Commissioning:	2000–2006

To garner opinions on the railjet's external color scheme, ÖBB presented three different versions on electric locomotives 1016 034, 1016 035, and 1116 200. Then, in early 2007, Austria's version of the picture tabloid *Bild Zeitung* (*Kronen Zeitung*) ran on their website an opportunity to vote on what color the railjets should be painted. The color the author considers the worst—because it was darkest—won narrowly: a combination of burgundy, bright red, and gray. So far, units 1116 201 to 236 have been painted in the railjet colors. More will follow.

The railjet trainset 1116 232, replacing an out of service ICE, is commuting between Munich and Stuttgart, and here passes through Stuttgart-Untertürkheim on January 02, 2011.

PORTUGAL

In February 1996, the Portuguese State Railways CP ordered ten six-car electric Series 4000 "Penduloso" (= pendulous) railcars, similar to the Italian ETR.460, to run on CP's flagship Lisbon-Porto route. The tilting technology and trucks came from Fiat Ferroviaria, Siemens delivered the 25 kV AC electrical equipment, and the railcar parts were manufactured by ADtranz in Amadora, Portugal, where final assembly was done between 1998 and 2000. This allowed the Portuguese to generate at least some national value in making the "Penduloso." Two unpowered cars each run between two powered cars. The outer axles of each powered truck are equipped with a 684 hp [510 kW] three-phase asynchronous motor. The trucks, with their under-floor engines, had to be adapted and modified for use on Portugal's broad gauge (5.4 ft [1,668 mm]) tracks. As usual with the Pendolino, each truck has a side-mounted, active tilting mechanism. For easier maintenance, each engine and trailer truck can be replaced individually. As on the ETR.460, the end car driver's cab is housed in the characteristic Giugiaro Design train front. The gyroscope is also there; it transmits its data to the electronic control unit, which, in turn, regulates the hydraulic tilting mechanism.

There are 96 First Class seats (*Conforto [comfort]*, seat layout 2 + 1) and 203 Second Class seats (*Turistica [tourist]*, seat layout 2 + 2) in each unit. There are also two wheelchair places. Of course, the open-plan passenger area and the driver's cab have independently working air conditioners.

On July 1, 1999, after more than a year's delay, CP finally began regular service with the Pendolino multiple-unit train—named the *Alfa Pendular*—between Lisbon and Porto. On its maiden run a day before, one unit made the 209 mile [336 km] stretch in 2 hours 50 minutes. To do this, it ran at 112 mph [180 km/h] on some sections, and, near Lisbon, even at its maximum speed of 137 mph [220 km/h]. In regularly scheduled service, it initially maintained a maximum speed of 99 mph [160 km/h], and an unaltered travel time of three-and-a-half hours—the same as the locomotive-pulled Alfa trains that previously travelled between the two Portuguese cities.

To operate the new trains at full capacity, extensive upgrading projects were needed on the tracks between Lisbon and Porto. These were begun in the first quarter of 1998 and to a large extent completed by summer 2001. The upgrades included extensive modernization of the existing tracks with new rails and concrete ties.

Series designation:	4000
Road numbers:	4001-4010
Wheel arrangement (six car):	(1A)(A1)+(1A)(A1)+2'2'+2'2'+(1A) (A1)+(1A)(A1)
Power system:	25 kV/50 Hz
Track gauge (ft [mm]):	5.4 [1,668]
Maximum speed (mph [km/h]):	137 [220]
Hourly output (kW):	
Nominal power (continuous power)(hp [kW]):	5469 [4,080 (8 x 510)]
Empty weight (t), six car:	2,983
Service weight (t), six car:	325
Maximum axle load (t):	14.6
Coupling length (ft [mm]), six car:	521.3 [158,900]
End car length (ft [mm]):	90.7 [27,650]
Intermediate car length (ft [mm]):	84.9 [25,900]
Distance between truck centers (mm):	6 x 19,000
Axle distance powered truck (ft [mm]):	8.8 [2,700]
Axle distance trailer truck (ft [mm]):	8.8 [2,700]
Driver wheel diameter (ft [mm]):	2.9 [890]
Trailer wheel diameter (ft [mm]):	2.9 [890]
Seats (six car):	299 (1st class: 96, 2nd class: 203.), ((75/239))
Commissioning:	1998-2000

A number of curves were straightened to some degree, and 161 new bridges had to be built to replace level crossings. Today, the Alfa Pendular runs between Lisbon and Porto in a nearly continuous every-two-hours service, with additional hourly trains during peak periods. The fastest travel time between the two cities is currently 2:43 h. North of Porto, the Alfa Pendular continues on to Braga 33.5 mile [54 km] away, four times a day, while two pairs of trains operate south of Lisbon on the 201 mile [323 km] route to Faro. Here, the Alfa Pendular can display its full capacity; it takes just three hours from Lisbon to Faro.

NEW HIGH SPEED LINES

Portugal has meanwhile developed a "master plan" for high-speed traffic. Although it only signed the first contracts to construct high-speed lines recently, Portugal, especially hard-hit by the financial crisis, had to cut spending and therefore will significantly delay construction of new lines. As already noted, the main railway corridor in Portugal is the south-north route from Lisbon (with a metropolitan area of some 2.8 million inhabitants) to Porto (around 2 million inhabitants in the metropolitan area). Over half the Portuguese population lives within commuting distance of this rail link. The master plan calls for building a 180 mile [290 km]

long, standard gauge high speed line for speeds up to 186 mph [300 km/h]. New train stations are to be built in Rio Maior (west of Santarem), Leiria, Coimbra-B, and Aveiro. In the future, non-stop trains will only take 1:15 hours between Porto and Lisbon. The costs for this project are estimated at $5 [€3.8] billion.

A standard gauge high speed line, Madrid-Lisbon, is also planned. When it is finished, a non-stop trip between the two capitals will take no more than 2:45 hours. Some six million future passengers per year are predicted for the early years; currently, the railway gets only a minimal share of national passenger travel. The 129 mile [207 km] long Portuguese section of this high speed line will first cross the Tejo river, over an 8 mile [13 km] long new bridge. It will run generally parallel to the existing line, via Poceirão to Vendas Novas. The line will then go directly east, to a new train station at Evora, and via the most direct route, to the border between Elvas and Badajoz in Spain. The high speed line will be electrified with 25 kV/50 Hz and allow the trains to run at speeds of up to 217 mph [350 km/h].

Also under discussion are a number of expanded lines, with the first priority being planned high speed lines. From Porto, a three-rail, 155 mph [250 km/h] expansion is being planned, to run via Braga and Valenca to Spanish Vigo. Constructing the first Porto-Braga section will cost an estimated $1 billion [€845 million]. There are further plans for high speed lines from Aveiro via Viseu in Spanish Salamanca and from Evora in the south to Faro on the Algarve coast, and on to Huelva in Spain.

In the Lisbon Apolonia station, the "Penduloso" 4007 is ready for its trip to Porto on July 12, 2010.

RUSSIA

Mainly for reasons of prestige, the Soviet State Railways SZD was also preoccupied with high-speed trains at the end of the 1960s. In 1970, the car factory in Tver (TYZ), in collaboration with the SZD and the Soviet Railway Research Institute, built the turbojet-propelled prototype train RR200 "*Reaktivnaya tyaga*" (= jet thrust). It was based on the car body of a Series ER22 railcar; on this, an aerodynamically shaped driver's cab was constructed at each end. The trucks were specially developed for this project. The vehicle was revved up with two Yak 40 turbojet engines, which weighed 59.4 tons, including the fuel, and made an awful lot of noise. Its interior was equipped with various testing facilities. The train was approved on October 20, 1970, and performed its first high-speed runs on the Golutvin-Ozeri track, where it reached up to 116 mph [187 km/h] in 1971. A year later, running between Balovnoyc and Beresowka, the rail flyer's speedometer stood at 166 mph [267 km/h]. In the late 1970s and 1980s, the train was sighted, mothballed in today's Ukraine. As a monument, the train front with the two turbines is still kept today in the Tver city park, where it commemorates the 110th anniversary of the TYZ railcar factory.

THE ER200

In mid-1971, the SZD announced that it wanted to develop a high-speed railcar for the 404 mile [650 km] Moscow-Leningrad (now St. Petersburg) connection. With a top speed of 124 mph [200 km/h], travel time between the two cities was to be cut from almost five to four hours, corresponding to a cruising speed of 101 mph [162 km/h]. Depending on the traffic requirements, the new ER200 trains comprise eight to fourteen cars. The first railcar left the Riga train carriage factory (RVR) in 1974. For an entire decade, the ER200 was extensively tested; on a trial run it reached up to 147 mph [236 km/h]. As of 1984, the first scheduled service between Moscow and St. Petersburg began, running once a week. Travel time was 4 hours and 39 minutes, about 90 minutes less than a locomotive-pulled train. But because it was so unreliable, the ER200 was usually an empty train; one of the 124 mph [200 km/h] fast Skoda Cl1S200 electric locomotives had to cover for it, and be available to step up in case of complete failure. In addition to technical, there were also logistical problems; at the time, many heavy freight trains ran on this main line, and it was difficult to find even a fast track for the ER200.

THE "SOKOL"

In 1998, the Soviet government approved the "Ecological High-speed Transport" project. With this, planning began for the first Russian high speed rail line from Moscow to St. Petersburg and construction of the prototype of a new Russian high speed train, named the "Sokol" (= falcon). The "Russian joint stock company high-speed lines" (*Rossijskoje Akcionernoje Obschschcestwo Vysokoskorostnije Magistral*—RAO VSM) was founded in 1991 to be responsible for manufacturing the train. The now-Russian Transport Ministry determined the technical details for the Sokol electric high-speed train in 1993. In addition to the Rubin Central Design Bureau for Marine Engineering, some sixty other companies in the railway sector and the military were involved in the project work.

Finally, construction of the prototype, with approximately 90% of the components of Russian origin, began in 1997 at Transmasch in Tikhvin. The prototype was built as six-cars, while the later-series trains were to be built as twelve-car units. The pre-series consisted of two half-trains that had identical drive technology, but were unable to run as separate units. Each half train had an unpowered control car, a motorized intermediate car, and an unpowered transformer car. For use on rail lines electrified with 3 kV DC and 25 kV/50 Hz AC, dual-voltage equipment had to be installed. To propel the train, there were four three-phase asynchronous motors with a selective output of 576 or 905 hp [430 or 675 kW] in each half-train. The continuous power of the multiple-unit train was appropriately 6,181 or 4,611 or 7,239 hp [4,611 or 3,440 or 5,400 kW]. Braking equipment consisted of an electrodynamic, a pneumatic, and a magnetic rail brake. The prototype's interior was quite luxurious. In each of the two control cars, there were 32 First Class seats in a 2 +1 layout and a First Class compartment with five seats. In one powered intermediate car were two open plan areas with 38 First Class seats, and in the other intermediate car, two open-plan areas with 80 Second Class seats. The first transformer car provided 30 Second Class seats and a bar; the second transformer car had two open-plan areas with a total of 76 Second Class seats.

The Sokol's equipment included numerous innovations for Russian Railways, such as the asynchronous traction motors, the aluminum car bodies, vacuum toilets, and an environmentally friendly air-conditioning system. The trucks were also newly developed, with four disc brakes per axle. The upgraded Russian rail lines are designed for a speed of 124 mph [200 km/h]; on the new rail lines, trains can run at 186 mph [300 km/h]. The Sokol, with its top

An ER200 unit in the depot on July 24, 2006, getting ready for its next trip.

At the beginning of the 1990s, two units—improved in many details—were built; these units started operating in 1996 as ER200–2 and –3, between Moscow and St. Petersburg. They were replaced in December 2009 by the new "*Sapsan*" (= Peregrine Falcon). One trainset was renovated, and now runs between the capital and Nizhny Novgorod. A small unit (two intermediate and two end cars) has now found a home in the Varsawsky Vokzal Railway Museum in St. Petersburg.

SERIES DESIGNATION:	ER200
Road numbers:	1-3
Unit configuration:	S+6T+S, S+8T+S
Wheel arrangement (end car):	2'2'
Wheel arrangement (intermediate car):	Bo'Bo'
Power system:	3kV DC
Track gauge (ft [mm]):	4.9 [1,520]
Maximum speed (mph [km/h]):	124 [200]
Hourly rating powered cars (hp [kW]):	1,287 [960 (4 x 240)]
Nominal power (continuous power) powered cars (hp [kW]):	1,153 [860 (4 x 215)]
Empty weight eight car/ten car (t):	442.4/557.4
Maximum axle load (t):	17
Length eight car/ten car (ft [mm]):	695.5/840 [212,000/256,000]
Distance between truck centers railcar (ft [mm]):	61.9 [18,880]
Distance between truck centers control car (ft [mm]):	61.9 [18,880]
Axle distance powered truck (ft [mm]):	8.2 [2,500]
Axle distance trailer truck (ft [mm]):	8.2 [2,500]
Driver wheel diameter (ft [mm]):	3.1 [950]
Trailer wheel diameter (ft [mm]):	3.1 [950]
Seats eight car/ten car:	416/544
Commissioning:	1974–1992

RUSSIA

Set aside, the "Sokol" awaits better times on August 24, 2009.

speed of 155 mph [250 km/h], was definitely intended for passenger travel over distances of 435–497 miles [700–800 kilometers]. Forecasts said that, by 2010, ninety twelve-car units would be required. Of these, two units were to be run in multiple unit control. Other potential versions under discussion included a Sokol with tilting technology and a double-decker Sokol.

SERIES DESIGNATION:	VSM250 (SOKOL)
Road numbers:	
Unit configuration:	S+T+2M+T+S
Wheel arrangement (end car):	2'2'
Wheel arrangement (intermediate car):	Bo'Bo' or 2*2'
Power system:	3kV DC and 25 kV/50 Hz
Track gauge (ft [mm]):	4.9 [1,520]
Maximum speed (mph [km/h]):	155 [250]
Hourly rating powered cars (hp [kW]):	3,619 [2,700 (4 x 675)]
Hourly rating unpowered cars (hp [kW]):	3,297 [2,460 (4 x 615)]
Empty weight entire train (t):	303
Service weight entire train (t):	356
Maximum axle load (t):	17
Entire train length (ft [mm]):	518 [158,000]
Distance between truck centers (ft [mm]):	
Axle distance powered truck (ft [mm]):	
Axle distance trailer truck (ft [mm]):	
Driver wheel diameter (ft [mm]):	3 [950]
Trailer wheel diameter (ft [mm]):	3 [950]
Seats:	350
Commissioning:	1999

On July 28, 1999, the Sokol prototype was ceremonially presented in Tikhvin, 124 miles [200 kilometers] east of St. Petersburg. In the beginning of November 1999, it undertook its first tests in the

Shcherbinka test center. Trial runs followed on the 406 mile [654 km] long Moscow–St. Petersburg rail line. There, during a trial run on June 30, 2001, the Sokol struggled to reach 147 mph [236 km/h], and shortly thereafter, broke down completely.

A little later, the trials were terminated. A subsequent investigation revealed in some cases over fifty serious faults, of which only two were dealt with. The train still ran for a while on the Yaroslavl-Rybinsk route, in secondary service. The Sokol project had failed completely. The RZD alone had invested around $20.4 million U.S. to build the trains, and the total cost of the project up to then had swallowed around $450 million.

THE "SAPSAN" (VELARO RUS)

Soon afterwards, the Russian state railway company RZD decided to acquire proven and well-tested western European high-speed trains. The choice quickly fell on Siemens' Velaro. In the first exuberance, RZD ordered sixty Velaro RUS trains in November 2005. In the spring of the next year, this contract was reduced to a realistic number. On May 18, 2006, Siemens agreed with RZD to supply eight high-speed Velaro RUS trains, along with maintenance for a period of thirty years. The entire package, including the trains and the service contract, was worth approximately $790 [€600] million. The Velaro RUS is based on the Siemens high-speed train "Velaro" platform; its development began with Deutsche Bahn's ICE 3 and continued with orders from Spain and China.

The trains, marketed under the name "Sapsan" (= Peregrine), had to meet both European and Russian standards. Above all, Russia's special requirements for electromagnetic compatibility made a variety of measures necessary. The special climatic conditions had to be taken into account: the trains are fully operable in outdoor temperatures down to -104° F [-40° C]; the safety systems, even down to -122° F [-50° C]. This was possible only by using special insulating materials, so that there would be no need for additional heating. At outside temperatures of -104° F [-40° C] to +80.6° F [+27° C], the air conditioning can maintain a comfortable +72° F [+22° C] inside. The driver's cabs are equipped with individual air-conditioning as well as floor heating. In case the on-board electrical system fails, the "Sapsan" can also be heated directly from the overhead line. To avoid problems with drifting snow, the under-floor components must be cooled via air ducts from the car roof. The headlights also had to be substantially more powerful. Four single-voltage trains (EVS 1) were manufactured, to operate with 3 kV DC (Moscow-St. Petersburg) and four dual-voltage trains that

The "Sapsan" (Velaro RUS) has enjoyed more success; it has been running since December 2009 in regular service between Moscow and St. Petersburg.

could also operate using 25 kV/50 Hz AC (Moscow-Nizhny Novgorod). On the latter, the voltage systems are completely separate electrically. In normal operation, the trains are driven with alternating current, using one of the two pantographs provided for this purpose. On DC power, two of four designated pantographs must be used. The two five-car half-trains are designed with self-sufficient traction equipment, so that if one set fails, the train, still with 75% of its traction and braking power, can continue to operate. The components of both traction systems are equally distributed under the floors, and have identical power units. Four powered cars with sixteen powered trucks ensure the required acceleration of the ten-car unit. Each powered truck has two transverse-positioned three-phase asynchronous motors, as well as gears and clutch. The primary brakes are wear-free regenerative brakes in the powered trucks, which allow for energy recovery. There are also pneumatic friction brakes with wheel discs in the powered trucks, and three-wave-disc-brakes on each axle of the trailer trucks.

In the meantime, a large part of the Moscow–St. Petersburg route has been upgraded to carry trains at 124 mph [200 km/h], with some sections even customized for trains running at 155 mph [250 km/h]. On such a section, the Velaro RUS achieved a new Russian speed record of 182 mph [293 km/h] during a test run. Scheduled service began in December 2009, with three pairs of trains per day. Today, seven pairs of Sapsan trains travel between Moscow and St. Petersburg; the fastest trains make the 404 mile [650 km] distance non-stop in 3 hours 50 minutes. An average speed of 106 mph [170 km/h] is nothing unusual for Western European conditions. However,

at over 90%, this utilization is far above that usual for the German ICE.

Series designation:	Sapsan (EVS1 and EVS2)
Road numbers:	01-04 (EVS2), 05-08 (EVS1)
Unit configuration:	T+M+T+4M+T+M+T
Wheel arrangement (end car):	Bo'Bo'
Wheel arrangement (intermediate car):	Bo'Bo' or 2*2'
Power system:	3 kV DC and 25 kV/50 Hz (EVS2), only 3 kV DC (EVS1)
Track gauge (ft [mm]):	4.9 [1,520]
Maximum speed (mph [km/h]):	300 (operating maximum speed: 250)
Output powered cars (kW):	4 x 500 (total train: 8,000)
Empty weight entire train (t):	
Loaded weight entire train (t):	662 (EVS1), 678 (EVS2)
Maximum axle load (t):	17 (EVS1), 18 (EVS2)
End car length (ft [mm]):	83.7 [25,535]
Intermediate car length (ft [mm]):	79.3 [24,175]
Entire train length (ft [mm]):	821 [250,300]
Distance between truck centers (mm):	8 x 17,375
Axle distance powered truck (ft [mm]):	8.2 [2,500]
Axle distance trailer truck (ft [mm]):	8.2 [2,500]
Driver wheel diameter (ft [mm]):	3 [920]
Trailer wheel diameter (ft [mm]):	3 [920]
Seats (1st/2nd class):	604 (104+500)
Commissioning:	2008–2009

Since July 2010, the Sapsan also has run on the somewhat modernized Moscow-Nizhny Novgorod route. Initially, there was only one pair of trains, but on October 31, 2010, a second pair of trains was added. However, the travel time is just under four hours, hardly earth-shattering for the 286 mile [461 km] long distance.

SWEDEN

Sweden also began to consider how to speed up rail transport in the 1970s. The Swedish State Railways (SJ) rejected the idea of building expensive high-speed lines relatively quickly, since the country's very sparse population and, therefore, relatively low traffic potential did not justify the new lines. The key requirement was to significantly shorten the time needed to travel the relatively long distances in the "golden triangle" among the cities of Stockholm, Gothenburg, and Malmo. Finally, SJ discovered its own version of "Columbus' egg," which was using tilting trains, combined with upgrading some sections of track, and building some new ones.

Today, Sweden has about 746 miles [1,200 km] of conventional lines, upgraded for trains to run at a maximum speed of 124 mph [200 km/h]. These include stretches from Stockholm to Gothenburg, Malmo and Gavle, and to Örebro via Vasteras or Eskilstuna. Some parts of the routes from Gothenburg to Malmo, Alvesta, and on to Kalmar, Karlstad, Hallberg, and Oslo have been modernized. In addition, there is the new Botnia railway line (Botniabanan), which runs along the Baltic coast from Sundsvall almost to Kramfors (to date, an upgraded route) and continues via Örnsköldsvik to the northern Swedish university city of Urneä. It became necessary to build this 118-mile-long [190 km-long] single-track line because the north-south route from Änge to Urneä, which runs more to the interior—also a single-track line—was completely overloaded by the heavy freight traffic, was badly laid out, and consistently bypasses the few larger settlements in northern Sweden. The need to double-track this line gave the Swedes the idea not to lay the second track alongside the first, but to do something much easier, given the topography: run it along the Baltic coast, where the larger northern

Swedish cities are located. The result was to develop, instead of a second track, another route altogether, with additional benefits for the region. Trains can run on the new Botnia railway line at a maximum speed of 155 mph [250 km/h] (regional transport at 112 mph [180 km/h]), and it is equipped with the ETCS Level 2 signaling system. On August 28, 2010, the Swedish royal family festively inaugurated the first link, between Umea and Ornskoldsvik. In December 2011, the entire route opened with the new X62.

The airport express train to Stockholm Arlanda Airport occupies a special place of its own. It was built for trains that travel at 124 mph [200 km/h], and began operation on August 20, 1999. The existing Stockholm–Uppsala main route between Stockholm and Rosersberg was also expanded from two to four tracks. The double-tracked airport loop, which branches at Rosersberg and Odensala from the main Stockholm–Uppsala line, is 13.6 miles [22 km] long. Some 5.7 miles [9.2 km] of the track run through tunnels. The northern section to Odensala is only for regional and Intercity traffic, while the southern section is also used for the Arlanda Express. There are now three different train stations located in the tunnel section beneath the airport. One is for regional and IC traffic, while the other two stations allow direct access from the Arlanda Express to the four airport terminals. The construction and operation contract, worth $790 [€600] million and including an operating license until 2040, was awarded to the Arlanda Link Consortium (ARL), as part of a "public-private partnership." The consortium included the companies NCC, Siab, Vattenfall, Mowlem, and Alstom. NCC and Siab carried out the civil engineering, Mowlem was responsible for track

construction, and Vattenfall installed energy supply facilities. Alstom undertook the signal technology for the tracks, telecommunications, and supplying of the Arlanda Express trains, along with maintenance facilities.

Sweden is also considering construction of the so-called "*Europabanan*," a new high-speed line from Stockholm via Jönköping to Gothenburg and further south to Malmö or Helsingborg. The route will then continue across the Oresund Bridge, through Denmark, and to Germany. It is still uncertain if this route—which would be 460 miles [740 km] long and cost at least $18 billion [€14 billion]—will be built.

Still in bright sunshine, an X2 unit departs from Lund train station, while storm clouds lurk in the background.

THE TRAINS

Although the Swedish rail speed record is 188 mph [303 km/h], only the following trains can even travel at up to 124 mph [200 km/h]: The Series X2 tilting trains (brand name X2000), the X3 (Arlanda Express), the X40 regional multiple unit train (Alstom double-decker railcars), the Regina Series X50, X52, and X54 trains from various operators, and the Norwegian state railway NSB's BM73B on the Oslo-Gothenburg connection. There are twenty Regina Series X55 railcars to be delivered, which the SJ wants to use in the future for long-distance transport, with the name SJ3000.

X2

It makes little sense to construct fast new railway lines in Sweden, with its very unusual population structure and hilly and mountainous landscape. The Swedish State Railways (SJ) chose a different way. After promising attempts using a two-car X1 trainset, with tilting technology based on air suspension, in 1973, SJ decided to develop—together with the manufacturer ASEA (later ABB Traction, then ADtranz, then Bombardier)—a 137 mph [220 km/h] fast tilting train. More tests with a three-car X5 trainset followed in 1975. Comparative tests of pneumatic and hydraulic tilting systems were done, and the hydraulic system prevailed. The drive configuration remained controversial for a long time; ultimately, the decision was in favor of electric power units without tilting technology. This made it possible to use a simple method to mount the pantograph, which cannot tilt along with the car. In August 1986, SJ ordered twenty six-car X2 multiple-unit trains. The standard configuration was to be one power car, four intermediate cars, and a control car. If necessary, these

could be supplemented by a fifth intermediate car. In principle, trains could also be set up using two power cars and up to twelve intermediate cars.

Each power car is driven by four 1,092 hp [815 kW] three-phase asynchronous motors, controlled by GTO thyristors. The tilting technology, in the intermediate and control cars, is controlled by an accelerometer in whichever vehicle is leading, depending on the direction the train is travelling. As usual, the tilt angle depends on speed and curve radius; the measurement is made on the trucks in each car and adjusted hydraulically. The X2's computer-controlled hydraulic tilt adjustment lies below the secondary suspension level. The operating cylinder, mounted low in the truck, is activated by a lateral accelerometer, and then tilts the car bodies when rounding curves in the track, into the curve. The tilt angle is a maximum of 6.5 degrees, so that the cars change their tilt angle at most four degrees per second. Special features on the X2 are the radial-steered individual axles on the truck. This allows each axle to adjust its alignment on Sweden's very curvy rail lines, significantly reducing friction, saving energy consumption, and lowering material wear. As already noted, the power cars themselves do not have tilt technology, but the special driver's seat is designed with reinforced lateral support, to offset increased lateral acceleration.

The ABB factory in Vasteras delivered the first X2 in August 1989. Just over a year later, in September 1990, scheduled service began, with just one trainset travelling between Stockholm and Gothenburg. After more units were completed from 1992 onward, the Stockholm-Malmö, Stockholm-Sundsvall and Gothenburg-Malmö routes have also enjoyed running the new trains. SJ created the new brand name "X2000" for the X2-driven trains; over time, this also became the name for the trains themselves.

The X2000 achieved considerable savings in travel time: in winter 1993–94, the fastest X2000, running at a top speed of 124 mph [200 km/h], needed just

2 hours 54 minutes to make the 283 mile [456 km] Stockholm-Gothenburg connection. In winter 1989–90, the fastest locomotive-pulled train had slunk along at a maximum 99 mph [160 km/h], taking 3 hours and 49 minutes on that route. Up to 1998, SJ acquired a total of forty-three X2 from ABB. These were, in part, combined into five or seven-car units. These trains allowed SJ to further extend the network serviced by the X2000. Between 2000 and 2001, some trains have been converted for service to Denmark via the Öresund connection, and to run in Norway. In addition to Danish and Norwegian train control systems, the power units intended for Denmark required dual-voltage equipment, since the Danish long-distance routes have a different system, 25 kV/50 Hz. There are now three sub-series:

• X2K (operating in Denmark): 2036, 2043
• X2N (operating in Norway): 2029, 2030, 2035, 2042
• X2NK (operating in Norway and Denmark): 2031, 2034, 2038

In autumn 2003, SJ decided to modernize all its X2 trains. The first train was given a makeover in February 2005. It emerged with a completely renovated interior, including Wi-Fi and cell phone amplifiers to improve reception. The new exterior gray color scheme, is, however, in the author's humble opinion, a big step backwards and, in fact, the "lowliest" color in the world. Refurbishment of all units was completed in spring 2007. From the very beginning, the X2 trainsets were intended to run in multiple unit operation. At first, this potential was used rarely. Scheduled service of double X2 units has only increased in recent years. To facilitate the now more frequently used coupling operations, starting in 2007, the noses of a number of power cars and control cars were reworked, in a "aesthetically unpleasant" way, that exposes the Scharfenberg couplers. So, the couplings, with the external casing on the nose outside

removed, were now exposed to wind and weather. It was soon realized that protection had to be improved. The first new nose casing and retractable couplers were tested in 2009. Although the X2 was allowed to run in Sweden—if at all possible—at 130 mph [210 km/h], SJ computed the schedules for a speed of 124 mph [200 km/h]. But this did not set limits for the X2 for long, as a trainset proved on its record run of July 21, 1993, when the speedometer stayed at 171 mph [276 km/h]. Export opportunities were also explored: In 1991, an X2 trainset created a great sensation with its demonstration runs on the German Federal Railroad's rail lines. One unit even ended up overseas. In 1992, Amtrak, responsible for long-distance rail travel in the U.S., tested the Swedish tilting train, among others, on the so-called Boston-New York-Philadelphia East Coast Corridor. Unfortunately, these efforts were to no avail, and only the neighboring country Norway, after trial runs of the X2, ordered tilting trains based on the X2.

SERIES DESIGNATION:	X2
Road numbers:	2001-2043
Wheel arrangement (six car):	Bo'Bo'+2'2'+2'2'+2'2'+2'2'+2'2'
Power system:	15 kV/16 2/3 Hz
Track gauge (ft [mm]):	4' 8.5" [1,435]
Maximum speed (mph [km/h]):	**130 [210]**
Hourly output (hp [kW]):	5,362 [4,000 (4 x 1,000)]
Nominal power (continuous power)(hp [kW]):	4,370 [3,260 (4 x 815)]
Empty weight (t):	344 (six car), 366 (seven car)
Maximum axle load (t):	18.5
Coupling length (ft [mm]):	457 [139,225 (six car)], 541 [165,000 (seven car)]
Power car length (ft [mm]):	58.2 [17,750]
Control car length (ft [mm]):	72.1 [21,980]
Intermediate car length (ft [mm]):	80 [24,400]
Distance between truck centers (mm):	8,975 + 4 x 17,700 +14,250
Axle distance powered truck (ft [mm]):	9.5 [2,900]
Axle distance trailer truck (ft [mm]):	9.5 [2,900]
Driver wheel diameter (ft [mm]):	**3.6 [1,100]**
Trailer wheel diameter (ft [mm]):	2.8 [880]
Seats (four car):	261 (six car), 309 (seven car)
Commissioning:	1989–1998

X55

SJ, the Swedish State Railways, ordered twenty new Regina trains from Bombardier in May 2008, this time for long-distance service. The four-car trainsets, including three powered cars, were designed with a more spacious interior layout than previous Regina units. In the Second Class, seating is now arranged 2 + 2 instead of 3 + 2.

Unit 3747, one of the first new X55s, in the Stockholm Hägalund depot on May 27, 2011, for start-up and personnel training.

SERIES DESIGNATION:	X55
Road numbers:	3344-3363
Wheel arrangement (four cars):	Bo'Bo'+Bo'Bo'+2'2'+Bo'Bo'
Power system:	15 kV/16 2/3 Hz
Track gauge (ft [mm]):	4' 8.5" [1,435]
Maximum speed (mph [km/h]):	124 [200]
Nominal power (continuous power) (hp [kW]):	4,263 [3,180 (12 x 265)]
Service weight (t):	274
Maximum axle load (t):	18.5
Coupling length (ft [mm]):	351.3 [107,100]
End car length (ft [mm]):	88.4 [26,950]
Intermediate car length (ft [mm]):	87.2 [26,600]
Distance between truck centers (mm):	19,000 + 19,000 +19,000 +19,000
Axle distance powered truck (ft [mm]):	8.8 [2,700]
Axle distance trailer truck (ft [mm]):	8.8 [2,700]
Driver wheel diameter (ft [mm]):	2.7 [840]
Trailer wheel diameter (ft [mm]):	2.7 [840]
Seats 1st /2nd class (four cars):	64/181
Commissioning:	2010 –

An "Arlanda Express" (X3) makes its way through the Stockholm Central Station railway yard.

SERIES DESIGNATION:	X3 (ARLANDA EXPRESS)
Road numbers:	1-7
Wheel arrangement (four car):	Bo'Bo'+2'2'+2'2'+Bo'Bo'
Power system:	15 kV/16 2/3 Hz
Track gauge (ft [mm]):	4' 8.5" [1,435]
Maximum speed (mph [km/h]):	124 [200]
Nominal power (continuous power) (hp [kW]):	3,003 [2,240 (8 x 280)]
Empty weight (t):	193.2
Maximum axle load (t):	16
Coupling length (ft [mm]):	305.3 [93,084]
End car length (ft [mm]):	78.7 [23,992]
Intermediate car length (ft [mm]):	73.9 [22,550]
Distance between truck centers (mm):	15,600 +15,600 +15,600 +15,600
Axle distance powered truck (ft [mm]):	8.3 [2,560]
Axle distance trailer truck (ft [mm]):	8.3 [2,560]
Driver wheel diameter (ft [mm]):	3 [920]
Trailer wheel diameter (ft [mm]):	3 [920]
Seats (four car):	190
Commissioning:	1998–1999

One of the intermediate cars also got a bistro area. The manufacturer named these railcars the "Intercity Regina;" in SJ service they are "Regina Alpha;" while the official series designation is X55. The car bodies, trucks, and electrical equipment, in general, correspond to those of the conventional Regina trainsets, while the interior design and color scheme reflect the X2 (X2000). This includes state-of-the-art Internet access and information systems. The new X55 will provide a top speed of 124 mph [200 km/h]. This can be increased, if required, after the appropriate modifications, to 155 mph [250 km/h]. The Intercity Regina will run mainly on the Stockholm-Borlänga/Falun, Stockholm-Karlstad and Gothenburg-Ämäl-Karlstad connections; this is intended to relieve several X2 trains, which then can be transferred to connections in greater demand, between Stockholm-Gothenburg, Sundsvall-Stockholm, and Malmö-Stockholm. The X55 will operate in the future as the "SJ3000." Although the first trains were to be delivered as early as April 2010, there were minor delays on the part of the manufacturer. The first train from Germany only started service in Vasteras, Sweden, in August.

X3 (ARLANDA EXPRESS)

For the "Arlanda Express," GEC Alsthom (now Alstom) supplied seven four-car, somewhat futuristic looking, X3 Series electric railcars. Around 305 feet [93 meters] long, they offer 190 seats and storage space for 250 large pieces of luggage. Drive power comes from four IGBT-controlled three-phase asynchronous motors in both end cars; the engines each have a capacity of 375 hp [280 kW] and can generate a top speed of 124 mph [200 km/h]. The welded aluminum construction car bodies were supplied by GEC Alsthom Transport in Barcelona. GEC's subsidiary Metro Cammell, in Birmingham, England, was in charge of the electrical equipment and final assembly. The X3 had to get a "nose job" in 2003–04, to make it easier to get at the couplings. In 2010, the trains got a full-scale renovation and a slightly changed color scheme—but still in the primary colors of yellow and gray.

The railcar's passenger area gives a very solid impression. A designer individually planned each of the seven units, including selecting colors and patterns. The trains, with their comfortable seats and equipped with several information systems, meet airplane Business

Class standards. There was also a good solution for wheeled luggage. There is a centrally located, large, and very visible luggage rack in one of the two boarding areas of each of the four cars, in which just about any suitcase can safely stand or lie down. The whole of the train is also well-designed for disabled people; everything is accessible: wheelchairs and their occupants have both extra-large "parking spaces" and their own restrooms on board. Between 5:05 AM and 10:35 PM, the Arlanda Express runs daily in 15-minute intervals, and even more frequently during peak hours from Monday to Friday. The train makes the 24 mile [39 km] long connection in just 20 minutes, and reaches a top speed of 124 mph [200 km/h] on many stretches.

Still without markings, the X52-2 3260 is on display for in-house photographers.

FAST RAILCARS FOR REGIONAL TRANSPORT: THE REGINA RAILCARS, SERIES X50 TO X54

The development of the Regina trains can actually be accredited to the restructuring of the Swedish railways, which started in the late 1980s. Until then, only the state railway SJ was responsible for regional and inter-regional train travel. After the deregulation of the Swedish railways, from 1990 on, regional authorities obtained the right to organize railway transport in their respective regions, using their own trains. The transport authorities quickly realized that it would be more economical to cooperate when acquiring a larger share of any new train series, which then could be adapted in their specifications, to fulfill the needs of each operator. As a result, in 1999 they founded, together with ADtranz, the joint venture "*Transitio*" (= transitioning), which was to undertake rail vehicle purchasing. Of course, it was still possible for the operators to obtain vehicles at their own expense, if this should prove advantageous.

With this as background, in the late 1990s, the manufacturer ADtranz (now Bombardier) developed a new electric railcar, named the Regina. The vehicles are specially adapted to the Swedish vehicle clearance profile, which allowed the trains to be wider and thus able to carry more people (with seating). The basic version of the Regina train was first designed with two cars (Series X50-2 to 54-2). To add an unpowered intermediate car, they also produced the Series X50-3, X52-3, and X53-3. A 2010 redesign created the four-car X55, which also has a powered intermediate car. The attractive front end is aerodynamically designed, and is made of fiberglass-reinforced plastic covering an underlying steel structure. The 11.3 ft [3,450 mm] wide car body is adapted to the Swedish clearance

gauge; the Second Class cars accommodate a 3 + 2 seat layout. The 4.2 ft [1,300 mm] wide doors have a lower access for 1.9 ft [580 mm] high platforms, and are equipped with wheelchair lifts. They also allow quick entry and exit for passengers with bulky luggage, shortening the time the train has to stop in the station and thus cutting travel time. In the two-car trains, six of the eight axles are powered. This generates good acceleration, at about 2.6 ft/s2 [0.8 m/s2], as well as fast and effective braking with the regenerative electromagnetic-dynamic brakes. The latter contribute significantly to the trains' low energy consumption. They are powered by three-phase asynchronous motors and controlled by IGBT rectifiers. Up to three units can run together in multiple traction operation.

On August 27, 2000, the first "Regina" was introduced to an admiring public. On January 18, 2001, the first unit went into service with *Västmanlands Lokaltrafik* (= VL, regional traffic around Vasteras). The rail operators ordered fifty trains at this point, six for *Västtrafik* (= VT, Gothenburg regional service) and the other forty-four for *Transitio*.

But the start up had its problems. Even the trains delivered during the winter were not cold-resistant. After most of the trains had been delivered, the operators suffered serious losses during the following cold season (winter 2001–02); *Tag i Bergslagen* (= TiB, Borlänge regional service) and *X-Trafik* (Gävle regional service) were especially hard hit. There were three different problems: the wheels wore out more quickly than expected, and the pantograph valves and the water pipes froze. Over time, however, Bombardier (which took over ADtranz in mid-2001) was able to resolve the difficulties, and the trains now run to their operators' satisfaction.

Regina railcars now carry a significant part of Swedish regional rail traffic, mainly for the central Swedish rail operators in Bergslagen (TiB), Gävle

Passengers disembarking from an X-Trafik Regina railcar.

Series designation:	X50-2 to X54-2	X50-3, X52-3, X53-3
Road numbers:	See next table	
Wheel arrangement:	Bo'Bo'+2'Bo'	Bo'Bo'+2'2'-i-Bo'Bo'
Power system:	15 kV/16 2/3 Hz	15 kV/16 2/3 Hz
Track gauge (ft [mm]):	4' 8.5" [1,435]	4' 8.5" [1,435]
Maximum speed (mph [km/h]):	See next table	
Nominal power (continuous power) (hp [kW]):	2131 [1,590 (6 x 265)]	2,842 [2,120 (8 x 265)]
Service weight (t):	142	203
Maximum axle load (t):	18.5	18.5
Coupling length (ft [mm]):	176.8 [53,900]	264 [80,500]
End car length (ft [mm]):	88.4 [26,950]	88.4 [26,950]
Intermediate car length (ft [mm]):	–	87.2 [26,600]
Distance between truck centers (mm):	19,000 + 19,000	3 x 19,000
Axle distance powered truck (ft [mm]):	8.8 [2,700]	8.8 [2,700]
Axle distance trailer truck (ft [mm]):	8.8 [2,700]	8.8 [2,700]
Driver wheel diameter (ft [mm]):	2.7 [840]	2.7 [840]
Trailer wheel diameter (ft [mm]):	2.7 [840]	2.7 [840]
Seats 1st /2nd class:	See next table	
Commissioning:	2001–2004	2001–2004

(*X-Trafik*), Uppland/Uppsala (*Upplands Lokaltrafik* = Upplands regional service, UL), Karlstadt/Värmland (*Värmlandstrafik* = VTAB) and Götaland (= VT). Regina units find themselves at home even in northern Sweden: for a time they ran between Lulea and Umea, and still do today as the "*Mittnabotäget*" between Sundsvall and Östersund.

From 2005, Bombardier began a series of trials, in collaboration with SJ, to develop a new, fast long-distance train to supplement the already proven X2. The trains were to use energy-saving drive technology and be built with environmentally friendly, ecological components. For this "*Gröna Taget*" (Green Train) project, Bombardier modified Regina railcar No. 9062 from the Transitio pool, using new permanent magnet motors, trucks, pantographs, and a new braking system. On July 26, 2006, the train set the new Swedish speed record of 175 mph [281 km/h], travelling between Skövde and Töreboda (on the Stockholm-Gothenburg route). The old record in Sweden, set by an X2, had

Type	Road no.	Former Road no.	Number	VU (operator)	Top speed	Seats (1st/2nd class + folding.)
X50-2	9001-9004	3242-3245	4	TiM (SJ)	200	0/166 + 28
X50-2	9053-9055	304-306	3	UL (SJ)	160	0/161 + 19
X50-2	9061	208	1	TKAB (X-Trafik)	200	0/166 + 28
X51-2	9007-9009	203-205	3	TiB	180	0/164 + 20
X51-2	9010, 9011	206-207	2	TKAB (X-Trafik)	180	0/164 + 20
X51-2	9012-15/18-25	3248-3259	12	TiB (Tägkompaniet)	180	19/127 + 19
X52-2	9066-9067	9066-9067	2	VTAB (Tägkompaniet)	200	19/129 + 23
X52-2	9032/33/51/52/63-65	3268/69, 9051/52/63-65	7	UL (SJ)	200	19/129 + 23
X52-2	9035	3271	1	Skänetrafiken (Arriva)	200	19/129 + 23
X52-2	9016, 9037, 9039	3260*), 3273, 3275	3		200	19/129 +23,*) 0/132 + 19
X52-2	9036/38/40/41	3272/74/76/77	4	VT	200	19/129 + 23
X52-2	9017, 9034, 9042	3261*), 3270, 3278	2	Mittnabotäget, Norrskenan (Veolia)	200	19/129 +23,*) 0/132 + 19
X52-2	9062 (Green train)		1	Transitio (test train Bombardier)	200	19/129 + 23
X53-2	9048-9050	3284-3286	3	VTAB (Tägkompaniet)	180	0/161 + 19
X54-2	9005/06/56/57	3246/47/87/88	4	TiB (Tägkompaniet)	200	19/122 + 20
X54-2	9068		1		200	19/122 + 20
X50-3	3262-3263, 3289-3296	3262-3263, 3289-3296	10	VT	200	0/304 + 35
X52-3	9043	3279	1	Mittnabotäget (Veolia)	200	19/226 + 27
X52-3	9044	3280	1	Reserve Transitio	200	19/226 + 27
X52-3	9045-9047	3281-3283	3		200	19/226 + 27
X53-3	3264-3267	3264-3267	4	VT	180	0/267 + 27

been 171 mph [276 km/h]. On September 14, 2008, the *"Gröna Taget"* was able to accelerate up to 188 mph [303 km/h], and reached that speed again on the Skövde-Töreboda section of the (conventional) Gothenburg-Stockholm main line. On August 30, 2010, service started on the first Umea-Örnsköldsvik section of the new Botniabanan, which is exclusively equipped with an ETCS Level 2 signaling system. Since the "Green Train" is the only train in Sweden that had this signaling system, it first had to undergo many test runs and provisionally started regular service in late August.

CORADIA DUPLEX X40

In December 2000, Alstom was awarded a contract from the Swedish State Railways SJ to supply sixteen two-car and twenty-seven three-car Type "CORADIA Duplex" units. This selection would make it possible to run up to six two-car trainsets in multiple-unit operation. Sweden's harsh climate required special features to ensure that trains function correctly, even in winter. The X40 is designed to operate in a temperature range between +104° F [+40° C] in summer and -95° C [-35° C] in an ice-cold winter, and it was necessary that the trains could be modified to operate at even lower temperatures, down to -104° F [-76° C]. Special precautionary measures were required to prevent the couplings, doors, and steps from icing up. The snow plow built into the head car can handle snow up to 1.9 ft [60 cm] deep and is so constructed that, in case of collision with a moose or an automobile, the railcars are still able to drive. Traction is generated by a powered truck equipped with two three-phase asynchronous motors, with a continuous power of 536 hp [400 kW] each in every car. The motors are controlled by a roof-mounted IGBT inverter. This creates enough drive power for a tolerable acceleration of 2 ft/s2 [0.64 m/s2]. The primary conventional coil-spring suspension and secondary air suspension ensure a comfortable ride. The car bodies are constructed of lightweight steel, so that it was possible to install a large part of the electrical equipment on the roof above the passenger compartment.

Passenger comfort was top priority for the interior design. A 2 + 2 seat layout was chosen, and the seats themselves resemble TGV seats, including armrests and headrests. There are tables for each four-seat group. All seats have an audio entertainment system. Important passenger information is displayed in extra-large lettering and is easily readable from every seat. Each trainset also has a multi-functional area, where there are vending machines for tickets, snacks, and drinks and enough storage space for strollers and bicycles.

The first Coradia Duplex was available for tests in Sweden by February 2004. Only a year later, the trains began scheduled service. But as is often the case with new vehicles, initially, the technical problems piled up. Non-functioning automatic door closings, air conditioners, and vending machines all caused frequent visits to the workshop.

In 2006, an attempt to use these trains for long-distance service between Stockholm and Gothenburg—for which they were never intended—ended up as a failure. Passengers complained about lack of space between seats and lack of luggage racks. The interiors were then converted to significantly reduce the number of seats in favor of more space. The original 182 seats in the two-car trains and 290 seats in the three-car trains, were cut by over 20%, satisfying passenger demand. The rail operators gradually got the problems under control, and the X40 now runs reliably in the Stockholm region, on the routes in Mälardalen, between Stockholm and Uppsala, and on the Linköping-Gävle-Ljusdal connection.

SERIES DESIGNATION:	X40-2 X40-3
Road numbers:	3301-3343 (16 two car, 27 three car)
Wheel arrangement (two-, three-car):	Bo'2'+2'Bo' or Bo'2'+2'Bo'+2'Bo'
Power system:	15 kV/16 2/3 Hz
Track gauge (ft [mm]):	4' 8.5" [1,435]
Maximum speed (mph [km/h]):	200
Hourly rating (hp [kW]):	2,681 [2,000 (4 x 500)], 4,021 [3,000 (6 x 500)]
Nominal power (continuous power) (hp [kW]):	2,145 [1,600 (4 x 400)], 3,217 [2,400 (6 x 400)]
Empty weight (t):	140 (two car), 205 (three car)
Maximum axle load (t):	22,5
Coupling length (ft [mm]):	180.7 [55,100] (two car), 267.3 [81,500] (three car)
End car length (ft [mm]):	90.3 [27,550]
Intermediate car length (ft [mm]):	86.6 [26,400]
Distance between truck centers (mm):	2 x 20,000, 3 x 20,000
Axle distance powered truck (ft [mm]):	8.2 [2,500]
Axle distance trailer truck (ft [mm]):	8.2 [2,500]
Driver wheel diameter (ft [mm]):	3 [920]
Trailer wheel diameter (ft [mm]):	3 [920]
Seats (two-, three car):	two car: 8/109 + 23, three car: 8/189 + 33
Commissioning:	2004-2008

Only in such a setting does the nondescript gray paint make sense: the three-car X40 3326 surrounded by forest, with blue sky and almost blue sea.

SWITZERLAND

Although Switzerland, with its curving rail lines in Alpine country, is literally predestined for tilting technology, the Swiss Federal Railways (SBB), at first, observed the development of tilting technology with only a passive interest. The "Railway 2000" program was adopted in 1985, which included making significant improvements in public transport. In 1991, Swiss railways began trial runs using the Italian Pendolino prototye ETR.401 and the Swedish X 2000. As early as 1993, the SBB recognized that its ambitious "Rail 2000" project could not be carried out by building new lines for higher speed, due to the high cost. Under the motto "technology instead of concrete," the SBB decided to achieve key cuts in travel time by using tilting trains. But instead of ordering a Pendolino derivative from Fiat, SBB wanted a completely newly designed tilting train, which, above all, would take into account the Pendolino's shortcomings: its tilting technology was too slow for the rapidly twisting Swiss railway network, and would not have made the desired acceleration possible.

The Swiss rail industry meanwhile had developed four versions of tilting systems, and their findings now flowed into the new project. To stay on the safe side, the consortium decided to build a four-car pre-series train. The ICN test train was already rolling over the Swiss rail tracks by July 1998, after a record construction time of only twenty-one months. Although the prototype met the test requirements, the level of vibration at high speeds forced changes in the design when the series was manufactured, such as reinforcing the car box construction with new sidewall profiles, and installing supporting bulkheads and cross bars in the car floors.

The ICN series trains consist of two end cars and five intermediate cars; in this configuration, there is an identical end car and one intermediate car in every half-train, so that overall there are five different types of cars: four Second Class cars, two of which are end cars, a First Class car, a half-dining car with First Class compartments, and a First Class car with a service and a luggage compartment. The ICN traction and auxiliary equipment are redundantly designed and distributed along the first three cars, i.e., the powered end cars, the powered intermediate converter car and the unpowered intermediate transformer car. In the event a traction unit fails, this system ensures that 50% of the drive power is still available, as well as 100% of the power for auxiliary and passenger comfort systems. The trucks were developed by FIAT-SIG for running on very curvy routes with tight curve radii, and on straight lines at high speed.

SWITZERLAND

The "NAVIGATOR" system lateral-car-body-control for the axles could cope equally well with contrary conditions, adhering to the rails when running around curves, and traveling steady and straight ahead at high speed. The tilt bolster is guided on rollers on the under-car frame and includes an integrated electromechanical tilt drive with passive box centering in case the tilting system fails. The eight powered axles are driven by a cardan shaft, which connects the under-floor three-phase asynchronous motors to the powered truck's final drive. In the FIAT-SIG technology electromechanical tilting system, the car body is supported on the truck with a central air spring suspension on a roller cradle and is secured against tipping by an anti-roll bar on each truck. The car body can tilt up to 8° going into the curve. To ensure the pantograph maintains secure contact with the overhead catenary wire as the car body tilts, there is a separate electromechanical pantograph tilting system, which always keeps it vertically aligned to the track middle.

The car body shells used integral construction of extruded aluminum profiles. The Italian design firm Pininfarina created the train front. The design is based on aesthetics and aerodynamics; the train front is essentially a fiberglass-reinforced plastic layer (GRP train head car). By May 2000, the SBB put the new trains, which had been delivered in rapid succession from December 1999 on, into regular service, but at first, so to speak, with the hand brake on. The tilting trains ran mostly in double traction and had to get to their destinations, just like regular trains. A tilting system failure would not have completely disrupted the timetable, but did not occur, anyway. Since the SBB timetable change in June 2001, the tilting trains have been running regularly, using this technology in a new schedule at shorter intervals. On the St. Gallen to Geneva route, passengers now saved at least nineteen minutes. The technology shortened travel time between Zurich and Lausanne/Geneva by fifteen minutes, and from Basel SBB to Geneva, by seven minutes.

To expand ICN service to another rail line (Basel-Geneva), the SBB decided on May 29, 2001, to buy a second series of ten ICN units. Differences with Bombardier concerning the factory in Pratteln, however, delayed the order to July 26. A little later, the SBB honored another option for ten trains, so that by 2005, the ICN fleet was up to forty-four units.

The ICN were also not immune to growing pains: on July 29, 2001, the RABDe 500 019 derailed in Zurich-Oerlikon, after a cardan shaft broke. Two weeks later, hikers found part of a navigator from an ICN truck on an open stretch of rail track. The entire fleet of ICN was taken out of service until all 54,600 screw

connections on the trucks were checked. In fact, some had to be tightened. By the end of August, all ICN units were running again. Since these incidents, the ICN has demonstrated its high-level operational availability and reliability. The ICN is also the culmination of a remarkable development: it was the last "customized" vehicle for rapid long-distance traffic, tailored to the needs of a railway company. Today, the picture is determined by global corporations with off-the-shelf products, which, with a few modifications, can be used all over the world.

ICN RABDe 500 002 "Annemarie Schwarzenbach" arriving at the Baden train station on October 10, 2009.

SERIES DESIGNATION:	RABDe 500
Road numbers:	500 000-043
Unit configuration:	T+T+M+M+M+T+T
Wheel arrangement (railcar):	(1A)(A1)
Wheel arrangement (intermediate car):	2'2'
Power system:	15 kV/16 2/3 Hz
Track gauge (ft [mm]):	4' 8.5" [1,435]
Maximum speed (mph [km/h]):	124 [200]
Power output powered cars (hp [kW]):	2 x 871 [2 x 650]
Nominal power (continuous power) (hp [kW]):	6,970 [5,200 (8 x 650)]
Empty weight (t):	355
Service weight (t):	395
Maximum axle load (t):	16.5
End car length (ft [mm]):	88.2 [26,900]
Intermediate car length (ft [mm]):	86.1 [26,270]
Entire train length (ft [mm]), seven car:	619.4 [188,800]
Distance between truck centers (mm):	7 x 19,900
Axle distance powered truck (ft [mm]):	8.8 [2,700]
Axle distance trailer truck (ft [mm]):	8.8 [2,700]
Driver wheel diameter (ft [mm]):	2.6 [820]
Trailer wheel diameter (ft [mm]):	2.6 [820]
Seats:	480 (125 + 326 + 23 + 6)
Commissioning:	1999-2005

76

SLOVENIA

To accelerate rail transport on their main Maribor-Ljubljana line, in 1998, the Slovenian Railways SZ (*Slovenske Zeleznice*) ordered three units of a train with tilting technology from Fiat Ferroviaria, in neighboring Italy. The train design corresponded to that of the FS ETR.460. The Slovenian 310, as an "off-the-shelf train," has only three cars, unlike the ETR.460. It consists of two powered end cars and an unpowered intermediate car. It runs using only 3 kV DC; a single pantograph on each end car is sufficient. On the end car trucks, as usual, the inner axles are powered by a 657 hp [490 kW] three-phase asynchronous motor. The interior design was adapted to the needs of the SZ. In the oddly numbered end cars, passenger space is divided into First and Second Class areas. After the driver's cab comes a First Class open-plan area with thirty seats arranged 2 +1. The Second Class also has an open-plan area with thirty seats (seat layout 2 + 2). The Bistro is in the intermediate car (facing the First Class), which takes up about one-third of the car. The whole setup is completed with another Second Class open-plan area with forty-two seats (seat layout 2 + 2). The second end car has a Second Class open-plan area with sixty-two seats (seat layout 2 + 2), two wheelchair spaces, and one restroom for the handicapped.

All three Pendolino trains were ready just in time for Slovenia's timetable change on September 24, 2000, and regular service using this new ICS train type (InterCity *Slovenija*) could be started between Ljubljana and Maribor. There was little change in this service in the 2011 timetable year: six pairs of ICS trains run Monday to Friday between Ljubljana and Maribor (ICS 11 to 14, 17 to 23, and 26). From late June to the end of August, one ICS runs daily, and a second on weekends from Ljubljana on to Köper and back (ICS 28–29 and 32–33). Using tilting trains made it possible to cut travel time on the 97 mile [156 km] Maribor-Ljubljana route to just under 30 minutes. The fastest ICS makes the trip in 1 hour 48 minutes, while the fastest locomotive-drawn trains take exactly 2 hours 14 minutes.

SERIES DESIGNATION:	310/316
Road numbers:	310 001-006, 316 001-003
Unit configuration:	T+M+T (310+316+310)
Wheel arrangement (railcar):	(1A)(A1)
Wheel arrangement (intermediate car):	2'2'
Power system:	3kV DC
Track gauge (ft [mm]):	4' 8.5" [1,435]
Maximum speed (mph [km/h]):	124 [200]
Power output powered cars (kW):	2 x 490
Nominal power (continuous power) (hp [kW]):	2,627 [1,960 (4 x 490)]
Empty weight (t):	152
Service weight (t):	164.5
Maximum axle load (t):	14.75
End car length (ft [mm]):	90.5 [27,600]
Intermediate car length (ft [mm]):	84.9 [25,900]
Entire train length (ft [mm]):	266.4 [81,200]
Distance between truck centers (mm):	3 x 19,000
Axle distance powered truck (ft [mm]):	8.8 [2,700]
Axle distance trailer truck (ft [mm]):	8.8 [2,700]
Driver wheel diameter (ft [mm]):	2.9 [890]
Trailer wheel diameter (ft [mm]):	2.9 [890]
Seats:	166 (30 + 134 + 2)
Commissioning:	2000

SPAIN

The history of Spanish high-speed rail transport began on October 11, 1986, when the government decided to increase investment in the nation's railroads. The first discussion was whether to modernize and expand the existing rail network, or take the plunge into the cold waters of high-speed transport. Ultimately, the decision was in favor of high-speed systems; for the first high speed rail line to be built, the government chose the Madrid-Seville connection. Before 1986, making the trip from Madrid to Seville required travelling a long, indirect route on a 356.6 mile [574 km], single-tracked line, and took nearly six hours. Technically, this was the worst bottleneck in the network. The 1992 Seville Expo gave the government both a point in time and a goal.

In addition, Spain was admitted to the European Union in 1986. This gave the Spanish government access to EU subsidies for improving infrastructure, while, at the same time, the government decided to invest in developing the relatively "poor" region of Andalusia.

On December 9, 1988, the decision was made to build the new high speed lines in standard gauge (4' 8.5" [1,435 mm]) rather than in Spanish broad gauge (5' 4" [1,668 mm]). Improved mobility of citizens and goods within the country, as well as direct links with its European neighbors, would be an excellent means to promote the integration of Spain into the European Community. The government also saw the rail expansion project as a means to strengthen Spain's own industry. The contract to build the 292.6 mile [471 km] long Madrid-Seville LAV (= *Linea de alta velocidad* = high speed transmission line) was finally signed on March 16, 1989. It was built in thirty-three months, including a construction period of twenty-four months, an unusually short time for a railway of this length. It cost about one-third less than similar routes—partly because of the stubborn efforts by the country and the national government—and the goal was achieved in time for the start of the World Expo. The route begins in Madrid's Atocha train station and runs over thirty-one bridges (total length 32,300 ft [9,845 m]) and through seventeen tunnels (total length 52,592 ft [16,030 m]) on the Castilian plateau, to the recently completed Santa Justa railway terminal in Seville. It ascends some 2,600 ft [800 meters] south of Toledo, crossing the Sierra Morena; towards Seville, the rail line again descends almost back to sea level. Instead of the usual Spanish 3,000 V DC current system, the rail power system used 25 kV/50 Hz alternating current. Twelve substations from the public network supply the overhead catenary wire. DC sections begin approximately eight kilometers from the two terminal train stations. The biggest obstacle to building the rail line was crossing the Sierra Morena mountains. "Spain is, after Switzerland, the most mountainous country in Europe," commented Juan Matias Archilla, Director of International Relations at the RENFE, the Spanish state railway. After the trial period was completed and trains were allowed to run at full speed, the RENFE was able to put the new Madrid-Seville link into operation in good time for the Expo opening on April 19, 1992. Now it takes just two hours and twenty minutes to reach Seville. Passengers soon flocked to the trains in droves and the new line proved to be the most crucial measure for economic development of the region.

After successful completion of the Madrid-Seville link, in 1993, the economic crisis struck Spain mercilessly, along with most of the world. It took Spain until 1997 to generate enough economic impact to be able to renew construction of the high-speed transport system. The focus now automatically turned to the connection between Madrid and Barcelona, with the aim to reduce travel time from six-and-a-half hours to about two-and-a-half hours. In 2003, the new AVE link from Madrid to the northeastern city of Lleida (Lérida) was finally opened. It provides both the first part of a new route to Barcelona, as well as to the French border. Travel time between Madrid and Lleida was cut in half.

In early 2005, the relatively short high-speed line running south from Madrid to Toledo went into operation. The southern extension from Cordoba to Antequera was opened on December 16, 2006, and reached the major tourist city of Malaga, its preliminary endpoint, on December 23, 2007.

Modernized, improved tunneling methods make it possible to build straighter routes. As a result, one of the longest railway tunnels in the world was dug in Spain; north of Madrid, the tunnel takes the new high-speed line under the Sierra de Guadarrama mountains. The Madrid to Valladolid link opened on December 22, 2007, and significantly improved overall rail transport in northwestern Spain.

On February 20, 2008, the now complete new Madrid-Barcelona rail line was opened. The 388 miles [625 kilometers] between the two largest cities of Spain are covered in just two-and-a-half hours.

...UTE	OPENING	LENGTH	MAXIMUM SPEED	TRAIN CONTROL SYSTEM
...thern corridor (Andalucia)				
...drid-Seville	04/14/1992	293.1 mi [471.8 km]	186.4 mph [300 km/h]	ASFA 200 AVE, LZB
...drid-) La Sagra-Toledo	11/16/2005	12.9 mi [20.8 km]	167.7 mi [270 km/h]	ETCS Level 1 + 2
...doba Malaga	12/23/2007	96.3 mi [155 km]	186.4 mph [300 km/h]	ETCS, LZB
...illa-Utrera-Jerez-Cadiz	2012 (planned)	76.4 mi [123 km]	186.4 mph [300 km/h]	
...adilla-Algeciras				
...ille-Antequera	2013 (planned)	99.4 mi [160 km]	186.4 mph [300 km/h]	
...equera-Granada	2013 (planned)	78.2 mi [126 km]	186.4 mph [300 km/h]	ETCS Level 2
...ante corridor				
...ejón de Velasco-Motilla del Palancar	12/19/2010	138.9 mi [223.6 km]	186.4 mph [300 km/h]	
...illa del Palancar-Valencia	12/19/2010	86.3 mi [139 km]	186.4 mph [300 km/h]	
...encia-Castellon de la Plana	2014 (planned)	34.1 mi [55 km]		
...illa del Palancar-Albacete	12/19/2010	39 mi [62.8 km]	186.4 mph [300 km/h]	
...acete-La Encina-Xàtiva	2012 (planned)	85.8 mi [138.2 km]		
...va-Silla		36.6 mi [59 km]		
...Encina-Alicante	2012 (planned)	119 km		
...diterranean corridor				
...nforte del Cid-Murcia	2012 (planned)	73.9 mi [150 km]		
...cia-Almeria	2014 (planned)	114.5 mi [184.3 km]	186.4 mph [300 km/h]	ETCS Level 2
...thwest corridor				
...drid-) Pantoja-Badajoz (-Portuguese ...der)	2013 (planned)	248.7 mi [400.3 km]	186.4 mph [300 km/h]	ETCS Level 2
...theast corridor				
...drid-Saragossa-Barcelona	02/20/2008	385.8 mi [621 km]	186.4 mph [300 km/h]	ETCS Level 2
...agoza-Huesca	12/23/2003	79 km	124.2 mi [200 km/h]	ASFA, LZB
...agoza-Teruel			124.2 mi [200 km/h]	
...celona-Figueres (41 mi [66 km] for ...dard gauge freight trains in service ...e 12/2010)	2012 (planned)	82 mi [132 km]		
...eres-Perpignan (France)	12/19/2010	27.5 mi [44.4 km]	217.4 mph [350 km/h]	
...thwest corridor				
...drid-Segovia-Valladolid	12/22/2007	111.5 mi [179.6 km]	186.4 mph [300 km/h]	LZB, ETCS Level 1+2
...adolid-Burgos-Vitoria	2014 (planned)	145.1 mi [233.6 km]	217.4 mph [350 km/h]	ETCS Level 2
...ria-Bilbao	2014 (planned)	56.4 mi [90.8 km]	142.9 mph [230 km/h]	ETCS Level 2
...edo-Ourense	2015 (planned)	212 mi [341.2 km]	217.4 mph [350 km/h]	ETCS Level 2
...ense-Santiago de Compostela	2012 (planned)	54.3 mi [87.5 km]		ETCS Level 2
...oruna-Santiago de Compostela-Vigo	2012 (planned)	105.6 mi [170 km]		
...ncia, León	2013 (planned)	75 mi [120.8 km]		ETCS Level 2
...obla-Pola de Lena (Variante de ...ares)	2013 (planned)	30.8 mi [49.7 km]	155.3 mph [250 km/h]	ETCS Level 2
...gara-San Sebastian-French border	2014 (planned)	55.7 mi [89.7 km]	142.9 mph [230 km/h]	ETCS Level 2

The first trains ran at a top speed of 186 mph [300 km/h], but in the future, they will travel at up to 217 mph [350 km/h]. Barcelona will not remain the ultimate destination of the Spanish high speed network, however. The Barcelona-Figueres high-speed link to Perpignan (France) has been under construction since 2005, including a five-mile [eight-kilometer] tunnel at Le Perthus. The Figueras-Perpignan section was opened to rail traffic on December 19, 2010, making a later connection to the French TGV *Mediterranee* line possible. This connection, however, will be finished, at the earliest, with the planned 2020 completion of the high-speed line between Perpignan and Montpellier.

On December 19, 2010, in a first phase of construction, the high speed Madrid-Levante link was opened. The first 272 mile [438 km] long section connects the Spanish capital with Valencia and with Albacete. Travel time on the 243 miles [391 km] between Madrid and Valencia, the third largest city in the country, was cut from almost four hours to ninety-five minutes. The trains run at 186.4 mph [300 km/h] top speed, but they will be able to reach up to 217.4 mph [350 km/h] in the future. By 2012 and 2014, the coastal cities of Alicante and Castellon were anticipated to be connected to the high-speed network. In northern Spain, high-speed lines between Valladolid and Bilbao, as well as Santander and Donostia/San Sebastian are under construction. The first route that is not oriented to Madrid, the so-called Mediterranean Corridor, should be completed by 2020. The table on page 79 provides an overview of the Spanish high-speed lines, although it is not likely that the planned opening dates will be met, since Spain is suffering badly from the aftermath of the global financial crisis.

THE PROBLEM: TOO MANY DIFFERENT TRACTION UNITS

"When traveling in Spain, aircraft was the transportation of the twentieth century; the railway is the twenty-first century," wrote the newspaper *El Pais*, "Spain is the land of the AVE." AVE stands for "*Alta Velocidad Espanola*" (= Spanish high speed), but also means "bird" and is the collective name for all Spanish high speed trains. The wide variety of Spain's high-speed trains makes the system every modern railway enthusiast's dream, but this is more of a nightmare for the Spanish National Railways RENFE. France ordered all its TGV units from Alstom, and despite significant improvements in the technology, this ensures interoperability among the—at times—over 100 trainsets designed for the TGV Sud Est, Atlantique, and Duplex. In Spain, however, the number of its AVE

model series and their brand names multiplied many times over. Only the interior design for the different series is somewhat similar. Despite the excellent performance of the first TGV derivatives, there were no repeat orders, and the Spanish fleet remained limited to eighteen standard gauge and six "Euromed" broad gauge trainsets. Instead, RENFE turned to Siemens' more expensive Velaro (Series S-103, based on the ICE 3) and the new Talgo Bombardier trains with their "duck bill" design (ninety-one units of Series 102, 112, and 130). The Series 102 and 103 are designed to run at 217 mph [350 km/h], but it remains to be seen whether they will ever achieve this. This scenario was completed with the Pendolino derivative, Series 490, S-104 and S-114, and the CAF variable gauge trains, Series S-120 and S-121. So while SNCF has some 450 high speed trains of similar design and usually technically compatible with each other, RENFE has ten series and some 225 trains, which generally cannot operate in combination!

Broad gauge AVE S-101 003, running as the "Euromed 1181" to Alicante, rushes by the Garraf train station on June 16, 2006.

THE AVE SERIES 100 AND 101

To run on their first high speed Madrid-Seville rail line, RENFE chose a modified version of the TGV "Atlantique;" in 1988 Spain ordered an initial 16 units of its new Series AVE S-100 from GEC Alsthom (now Alstom). While an Atlantique unit includes ten intermediate cars, each AVE set had only eight intermediate cars in an articulated train, with two power cars, one at each end. Except for a slightly different

In the newly built Santa Justa railway station in Seville, AVE S-100 09 and 17 await departure on their return trip to Madrid, on March 30, 2002.

SERIES DESIGNATIONS:	S-100, S-101
Fleet numbers:	100-001 TO 024, 101-001 TO 006
Wheel arrangement (ten car):	Bo'Bo'+2'(2)'(2)'(2)'(2)'(2)'(2)'2'+
Bo'Bo'	
Power system:	25kV/50Hz; 3kV DC
Track gauge (ft [mm]):	4' 8.5" [1,435] (S-100), 5.4 [1,668] (S-101)
Maximum speed (mph [km/h]):	S-100: 186 [300], S-101: 137 [220]
Hourly output (hp [kW]):	9,387 [7,000 (8 x 875)] with 3 kV DC
Nominal power (continuous power) (hp [kW]):	11,800 [8,800 (8 x 1,1000)] with 25 kV/50 Hz; 7242 [5,400 (8 x 675)] with 3 kV DC
Empty weight (t), ten car:	392.6
Service weight (t), ten car:	421.5
Maximum axle load (t):	17.2
Coupling length (ft [mm]), ten car:	656.5 [200,114]
End car length (ft [mm]):	72.6 [22,150]
Intermediate car length (mm):	21,845 + 6 x 18,700 + 21,845
Distance between truck centers (mm):	14,000 + 8 x 18,700 +14,000
Axle distance powered truck (ft [mm]):	9.8 [3,000]
Axle distance trailer truck (ft [mm]):	9.8 [3,000]
Driving wheel diameter (ft [mm]):	3 [920]
Trailer wheel diameter (ft [mm]):	3 [920]
Seats ten car (Club/Preferente/Turista):	S-100 before conversion: 328 (38 +78 +212),
S-100 after conversion: 330 (41 + 78 + 211),	
S-101: 320 (0 + 108 + 212)	
Commissioning:	1992–1997, conversion 2007–2009

head car shape, these power cars are identical to the Atlantique power cars. They were designed to operate using 25 kV/50 Hz AC and 3 kV DC. There are eight three-phase synchronous motors on the power cars' four powered trucks, each delivering 1475 hp [1,100 kW] using 25 kV/50 Hz. Under DC operation, the motors generate 7,242 hp [5,400 kW].

The trainsets have three levels of accommodations: In the Club Class, the seats are in half-compartments. The Preferred Class has 78 seats, arranged 2 + 1 in the open-plan area, while Tourist Class has 213 seats (seat layout 2 + 2) in open-plan areas. A cafeteria car separates the economy class from the two more expensive classes, and offers a spacious bar with stylish decor.

RENFE made a second order for another eight units in December 1993. The first two units of this order were used to reinforce the Series S-100 fleet. The other six were given broad-gauge axles (5.4 ft [1,668 mm]) and were used as "Euromed" trains to run from June 1997 to 2009 between Barcelona and Valencia, at a top speed of 137 mph [220 km/h]. By the end of 2009, as a number of other high-speed trains started operating, and as the Spanish high speed network continued to expand, the Euromed units were adapted to match the standard gauge S-100 and given fleet numbers 100-019 and 100-024.

THE HIGH-SPEED TALGO TRAINS

The Talgo articulated trains are an invention of the Spanish engineer Alejandro Goicoechea, who, during the late 1930s, worked to develop a new vehicle concept that could compensate for all the problems posed by heavy and not very track-friendly passenger coaches. In 1942, Goicoechea and the financier Oriol founded the Patentes Talgo S.A. company of Madrid. With his Talgo I, he created a first prototype, with an articulated three point mounted train car elements and individual wheels. "Talgo" stands for "*Tren articulado ligero Goicoechea Oriol*" (= Goicoechea-Oriol light articulated train). In the Talgo, each car body has a truck with independent wheels, only at one end, while the other end is supported on the neighboring car. Only the leading end car has two trucks. Due to the short car bodies, the wheel stub axles are almost radially positioned when rounding curves, so that, compared to conventional vehicles, the wheel flanges run less heavily and so there is less wear and tear on the tracks. This design allowed the Talgo trains to roll around bends very easily and smoothly. This basic Talgo train concept has not changed over the years, although it has of course been continuously developed. So they added a radial truck steering, the "Talgo Pendular" passive tilting facility, and the "Talgo RD" variable gauge axles.

In the "Talgo Pendular" the axles and tilting technology are structurally connected. The radial-controlled independent wheels' air suspension is just below the roof. This high suspension works together with the car body suspension, to turn the car body on a virtual axis of rotation over the roof. The centrifugal force from rounding a curve tilts the car body away from the curve, thus considerably reducing centrifugal force on the passengers. The independent-wheel design eliminates the lateral instability motion caused by a rigid axle, creating a vehicle that runs with comparatively less vibration, less wear, and less noise.

Talgo also developed a variable gauge system, which makes it possible to switch the trains from the Spanish broad gauge, without having to change to standard gauge trucks or wheels on the cars; this system adjusts the distance between the wheels. Talgo trains with this equipment were given the additional designation RD (= *Ruedas Desplazables* = adjustable wheels). The gauge change is done in a gauge changing installation, where the weight is taken off the wheels, they are unlocked, pushed by guide bar into the new position, and relocked.

THE TEST TRAIN TALGO XXI (SERIES 355)

As part of the 150th anniversary celebrations for the Spanish National Railways RENFE, a prototype "Talgo XXI" was presented to an admiring public in October 1998. The test train was equipped with diesel-hydraulic power cars at both ends; these had, for the first time, powered trucks designed for variable gauges, making it possible to change gauges automatically. The modern lightweight power cars and special tilting technology allows the train to run on very winding routes. These "BT" power cars, with 2000 hp [1,500 kW] diesel engines and two-speed turbo transmissions from Voith can reach a top speed of 137 mph [220 km/h]. They were supplied by Krauss-Maffei, while the Talgo 7 cars were designed in-house at Talgo. The power cars have only one powered truck, while the car's other end is supported by the Talgo truck of the neighboring car. The aerodynamically designed profile of the train's molded front is a single GFK component.

On April 3, 2000, a test train, consisting of a BT power car and seven cars, made a demonstration run from Madrid to Puente Genil. The gauge change process, while the train was still underway, was demonstrated for the first time in Cordoba, as the train

Talgo XXI train "Virgen del Rocio" with power car BT-001, photographed during a test run by Talgo plant photographers.

ran through the gauge change installation at 10 mph [15 km/h] in 60 seconds. In a test run on June 12, 2002, the Talgo XXI (power cars 355 001 and 002, and three intermediate cars) set a new world's record of 159.3 mph [256.38 km/h] for diesel-powered trains. Both power cars were given appropriate inscriptions to commemorate this record-breaking trip. After two control cars were delivered, two four-car trainsets were created, each consisting of a power car, two intermediate cars, and a control car. Both trains later became the property of the Spanish infrastructure authority GIF (now ADIF), which uses them, as before, to make trial runs on high speed lines.

SERIES DESIGNATION:	355 "TALGO XXI"
Road numbers:	355 001 and 002
Wheel arrangement (power car):	B'(1)'
Drive:	diesel-hydraulic
Track gauge (ft [mm]):	4' 8.5" [1,435] and 5.4 [1,668]
Maximum speed (mph [km/h]):	137 [220]
Hourly output (kW):	
Nominal power (continuous power) (kW):	1,500 (+ 200 auxiliary engine)
Service weight (t), power car:	44
Maximum axle load (t):	18
Power car length (ft [mm]):	48.2 [14,700]
Axle distance powered truck (ft [mm]):	9.1 [2,800]
Driving wheel diameter (ft [mm]):	3.6 [1,100]
Trailer wheel diameter (ft [mm]):	2.8 [880]
Commissioning:	1998

THE AVE SERIES S-102 AND S-112 "EL PATO"

Project "Talgo 350," for Talgo and ADtranz to cooperate in developing a high-speed power car for the Talgo articulated trains, was launched in May 1998. The prototype consisted of a power car and six intermediate cars. ADtranz was responsible for the power car and drive equipment, the trucks and the control and safety technology. Krauss-Maffei, as

A Spanish AVE S-102 (El Pato) speeding through the barren landscape.

Velaro trains, to allow basically uniform operation. Twelve low-floor Talgo XXI type lightweight aluminum cars are lined up between the two power cars.

Since the floor level throughout is only 2.4 ft [760 mm], this makes boarding from a standard platform more convenient. The car bodies' relatively low weight comes from the Talgo articulated train concept and the resulting car length of only 43.11 ft [13.14 m]. This means an interim truck can have a monoaxle at every 43.11 ft [13.14 m]. Compared to an 86.6 ft [26.4 m] long conventional car, these trucks can be made considerably lighter and are less technically complex. An S-102 provides 316 seats in three classes, with six Tourist Class cars, three Preferred Class, and two Club Class. There is also a bar coach. All seats can be rotated in the travel direction and interestingly, in all three classes, the distance between seats is three feet [one meter]. In late February/early March 2004, the RENFE Board of Directors decided to procure additional Talgo 350 trains, with the new series designation S-112. These trains were designed for the Madrid-Cordoba-Mälaga and Madrid-Valencia routes. In configuration and structure, outer dimensions and technical data, the S-112 corresponds broadly to its predecessor, the S-102. The most important alterations included eliminating the Preferred Class (increasing Tourist class seats to 292), equipping all seats with 220 V electrical outlets, installing lighter seats, better

an ADtranz subcontractor, supplied the mechanical components and the brakes. Talgo produced the intermediate cars, using a design based on the Talgo XXI car.

In March 2000, the pre-series train was presented in Madrid, made up of one power car and six Talgo cars. The first trial runs began shortly afterwards on the high-speed Madrid-Seville railway. After a slow powering up, the prototype set a new Spanish speed record of 223 mph [359 km/h]. In addition, the power unit data certified the train's excellent features for stability and comfort. After the trials, the prototype was set aside at first. It was later taken over by the Spanish infrastructure operator GIF (now ADIF) and was rebuilt by Talgo in 2003 into a five-car Series 330 train to test catenary wires and tracks. Since then, the train has consisted only of the power car, three intermediate cars, and a new purpose-built control car, which corresponds to a power car without traction motor.

In early 1999, RENFE announced it would acquire thirty-two high-speed trains for the planned opening of the high-speed line between Madrid and Barcelona in 2004. The consortium of Talgo and ADtranz (later Bombardier) participated in the tender with the "Talgo 350," and in March 2001 was awarded the contract to make sixteen multiple-unit trains of the future Series S-102, with two power cars and twelve Talgo intermediate cars. The characteristic "duck bill" design (*el pato* = the duck) of the power cars was the result of aerodynamic optimization. This was to reduce susceptibility to crosswinds and the tunnel boom effect. Each power car has four three-phase asynchronous motors, controlled by two water-cooled IGBT power converters. The maximum braking power is 5,600 hp [4,200 kW]; braking resistors provide for braking power independent of the overhead catenary wire. Both power cars are connected with a high-voltage roof cable, so that only one pantograph has to be in contact with the catenary wire. The controls in the driver's console are broadly similar to those in the Series S-103

SERIES DESIGNATIONS:	S-102, S-112 "EL PATO"
Road numbers:	102-001 to 102-016, 112-001 to 112-030
Wheel arrangement (14 car):	Bo'Bo'+1'(1)'(1)'(1)'(1)'(1)'(1)'(1)'(1)'(1)'(1)'(1)'(1)'+Bo'Bo'
Power system:	25 kV/50 Hz
Track gauge (ft [mm]):	4' 8.5" [1,435]
Maximum speed (mph [km/h]):	205 [330]
Hourly output (kW):	
Nominal power (continuous power) (hp [kW]):	10,700 [8,000 (8 x 1,000)]
Empty weight (t), 14 car:	329
Service weight (t), 14 car:	S-102: 350, S-112: 357
Maximum axle load (t):	17
Coupling length (ft [mm]), 14 car:	657 [200,250]
Power car length (ft [mm]):	68.4 [20,870]
End intermediate car length (ft [mm]):	45.5 [13,890]
Intermediate car length (ft [mm]):	43.1 [13,140]
Distance between truck centers (mm):	11,000 + 10,520 + 10 x 13,140 +10,520 + 11,000
Axle distance powered truck (ft [mm]):	8.6 [2,650]
Driving wheel diameter (ft [mm]):	3.4 [1,040]
Trailer wheel diameter (ft [mm]):	2.8 [880]
Seats (Club/Preferente/Turista):	S-102: 316 (45 + 76 + 195) S-112: 363 (71 + 0 + 292)
Commissioning:	S-102: 2004–2005, S-112: 2008–2010

impact protection on the power car noses, and a more differentiated distribution of the drive power between the pulling and pushing power cars, so that in respective driving dynamics, the front power car delivers more power than the rear one.

THE AVE SERIES S-130 AND S-130H "EL PATITO"

In April 2004, RENFE gave the Talgo-Bombardier consortium a contract to produce twenty-two high-speed Series S-130 dual-voltage, variable gauge trains. In mid-September 2005, the consortium got the contract to supply a further forty-six identical high-speed power cars and new Talgo cars, for more S-130 trains. The dual-voltage equipment (25 kV/50 Hz and 3 kV DC) created a special challenge, as did the four train control systems required and the variable gauge trucks for the power cars. The developers had to keep within the maximum eighteen-ton axle load, even while giving the trains the stipulated drive power. To save space and weight, an asymmetric layout was selected to house the equipment in the engine room. The power car converters were set in a common container with common cooling, which optimized use of space and weight. Design and mounting of the three-phase asynchronous traction motors and transmissions in the Talgo variable-gauge truck also had to be very sophisticated, given the very limited space available. The power systems and gauges are changed in stationary gauge-changing installations at the transition points between two networks. Trains can drive through these installations at up to 10 mph

[15 km/h], while the actual gauge switch is done mechanically by the stationary installation. The power car remains passive during this process and meanwhile is prepared to change its power system. The power car design leaned heavily on the Series S-102 "duck bill," but is a bit more angular.

SERIES DESIGNATION:	S-130 "EL PATITO"
Road numbers:	130-001 to 130-090 (power cars)
Wheel arrangement (13 car):	Bo'Bo'+1'(1)'(1)'(1)'(1)'(1) (1)'(1)'(1)'(1)'(1)'(1)'1'+Bo'Bo'
Power systems:	25 kV/50 Hz and 3 kV DC
Track gauge (ft [mm]):	4' 8.5" [1,435] and 5.4 [1,668]
Maximum speed (mph [km/h]):	155 [250] (at 4' 8.5" [1,435 mm]), 137 [220] (at 5.4 [1,668 mm])
Hourly output (kW):	
Nominal power (continuous power) (hp [kW]):	6,434 [4,800 (8 x 600)] with 25 kV/50 Hz, 5,362 [4,000 (8 x 500)] with 3 kV DC
Empty weight (t), 13 car:	312
Service weight (t), 13 car:	335.9
Maximum axle load (t):	18
Coupling length (ft [mm]), 13 car:	604 [184,158]
Power car length (ft [mm]):	67 [20,434]
End intermediate car length (ft [mm]):	40 [12,200]
Intermediate car length (ft [mm]):	43.1 [13,140]
Distance between truck centers (mm):	10,650 + 8,970 + 9 x 13,140 + 8,970 +10,650
Axle distance powered truck (ft [mm]):	9.1 [2,800]
Driving wheel diameter (ft [mm]):	3.3 [1,010]
Trailer wheel diameter (ft [mm]):	2.8 [880]
Seats (Preferred/Tourist):	298 (62 + 236)
Commissioning:	2006–2009

As a result, the vehicles were quickly nicknamed "patito" (= duckling). A total of forty-five trainsets were manufactured, each with two power cars and eleven intermediate cars designed as modified Talgo 7 cars. All cars are pressure-sealed, air-conditioned, and have GPS-based passenger information systems, video screens, and audio modules at each seat. Thanks to a continuous floor level of 2.4 ft [760 mm] (= platform height in Spain), the cars have low floors and are fully stair-free. Talgo was responsible for the cars and mechanical parts of the power units (boxes and trucks, construction, and manufacturing), while Bombardier's share included the electrical engineering and power unit electronics. Since the trains are intended for service on all the Spanish lines, the ERTMS Level 1 and 2, LZB, EBICAB, and ASFA signaling systems were all installed. To offer high quality service in those areas of Spain not connected to the electrified rail network, fifteen trainsets were converted into hybrid units, at a cost of $102 [€78] million. Instead of the two end

An AVE S-130 (El Patito) passes through the Sitges train station, as the Euromed 1161 (Barcelona-Alicante) on May 14, 2011.

intermediate cars, the hybrid trains have two end cars without driver's consoles, with an additional powered truck each. These power cars each have a 2,400 hp [1,800 kW] diesel engine, housed with its dedicated generator. From 2012 on, these trains will run on the routes from Madrid to Murcia and from Madrid to Galicia.

Barcelona's Estació de França is often used for parking and cleaning broad-gauge high speed trains. Units S-130 43 and 03 awaiting their next trips on May 15, 2011.

SERIES DESIGNATION:	S-130H "EL PATITO"
Road numbers:	
Wheel arrangement (13 car):	Bo'Bo'+ Bo'(1)'(1)'(1)'(1)'(1)'(1)'(1)'(1)'(1)' Bo'+ Bo'Bo'
Power systems:	25 kV/50 Hz and 3 kV DC
Auxiliary drive:	diesel-electric
Track gauge (ft [mm]):	4' 8.5" [1,435] and 5.4 [1,668]
Maximum speed (mph [km/h]):	155 [250] (at 4' 8.5" [1,435 mm]), 220 (at 5.4 [1,668 mm]), 180 (for diesel operation)
Hourly output (kW):	
Nominal power (continuous power) (hp [kW]):	6,434 [4,800 (8 x 600)] at 25 kV/50 Hz,
5,361 [4,000 (8 x 500)] at 3 kV DC,	
hybrid operation: 4,826 [3,600 (2 x 1,800)]	
Empty weight (t), 13 car:	312
Service weight (t), 13 car:	335.9
Maximum axle load (t):	18
Coupling length (ft [mm]), 13 car:	604 [184,158]
Power car length (ft [mm]):	67 [20,434]
End railcar length (ft [mm]):	
Intermediate car length (ft [mm]):	43.1 [13,140]
Distance between truck centers (ft [mm]):	
Axle distance powered truck (ft [mm]):	9.1 [2,800]
Driving wheel diameter (ft [mm]):	3.3 [1,010]
Trailer wheel diameter (ft [mm]):	2.8 [880]
Seats (Preferente/Turista):	264 (48 +216)
Commissioning:	2012

THE AVE SERIES S-103 "VELARO E"

In July 2001, Siemens and RENFE signed a contract to build sixteen high-speed type "Velaro E" trains. The contract was worth $921 [€705] million, including $524 [€401] million for the trains and $397 [€304] million for their maintenance for a period of fourteen years. In March 2004, RENFE entrusted Siemens with the delivery of ten more trainsets.

The "Velaro" platform was created in response to the needs of the global high-speed-transport market and represents a further development of the German ICE 3. To survive in the world market, the new vehicles must meet the technical specifications for interoperability of high speed trains (TSI), and be multi-system capable and equipped with the ETCS European Train Control System. Furthermore, the manufacturers require experience with international approval processes. The main features of the "Velaro" platform are:

- reliable technology,
- spaciousness,
- high-level ride comfort,
- fascinating design,
- low life-cycle costs,
- modern multiple-unit train technology,
- operating speed of 217 mph [350 km/h],
- a modern, permanently coupled, multi-unit train.

As in the ICE 3, the S-103 drive components and system modules are housed under the floor, providing about 20% more space for passengers within the same train length. Direct propulsion from the three-phase asynchronous motors to half of all the axles ensures safe acceleration, due to better adhesion utilization. Beyond this, the new drive concept makes it possible to travel on tracks with gradients of up to 40%. As a result of better weight distribution over the entire multiple-unit train, less weight is put on the individual axles, complying with the international specification for a maximum of a seventeen-ton load per axle. Compared to the ICE 3, the Velaro E's maximum operating speed was increased to 217 mph [350 km/h] and the drive power by 10% to 11,796 hp [8,800 kW]. Instead of eddy current brakes, this train has an electric rheostatic brake. The powerful air conditioning system ensures a pleasant ride, even with outdoor temperatures up to 122° F [50° C]. The ETCS Level 2 train control system is standard equipment on the S-103, and is also the basis for cross-border operation. For trips on the first Spanish high speed Madrid-Seville line, which was opened in 1992, it also has the Linear Train Control (*Linienzugbeeinflussung* LZB) system. The AVE

The AVE S-103 23 from Barcelona to Madrid, making a stopover at Zaragoza Delicias train station on June 27, 2008.

SERIES DEDESIGNATION:	S-103 VELARO E
Road numbers:	103-001 to 103-026
Wheel arrangement:	Bo'Bo'+2'2'+Bo'Bo'+2'2'+2'2'+Bo'Bo'+2'2'+Bo'Bo'
Power system:	25 kV/50 Hz
Track gauge (ft [mm]):	4' 8.5" [1,435]
Maximum speed (mph [km/h]):	217 [350]
Nominal power (continuous power) (hp [kW]):	11,796 [8,800 (16 x 550)]
Empty weight (t):	425
Service weight (t):	462
Maximum axle load (t):	17
End car length (ft [mm]):	83.7 [25,535]
Intermediate car length (ft [mm]):	79.3 [24,175]
Coupling length (ft [mm]):	657.2 [200,320]
Distance between truck centers (mm):	8 x 17,375
Axle distance powered truck (ft [mm]):	8.2 [2,500]
Axle distance trailer truck (ft [mm]):	8.2 [2,500]
Driving wheel diameter (ft [mm]):	3 [920]
Trailer wheel diameter (ft [mm]):	3 [920]
Seats (Club/Preferred/Tourist):	405 (38 +103 + 264)
Commissioning:	2005–2008

S-103 has space for 405 passengers in three classes, Club, Preferred, and Tourist. The new train features exceptional comfort, video and audio entertainment, and catering by four kitchen compartments (galleys).

One Club class end car has conference and VIP rooms, along with a separate galley. The adjacent Preferred Class shines with its high-quality facilities and personalized business class-level service. The transition to Tourist Class is through the cafeteria car, where the customer service center and rooms for the crew and for

unaccompanied baggage are also located. Almost all the seats in the Velaro E can be turned in the travel direction before departure. All classes enjoy large video screens with entertainment programs and there are six different stereo quality audio programs at each seat. LED indoor and outdoor displays provide passenger information in Spanish, Catalan, and English. The Velaro E was the first German high speed train Siemens sent abroad to a foreign railway. Already, in September 2006, the S-103 set a new world speed record of 250.8 mph [403.7 km/h] for a series train, on a test run between Madrid and Barcelona. Since June 22, 2007, the first trains have been in regular service on the Madrid-Tarragona and Madrid-Seville routes. After the Tarragona-Barcelona section was completed, after February 20, 2008, the Velaro E has provided passenger service between Madrid and Barcelona and makes the 386 mile [621 km] trip in two hours and thirty-eight minutes.

THE SPANISH PENDOLINO

Four different types of trains based on the Italian "Pendolino" design have found their way onto Spanish tracks: a prototype and three series trains. They were acquired at very different points in time, for different ends and purposes. These trains have a common ancestry, but no common history, since they were bought based on different initiatives. Today, the prototype "El Platanito" (S-443) has been taken out of service; meanwhile, the ten first Series "Alaris" (S-490) trains have formed the backbone of the service between Barcelona and Valencia. The high-speed Series S-104 regional trains began their career with the development of new routes and efforts to establish a new product. This high-speed regional rail transport product, will be further upgraded with the new S-114.

SERIES 443 "EL PLATANITO"

The first unit of the Spanish "Pendolino" was called the *"electrotren basculante"* (= electric tilting railcar), and soon popularly became known as *"el platanito"* (= plantain [small banana], because of its yellow color and its long, narrow shape). Officially, the train got road number 443 001. This train was built in the mid-1970s to analyze the practicality of using tilting trains. It served as an experimental train for many years, for this and other innovations. Sometimes it was even used for regular service. The train was taken out of service in the late 1980s and is currently preserved as a historic vehicle in Castejön de Ebro (Navarra).

Parked on its side line, the 443 001 (El Platanito) awaits things that are to come.

During the 1970s, RENFE consistently opted to continue research and development, and created a so-called "innovation" department to introduce advanced knowledge in various areas of rail transport into Spain. Developments in this period included construction of the Calatayud and Ricla link, early studies of a high-speed line from Madrid to Barcelona, and acquisition of an electric tilt train. This last component was implemented to ascertain the potential tilting trains represented for increasing speed when rounding curves, an especially attractive option in a country like Spain, with its challenging terrain that creates many difficulties for increasing train speed.

At that time, the Italian manufacturer Fiat first developed trains with a hydraulic tilting system. The four-car prototype ETR.401 railcar attracted significant attention when it first ran in 1976. RENFE bought a very similar train (actually two half-trains) at that time to test the potential of tilting technology. Talgo also had been tinkering with an improved tilting system since 1972–73, which proved itself best in the "Talgo Pendular," which became available beginning in 1980.

The two systems were based on very different principles. The Talgo technology proved to be simpler, more efficient, and more cost-effective (even if the 35-degree tilt angle was slightly less than the eight degrees of the "Platanito," allowing less acceleration on curves). The introduction of the new Talgo Pendular meant, in practice, foregoing active

tilt technology and the "Platanito" with it. Only years later did RENFE decide to acquire series 490 trains, although it appeared that the basis of this decision was less the tilt technology itself, and rather the train's potential speed.

The "electric tilting railcar" consisted of two powered end cars, each with a cab, and two powered intermediate cars. From a technical point of view, the train could be divided into two autonomous half-trains, each half-train having a set travel direction. The drive power is provided by eight 295 hp [220-kW] DC motors, which gave the train a total output of 2,359 hp [1,760 kW]. The most important innovations were: the tilt capability (from a system of gyroscopes and accelerometers that tilt the car bodies mechanically by up to eight degrees on the curves), introducing a static converter, presetting the selected travel speed, and regulation of the traction motors' magnetic fields. The trains also got the new ASFA system, electromagnetic brakes with anti-skid protection, and engines suspended from the car body rather than built into the truck. This was a wide range of new features—which some people considered to be the reason for its failure: "There were a number of innovations that could not be all digested at once…".

After the "Platanito" had demonstrated ample evidence of its driving and tilt technologies between 1976 and 1979, it was used for regular service between Madrid and Albacete between October 1979 and May 1980. Between 1980 and 1982, it was used for regular service between Madrid and Jaen (the train arrived in Madrid in the morning and returned in the evening). Finally, the train was taken out of service to await better times. In 1984, it was taken back out of the mothballs for various tests. After a general inspection at CAF in Zaragoza, in 1986 it was used for the "Murallas de Avila" (Madrid-Avila) and "Doncel de Sigüenza" (Madrid-Sigüenza) tourist service. In the 1987 season, it ran in a new service to Avila. The train had also furnished proof that a direct-current overhead contact line works for high-speed transport. These efforts culminated when it set the speed record for electric traction (128 mph [206 km/h] in May 1987 at 12:26 PM, between 136.7 and 137.3 mph [km 220 and 221] on the Madrid to Alicante route). Finally, it was returned to Fuencarral and parked for several years. The idea of using the railcars for regional transport also was rejected. In 1994, the train came into the hands of railway enthusiasts in Castejón (*Asociación de Amigos del Ferrocarril de Castejón*), where it is preserved at the local railway station.

SERIES DESIGNATION:	443
Road number:	443 001
Wheel arrangement:	(1A)(A1)+(1A)(A1)+(1A)(A1)+(1A)(A1)
Power system:	3kV DC
Track gauge (ft [mm]):	5.4 [1,668]
Maximum speed (mph [km/h]):	111.8 [180]
Power output (hp [kW]):	2,359 [1,760 (8 x 220)]
Service weight empty (t):	200
Maximum axle load (t):	15
End car length (ft [mm]):	91.4 [27,875]
Intermediate car length (ft [mm]):	84.6 [25,800]
Entire train length (ft [mm]):	351.6 [107,170]
Distance between truck centers (mm):	4 x 18,900
Axle distance, powered truck (ft [mm]):	8 [2,450]
Driver wheel diameter (ft [mm]):	2.8 [880]
Trailer wheel diameter (ft [mm]):	2.8 [880]
Seats (1st/2nd class):	167 (51 + 116)
Commissioning:	1976

Passing through the Garraf train station on May 14, 2011, a Series 490 unit "Alaris 1142" from Valencia runs elegantly around a curve.

SERIES 490 "ALARIS"

In the mid-1990s, RENFE took the necessary steps to replace the Talgo III, which had been in operation for nearly thirty years. Those responsible decided, however, not to replace the vehicle with new Talgo trains, but with electric railcars. Why they chose a tilting train is not known. It is possible they were thinking of expanding the operation and extending it throughout Spain, or (more likely) they got the trains from Alstom and Fiat for a good price, for a well-known product, which was already operating in various European railway systems. In any case, they ordered ten single-class trains (the reason is unknown) with a total of 186 seats and a top speed of 136.7 mph [220 km/h].

RENFE quickly found a place for these trains: there were several stretches between Madrid and Valencia where the new train could reach speeds of up to 124 mph [200 km/h]. In addition, since its inception in 1980 until the mid-1990s, Intercity traffic from Madrid to Valencia had been using conventional electric railcars: first the Series 444 (87 mph [140 km/h]) and then the derived Series 448 (99 mph [160 km/h]). So RENFE decided that the new trains should indeed be laid out in the standard two-class system. But the new railcars still did not provide the seating capacity their predecessors had, making it necessary to both increase train frequency and track capacity on the line to Valencia.

The three-car trains are based on the Italian ETR.460, including the aluminum car bodies with their characteristic Giugiaro design and electrical

equipment. The trucks, with tilting technology, had to be adapted for the Spanish broad gauge. The tilt technology allows the trains to round curves with a lateral acceleration of 5.9 ft/s2 [1.8 m/s2] (instead of 3.2 ft/s2 [1.0 m/s2]). As usual, four 684 hp [510 kW] power traction motors were mounted on the car body's drive end car trucks' inner axles via a cardan shaft. The unpowered intermediate car, with two pantographs for power supply, was something rather unusual for the Pendolino concept. Up to three units can run in multiple unit operation.

Since starting service on February 1, 1999, up to 2009–10, these trains were only used in regular service from Madrid to Valencia, with some further connections to Castellön and Gandia. RENFE again followed their custom of creating a brand name for a service on their important connections (grandes lineas = great lines), which is also connected with a type of train. The new connection between Madrid and Valencia was named "Alaris," which immediately was associated (as so often happened) with the trains themselves; hence the name "Alaris" is commonly used for these units. Occasionally, RENFE has reviewed the possibility of increasing capacity by adding more intermediate cars or more trips, by obtaining more trains, but the prospect of finishing new high-speed lines put the brakes on these considerations. As a result, the supply of new trains for the Madrid-Valencia connection has stagnated; the train has a rather Spartan interior anyway. With the conversion of the Euromed trainsets (Series 101) to standard gauge units, the "Alaris" has been running more and more between Valencia and Barcelona. When the new Madrid-Valencia link opened in December 2010, this train lost its traditional base of operations.

SERIES DESIGNATION:	490
Road numbers:	9-490 001-10/ 7-490101-10/ 9-490201-10
Wheel arrangement:	(1A)(A1)+2'2'+(1A)(A1)
Power system:	3kV DC
Track gauge (ft [mm]):	5.4 [1,668]
Maximum speed (mph [km/h]):	136.7 [220]
Hourly output (hp [kW]):	2734.5 [2,040 (4 x 510)]
Nominal power (continuous power) (hp [kW]):	2,614 [1,950]
Service weight empty (t):	159
Maximum axle load (t):	15
End car length (ft [mm]):	89.2 [27,200]
Intermediate car length (ft [mm]):	82 [25,000]
Entire train length (ft [mm]):	260.4 [79,400]
Distance between truck centers (mm):	3 x 18,900
Axle distance, powered truck (ft [mm]):	8.8 [2,700]
Axle distance, trailer truck (ft [mm]):	8.8 [2,700]
Driver wheel diameter (ft [mm]):	2.9 [890]
Trailer wheel diameter (ft [mm]):	2.9 [890]
Seats (1st class/2nd class):	161 (49 + 111 + 1)
Commissioning:	1998–99

AVE SERIES S-104

The Series 104 trains have four cars, also based on the Pendolino family, but have no tilting system. Since the end of 2004, they have been used for regional transport on high speed

High praise and fine speeches: Many political notables and a Series S-104 trainset at the opening of the high speed Madrid-Toledo line.

SERIES DESIGNATION:	S-104
Road numbers:	104001-020
Wheel arrangement:	(1A)(A1)+(1A)(A1)+(1A)(A1)+(1A)(A1)
Power system:	25 kV/50 Hz
Track gauge (ft [mm]):	4' 8.5" [1,435]
Maximum speed (mph [km/h]):	155 [250]
Power output (hp [kW]):	5,898 [4,400 (8 x 550)]
Empty weight (t):	221.5
Service weight (t):	240
Maximum axle load (t):	17
End car length (ft [mm]):	90.5 [27,600]
Intermediate car length (ft [mm]):	84.9 [25,900]
Entire train length (ft [mm]):	351 [107,000]
Distance between truck centers (mm):	4 x 19,000
Axle distance, powered truck (ft [mm]):	8.8 [2,700]
Driver wheel diameter (ft [mm]):	2.9 [890]
Trailer wheel diameter (ft [mm]):	2.9 [890]
Seats:	237 (31 + 205 + 1)
Commissioning:	2004-2005

lines (Cordoba-Seville and Madrid Puertollano), and were included in the package to buy new trains for the opening of the second generation high-speed lines. These trains are outwardly very similar to the "Alaris" Series 490, but have four cars (two powered end cars and two powered intermediate cars) instead of three; the cars have a continuous roof panel and two doors per car (with the exception of the cafeteria car). There are greater technical differences: no tilting system, a 25 kV/50 Hz power system, and standard gauge (4.7 ft [1,435 mm]).

Regional transport on high speed lines is a Spanish novelty, which does not exist in the same way in other countries. The general demand and supply structure in other countries—where there is much higher-capacity utilization of the high speed lines than in Spain—is not comparable to that in Spain. As early as 1992, the rail authorities were already testing the possibility of setting up regional connections from Madrid to Ciudad Real and Puertollano, on the new Madrid-Seville line, especially since utilization of the track was low. So, in September 1992, the so-called "Lanzaderas" (= shuttles) began this service using AVE Series 100 trains; they were also used for long-distance travel between Madrid and Seville and were moderately over-spacious. In 1997, RENFE started negotiations with the train manufacturers to try to define a train that did not yet exist. It was to be suitable for regional high-speed rail transport, have about 220 seats and a top speed of 168 mph [270 km/h], offer less on-board service and less restaurant space, since travel times would be shorter, and allow very easy outside access. A tender was issued in 2000, which CAF-Alstom won with a four-car railcar (based on the Pendolino); in 2001 they got a contract to supply twenty trains, which were delivered by November 2004. The new regional rapid transit service between Cordova and Seville (six trips per day in each direction) began using eleven units on December 29, 2004. A few days later, on January 3, 2005, the new trains started running between Madrid and Ciudad Real and Puertollano, so that service was increased from nine to thirteen trips, in both directions per day. After the Madrid-Toledo link opened in November 2005, the new trains were also used there.

AVE S-114 SERIES

As more high speed lines started operating, demand increased for regional train service on lines such as Cordoba-Malaga, Madrid-Valladolid, Barcelona-Lleida, or Zaragoza-Calatayud. RENFE then ordered another thirteen trainsets from the Alstom-CAF consortium, for fast regional transport; their product name is "Avant." The Pendolino was again the basic model, but this time, the latest generation ETR.600. Externally, the new AVE Series S-114 railcars' broadly resemble their Italian relatives. They have four powered cars; as always, three-phase asynchronous motors drive the truck inner axles. Again, a top speed of 155 mph [250 km/h] was considered sufficient; tilt technology was omitted. Of course, there were inevitable small alterations in dimensions: the Spanish version got a 9.5 ft [2,920 mm] wide car body, instead of the Italian original's 9.2 ft [2,830 mm].

There were significant changes in Series 104, so that this train got the improved MEGA (*Modulo Energetico de Gran Absorcion* = high absorption power module) passive collision safety system, a pneumatic secondary suspension instead of coil springs, and all seats were equipped with power outlets. Like the S-104, the S-114 only has Second Class seats. There is no cafeteria area, but vending machines are available for snacks or drinks. There are also places for people with restricted mobility and for bicycles.

SERIES DESIGNATION:	S-114
Road numbers:	114-601/602 to 114-625/626
Wheel arrangement (four car):	(1A)(A1)+(1A)(A1)+(1A)(A1)+(1A)(A1)
Power system:	25kV/50Hz
Track gauge (ft [mm]):	4' 8.5" [1,435]
Maximum speed (mph [km/h]):	155 [250]
Hourly output (kW):	
Nominal power (continuous power) (hp [kW]):	5,362 [4,000 (8 x 500)]
Empty weight (t), four car:	228.8
Service weight (t), four car:	247.8
Maximum axle load (t):	17
Coupling length (ft [mm]), seven car:	354 [107,900]
End car length (ft [mm]):	90.5 [27,600]
Intermediate car length (ft [mm]):	82 [25,000]
Distance between truck centers (mm):	4 x 19,000
Axle distance, powered truck (ft [mm]):	8.8 [2,700]
Driver wheel diameter (ft [mm]):	2.9 [890]
Trailer wheel diameter (ft [mm]):	2.9 [890]
Seats (four car):	236
Commissioning:	2008–2010

AVE SERIES S-120 AND S-121

In September 2001, RENFE gave the CAF Alstom consortium a contract to manufacture twelve four-car variable gauge trains for the Madrid-Barcelona high speed line and its branch lines. A second contract to manufacture another forty-five trains followed in February 2004. The RENFE Series S-120 includes the twelve trains in the first order and sixteen trains in the second; the remaining twenty-nine units were assigned to the second series, the AVE S-121. The main difference from the Series S-120 is that both first class and cafeteria car were omitted, increasing seating capacity from 237 to 281. The first trains from the first order were delivered in autumn 2005, while the first S-121 started running in January 2009.

Unit S-114 01 taking its first steps near Zaragoza Deliciason, October 19, 2008.

S-120 306 and another trainset waiting in Barcelona's "Estacio de Franga" rail yard on June 16, 2006, for their next trips in the "Alvia" service to the capital, Madrid.

The freshly painted S120 304 is ready for an in-house photo shoot.

All trains were manufactured by the CAF-Alstom consortium, and got the automated CAF variable-gauge BRAVA trucks (= *Bogie du Rodadura de Ancho Variable Autopropulsado* [self propelled rolling variable gauge truck]). The four-car dual-voltage electric railcars have only powered trucks and two end car driver's cabs. Their top speed is 155 mph [250 km/h] on normal gauge high-speed lines, but only 137 mph [220 km/h] on conventional broad gauge lines. The units are designed for 25 kV/50 Hz alternating current and 3,000 volt DC; the system changes automatically. They are equipped for two signal systems and can operate as double headers.

Using alternating current, a unit has about 4,000 kW power; using the DC overhead contact wires, only 2,700 kW. Eight self-ventilated 670 hp [500 kW] three-phase asynchronous motors with IGBT inverters propel the train. The motors are suspended under the car bodies, and the axles driven by cardan shafts. The inner axle is powered on all trucks; the second is designed as a trailing axle. The gauge change operation can be performed at up to 10 mph [15 km/h]. The braking system is a combination of electric rheostatic and regenerative dynamic brakes, supplemented by pneumatic disc brakes. These systems allow the following braking distances: 0.6 miles [1 km] at 62 mph [100 km/h]; 1.2 miles [2 km] at 137 mph [220 km/h]; and 1.6 miles [2.7 km] at the maximum speed of 155 mph [250 km/h]. A primary set of coil springs and a secondary air suspension provide the necessary ride comfort.

Each car has central access doors, which create two open-plan areas per car, so that the cars do not look like

SERIES DESIGNATION:	S-120, S-121
Road numbers:	120-301/601 to 120-312/612, 120-351/651 to 120-366/666, 121-001/501 to 121-029/529
Wheel arrangement:	(1A)(A1)+(1A)(A1)+(1A)(A1)+(1A)(A1)
Power system:	25 kV/50 Hz, 3 kV DC
Track gauges (ft [mm]):	4' 8.5" [1,435] and 5.4 [1,668]
Maximum speed (mph [km/h]):	155 [250] (25 kV/50 Hz), 137 [220] (3 kV DC)
Power output (hp [kW]):	5362 [4,000 (8 x 500)] with 25 kV/50 Hz; 3,619 [2,700 (8 x 338)] with 3 kV DC
Empty weight (t):	S-120: 233, S-121: 251.4
Service weight (t):	S-120: 259
Maximum axle load (t):	17
End car length (ft [mm]):	90.8 [27,700]
Intermediate car length (ft [mm]):	84.5 [25,780]
Entire train length (ft [mm]):	352.2 [107,360]
Distance between truck centers (mm):	4 x 19,000
Axle distance, powered truck (ft [mm]):	9.1 [2,800]
Driver wheel diameter (ft [mm]):	2.7 [850]
Trailer wheel diameter (ft [mm]):	2.7 [850]
Seats (1st/2nd class):	S-120: 237 (81 + 156), S-121: 281
Commissioning:	S-120: 2004–2010, S-121: 2009–2010

large tubes. Restrooms and luggage racks are in the entry areas. The car bodies are made of self-supporting aluminum tubing and feature a shock-absorbing safety system. Inside, two-panel sliding doors close off the open-plan seating areas, while the 3.2 ft [1,000 mm] wide outer doors are just one panel. All sliding doors are electric. The trains are equipped with air conditioning, public address systems, and video displays. The information system includes 17" TFT screens in the passenger areas; passengers can play DVD videos, audio CDs, and MP3 format files. Each seat has its own audio connection.

The AVE-Series S-105 "Oaris"

After four years of development, the Spanish train manufacturer CAF presented its OARIS platform—the first real Spanish high-speed train—at the "International Rail Forum 2010" in Valencia, in May. The OARIS platform is a modular vehicle concept, which makes it possible to set up four, six, or even eight-car units. An eight-car OARIS is 662.7 feet [202 meters] long and can operate as a double-header; this gives a maximum train length of 1,325 ft [404 m]. Each car has a powered truck with two three-phase asynchronous motors and an electronic frequency converter, so that the installed capacity increases proportionally with the number of cars. Its multiple-traction system allows the train to run using both 1.5 or 3 kV direct current, and either 15 kV/16 2/3 kV or 25 kV/50 Hz AC. An eight-car trainset has two transformers, which each feed four inverters; in a turn, one inverter powers the car's two motors.

The aluminum car bodies were designed to meet all European TSI and crash safety standards, and to ensure weight reduction. The primary coil spring and second-day air suspension between truck and car provide the necessary ride comfort. The traction motors rest on the trucks to minimize unsprung weight.

The OARIS railcars can function both on normal and broad gauge and, of course, can also be equipped with their own BRAVA system variable-gauge trucks. It can also accommodate the European signaling systems, including ETCS. The cars can be finished in various interior designs. Access can be via either two or four doors per car. A typical trainset will have seats in two comfort classes and a bistro area. There is easy access for passengers with reduced mobility.

This is how it will look: the CAF AVE S-105 (Oaris). We cannot completely rule out similarities with the ETR.600 or Alstom's S-114.

In September 2010, CAF began production of a four-car prototype, which RENFE will give the series designation S-105, and CAF announced that the prototype was ready on January 14, 2011. The first driving dynamics tests began in early 2011.

Series designation:	S-105
Road number:	"Oaris" prototype
Wheel arrangement:	Bo'2'+Bo'2'+2'Bo'+2'Bo'
Power system:	25kV/5oHz,3kV DC
Track gauges (ft [mm]):	4' 8.5" [1,435] and 5.4 [1,668]
Maximum speed (mph [km/h]):	199 [320 (25 kV/50 Hz)]
Power output (kW):	7,078 [5,280 (8 x 660)] with 25 kV/50 Hz
Empty weight (t):	
Service weight (t):	
Maximum axle load (t):	
End car length (ft [mm]):	87.8 [26,780]
Intermediate car length (ft [mm]):	81.2 [24,780]
Entire train length (ft [mm]):	338.3 [103,120]
Distance between truck centers (ft [mm]):	
Axle distance, powered truck (ft [mm]):	
Axle distance, trailer truck (ft [mm]):	
Driver wheel diameter (ft [mm]):	3 [920]
Trailer wheel diameter (ft [mm]):	3 [920]
Seats (1st/2nd class):	216
Commissioning:	2011

THE CZECH REPUBLIC

Already, by the mid-1990s, the Czech National Railways (CD) had ordered ten Pendolino trains based on the Italian ETR.460, from the CKD-MSV Studenka-Fiat-Siemens consortium. Economic turmoil—in both the railway and the participating companies—delayed production for several years before Alstom finally took the contract. Due to the cost, CD had to decrease the order to seven trains.

On March 26, 2003—a full month before the agreed date—the first Czech Pendolino Series CD-680 rolled out of the Alstom factory in Savigliano, Italy. These tilting trains were actually intended to take over international long-distance service on the Berlin-Prague-Vienna connection by 2004. To do this, the trains, equipped with the proven Fiat hydraulic tilt system, got triple-voltage systems (3 kV DC, 16.7 kV Hz/15, 50 Hz/25 kV). The seven-car trains, 605 ft [184.4 m] long, have eight three-phase asynchronous motors, each with 657 hp [490 kW] power output. They can travel at a top speed of 143 mph [230 km/h] and seat 331 passengers. The self-supporting body shells are light metal, and the end car driver's cabs are built of an aluminum framework with fiberglass-reinforced plastic casing.

Only the inner axle of each powered truck is driven, via cardan shaft and final drive. The 680's active tilting system works on a tilting bolster with four pendulums and two hydraulic cylinders. The tilting bolster lies on the coil springs and is, in turn, connected to the car body cross-bar. The train has four pantographs: a DC-pantograph on each end car (Series 681 and 682) as well as an AC pantograph on each adjoining intermediate car (series 081 and 082). To ensure that the pantograph does not tilt with the train, they are directly supported on the truck tilting rod. The trains have ETCS Level 2 and GSM-R equipment, and the current train control systems used in Germany, Austria, Slovakia, and the Czech Republic.

However, after the encouragingly early delivery, all sorts of problems emerged. These began with the unacceptably long time required for the various approval procedures. Initially, the Pendolino could operate in the Czech Republic only under their own power using 3 kV DC; for 25 kV AC, they had to be towed, because only limited interference currents were allowed. The need to comply with the Czech Republic's low interference current limit in the AC network was only one of the reasons

THE CZECH REPUBLIC

A Pendolino series 680 makes a stop at the Bohumín station during its trial runs.

given approval in Austria and Slovakia, six pairs of trains have been travelling from Prague to Ostrava, two pairs of trains to Vienna, and a pair of trains to Bratislava. In the annual 2010 timetable, the pair of trains between Prague and Bratislava was stopped, due to low demand, and service was reduced to one pair of trains between Vienna and Prague. Since June 12, 2009, the "Pendolino SC Sprinter" has run on Fridays between Prague and Trinec. This does not stop between Prague and Ostrava, but does at Bohumin, Karvina, Cesky Tesin, and at Trinec, the country's east terminus. Seven pairs of trains run every two hours from Prague to Ostrava, with some connections to Bohumin; in the 2011 timetable, the Sprinter ran to Trinec and service of a pair of trains between Prague and Bratislava was restarted. In Vienna, however, you will look in vain for a Czech Pendolino.

Due to a lack of existing high-speed rail lines, the Pendolino currently run only at a maximum speed of 99 mph [160 km/h] in the Czech Republic. Since the timetable change, the fastest train between Prague and Ostrava takes just three hours and three minutes. At 82 mph [132 km/h] on the Olomouc main station to Ostrava-Svinov stretch, it reaches the highest average speed of a scheduled train in the Czech Republic.

for the long approval process. The others included technical problems in meeting other Czech standards, and making various modifications and adaptations. Scheduled Pendolino service began in the 2005 timetable year, but this was using only one pair of trains (R 772-777) running between Prague and Decin. In November 2005, Alstom finally delivered the last multiple-unit train to the Czech railways. Regular service was to start as of the timetable change on December 11, 2005. This timetable included six pairs of Type "SC Pendolino" (SC = SuperCity) trains running from Prague to Ostrava. Two more train pairs (EC 134-135 and IC 570-571) were also to be driven by a Pendolino on the Prague-Breclav, depending on availability. The EC pair had to stop running at Breclav, because the Series 680 had not been approved for use on the Slovak railway network.

Yet, as early as January 25, 2006, the trains had to be taken out of service again, due to some serious technical and software problems. The pride of Czech Railways had become a laughing stock. Aside from the fact that it was only possible to import the trains after almost six years' delay, they only made negative headlines after they started running in December 2005. They even got the dubious honor of being the target of several jokes, such as: "What do Italian shoes, men, cars, and the Pendolino have in common? They're very attractive—at first glance. But their staying power leaves something to be desired."

After Alstom Ferroviaria was able to eliminate the problems and successfully stabilize the trains, they were gradually reentered in the service plan over the year. Since then, operation has been fairly stable. As of the 2007 annual schedule, and after the Series 680 was

SERIES DESIGNATION:	680
Road numbers:	681/081/683/084/684/082/682001-007
Unit configuration:	T+M+T+M+T+M+T
Wheel arrangement (railcar):	(1A)(A1)
Wheel arrangement (intermediate car):	2'2'
Power system:	25 kV/50 Hz, 15 kV/16.7 Hz, 3 kV DC
Track gauge (ft [mm]):	4' 8.5" [1,435]
Maximum speed (mph [km/h]):	142 [230]
Hourly output (kW):	5,496 [4,100]
Nominal power (continuous power) (kW):	5,255 [3,920 (8 x 490)]
Empty weight (t):	385
Maximum axle load (t):	15.6
End car length (ft [mm]):	90.7 [27,650]
Intermediate car length (ft [mm]):	84.9 [25,900]
Entire train and coupling length (ft [mm]):	607.9 [185,300]
Distance between truck centers (mm):	7 x 19,000
Axle distance, powered truck (ft [mm]):	8.8 [2,700]
Axle distance, trailer truck (ft [mm]):	8.8 [2,700]
Driver wheel diameter (ft [mm]):	2.9 [890]
Trailer wheel diameter (ft [mm]):	2.9 [890]
Seats 1st/2nd class:	333 (105 + 226 + 2)
Commissioning:	2003-2005

TURKEY

Turkey followed the European model in developing its railways; in the coming years, the country wants to build a high-speed network connecting all its major cities. According to Suleyman Karaman, Director General of Turkish State Railways (*Türkiye Cumhuriyeti Devlet Demiryollari*—TCDD [State Railways of the Republic of Turkey]), under this ambitious program, a total of some 10,560 miles [17,000 km] of railway lines are to be built or upgraded for rapid transport in the medium term. Of these, 7,456 miles [12,000 km] will be designed for speeds of 155 mph [250 km/h] or more.

THE ANKARA-ESKIŞEHIR-ISTANBUL
HIGH SPEED RAIL LINE

The first connection is between the cities of Ankara and Istanbul. The purpose of this ambitious project to build a new high-speed route between the two cities was to cut travel time by more than half; it is the precursor to a new wave of railway service modernization in this rapidly growing country. Ankara is the Turkish capital, with about five million inhabitants, while Istanbul, the largest city in the country, has nearly twelve million people. There is heavy traffic between these cities, and this connection is the most overburdened in the country. There are also many cities on the Ankara-Istanbul corridor that contribute to the increasing congestion on this artery.

The new project was created in two phases. The first 128 mile [206 km] section from Esenkent to Eskişehir cost $835 million. Construction was two-thirds completed by April 2006, and was finished in late 2007. The second phase, the 117 mile [188 km] long section between Eskişehir and Köseköy, includes thirty-nine tunnels and thirty-three bridges and viaducts. Completion was expected in 2012, after investment of some $1.32 billion. The two remaining sections, Esenkent-Ankara and Köseköy-Gebze, will be completed in 2014 at the latest. The latter is expected to cost around $136 million.

The TCDD started trial runs in April 2007, using two ETR.500 trains rented from Trenitalia on the first section of the Ankara-Istanbul high-speed line. The testing program focused on the 128 mile [206 km] stretch between Esenkent, west of Ankara, and Eskişehir, where the trains travel at up to 155 miles [250 km/h]. This section was finally opened for regular service on March 13, 2009.

When the entire route starts operation, it will be possible to shorten travel time between Ankara and Istanbul from at least 6 hours 30 minutes (the old route), to only three hours. The new line will be 27 miles [43 km] shorter, fully double-tracked, and electrified at 25 kV/50 Hz. Inauguration of the entire route is planned for 2014.

TURKEY

HIGH-SPEED LINE	LENGTH (MI [KM])	MAXIMUM SPEED (MPH [KM/H])	COST (U.S. $ MILLION)	CONSTRUCTION COMPLETED	FUTURE TRAVEL TIME	STATUS
Ankara-Istanbul	331 [533]	155 [250]		2014	3 h	under construction
- Ankara-Eskişehir	152 [245]	155 [250]		2007	1 h	completed
(Ankara) Polatli-Konya	132 [212]	155 [250]	375	2011	1 h 15 min	completed
- Konya-Istanbul	463 [745]	155 [250]		2014	3 h 45 min	
Ankara-Sivas	293 [471]	155 [250]	1,300	2015	2 h	under construction
- Sivas-Istanbul	624 [1,004]	155 [250]			5 h	
(Ankara-) Kocahacili-Izmir	376 [606]	155 [250]	1,850	2015	3 hrs 20 mins	Planning completed
Bursa-Osmaneli	65.5 [105.5]	155 [250]	250	2013	30 min	under construction
- Ankara-Bursa		155 [250]			2 h 15 min	
- Ankara-Istanbul		155 [250]			1 hr 30 mins	
Istanbul-Edirne (Bulgarian border)	143 [230]	155 [250]	545	2017	1 h 20 min	Planning completed
Ankara-Kayseri		155 [250]				projected
Eskişehir-Antalya		155 [250]				projected
Sivas-Erzincan-Kars		155 [250]				projected

MORE HIGH-SPEED LINES

Construction has begun, or will begin shortly, on other routes departing from the capital. First, the Black Sea city of Sivas, the third largest Turkish city of Izmir, and the emerging city of Konya in the south will get express connections to Ankara. The central Anatolian hinterland presents less challenging requirements for train tracking than the mountainous coastal regions. The Konya region is one of the more densely populated areas in Turkey. It has the largest surface area in the country and is both a concentration of industry and the center of grain production. The current Ankara-Eskişehir-Afyon-Konya rail line is 613 miles [987 km] long and trains now take at least 10 hours and 30 minutes. By road, the distance between Ankara and Konya is only 160 miles [258 km]. As a result, both passenger and freight transport are on the highway, and the railway is rarely used. On the new, just 190 mile [306 km] long high-speed line, trains will only take one hour and 15 minutes, a drastic reduction in travel time. The new, 132 mile [212 km] long, high speed line to Konya branches from the Istanbul-Ankara high speed line in Polatli; it was opened by Turkish Prime Minister Erdogan on December 17, 2010. It is also electrified using 25 kV/50 Hz, designed for 155 mph [250 km/h] and equipped with ETCS Level 1 signaling. Scheduled service began in April 2011, and with that came a drastic reduction in travel time: in future, the travel time on the Istanbul-Konya connection will be 3 hours and 30 minutes. Today, the fastest trains take 12 hours and 30 minutes.

The existing line between Ankara and Sivas is 374 miles [602 km] long and the trip takes twelve hours.

The planned, only 293 mile [471 km] long high-speed line will be an important part of the East-West Corridor when it is finished; trains will only need two hours to make the trip. Unlike the current single tracking, the new lines will be double-tracked; this will significantly increase capacity on the rails between the two cities, both for passenger and freight traffic. Between Ankara and Izmir, the current distance by rail is 512 miles [824 km] and travel time is 14 hours. The new high speed line will be only 387 miles [623 km] long, with a scheduled service of just 3 hours 30 minutes. Project planning has been completed and construction will begin as soon as possible.

With its high-speed rail projects, Turkey is taking on the target formulated by the EU: to connect all major cities by 2020 with express train lines. After the initial project series are completed, the TCDD next plans to connect the cities of Bursa, Isparta, Antalya, and Erzincan to the network. It is still being considered, whether the TCDD will invite tenders to operate on the routes after construction is completed. The privatization of ports that were previously operated by the TCDD

HT65002 poses on the new rail line for the TCDD photographers.

is playing an important role in financing the railway projects planned for up through 2017. The license to operate the ports of Izmir and Mersin alone has brought about $2 billion U.S. into the state railway's coffers. The TCDD hopes to obtain another $2 billion U.S. from the forthcoming privatization of the loading facilities at Samsun, Derince, Bandirma, and Iskenderun. This amount should cover construction costs for the Ankara-Istanbul (about $3 billion U.S.), and Ankara-Konya (about $500 million U.S.) routes.

New TRAINS

The high speed rail lines require new rolling stock. Spain's CAF has manufactured 12 Series HT65000 high-speed trains. The six-car electric railcars can travel at a maximum speed of 155 mph [250 km/h], seat 409 passengers, and operate using 25 kV/50 Hz. One unit consists of two end control cars and four powered intermediate cars; it can be expanded to an eight car unit by adding two more intermediate cars as required. These multiple-unit trains can work in double traction, creating a twelve-car train.

Each intermediate car has two three-phase asynchronous motors under the floor, controlled by an IGBT (insulated-gate bipolar transistor). One axle of each truck is powered via a cardan shaft. The trains also have regenerative electric brakes, supplemented with an anti-skid system through pneumatically actuated disc brakes. One traction inverter per car feeds the two drive motors. Each train has three auxiliary current converters, two needed to run the train and the third as a reserve.

The axles are designed for a 4' 8.5" [1,435 mm] track gauge; each powered truck has one powered and one trailing axle. The monoblock wheels are made of non-alloy, low-carbon-content steel with hardened surfaces. The aluminum car bodies are set on a welded steel frame. The primary coil spring and secondary pneumatic suspension ensure a comfortable ride. Operating and emergency brakes are made of steel discs mounted on the axles. The trains also have emergency brakes.

The interiors are modern and functional. In the most expensive category (Business Class), the seating layout is 2 + 1; in the less-expensive class (First Class) seating is 2 + 2. Eight restrooms are available in each unit, one of which is designed for disabled passengers. The entry doors are located in the center of the car and open to the two open-plan areas to the right and left of the entrance area. There is an audio-video system for passengers. Both the driver's cabs and passenger open-plan areas are air conditioned. The safety equipment includes a black box. The trains also have the appropriate control, data transmission, and communication systems. Refreshments are available in the buffet car.

After regular service to Konya began, of the twelve units, four are running between Ankara and Eskişehir and another four between Ankara and Konya. Two trainsets travel the Konya to Eskişehir connection, and two multiple-unit trains are kept in reserve. Eleven pairs of new trains currently offer a nearly continuous hourly service between Eskişehir and Ankara, with a travel time of 90 minutes.

The TCDD is now planning to order up to 48 new high-speed trains to meet future demand on the high-speed network. In the long run, of course, the twelve CAF Series HT65000 trains will not be sufficient.

A just-delivered HT65000 (650 016) is in the new depot, ready for its trial run.

SERIES DESIGNATION:	HT65000 (S+T+T+T+T+S)
Road numbers:	001-024
Number of units:	12
Wheel arrangement:	2'2'+(1A)(A1)+(1A)(A1)+(1A)(A1)+(1A)(A1)+2'2'
Power system:	25 kV/50 Hz
Track gauge (ft [mm]):	4' 8.5" [1,435]
Maximum speed (mph [km/h]):	155 [250]
Power output (hp [kW]):	6,434 [4,800 (8 x 600)]
Empty weight (t):	
Maximum axle load (t):	17
Length (end car) (ft [mm]):	89.7 [27,350]
Length (intermediate car) (ft [mm]):	84.5 [25,780]
Entire train length (ft [mm]):	520 [158,520]
Distance between truck centers (mm):	6 x 19,000
Axle distance powered truck (ft [mm]):	9.1 [2,800]
Axle distance trailer truck (ft [mm]):	9.1 [2,800]
Driver wheel diameter (ft [mm]):	2.7 [850]
Trailer wheel diameter (ft [mm]):	2.7 [850]
Seats (Business/First):	409 (354 + 55)
Commissioning:	2007-2010

AUSTRALIA

THE XPT IN NEW SOUTH WALES

For many years, Australia was hardly a promising hunting ground for high-speed rail exporters. However, the British HST had achieved a critical success, in that its Australian brethren, named the XPT, succeeded in reviving long-distance travel in the Australian state of New South Wales. But its top speed of just 99 mph [160 km/h] didn't qualify the XPT for the high-speed badge. From 1986 on, however, it did look as if high-speed transport would move forward. Up until 1990, feasibility and viability studies had been done for a 544 mile [876 km] long high-speed rail line from Sydney via Canberra to Melbourne. The route was to include about 31 miles [50 km] of existing tracks in suburban Sydney and Canberra, as well as about 168 miles [270 km] of newly built high-speed line. Stations were planned at Mascot Airport, Southern Highlands, and Goulburn. The route would be mostly built close to or right next to existing highways, and designed for a maximum speed of 217 mph [350 km/h]. That would make travel time from Canberra to Sydney about 80 minutes. Yet in mid-December 2000, quite surprisingly, this $4.5 billion project was halted, which the government in Canberra justified as mainly due to financial difficulties.

Public transport was one of the major campaign issues in the 1976 elections in the Australian state of New South Wales. Between September 1977 and January 1978, the new government accepted offers for the construction of forty passenger coaches for long-distance travel, sixteen two-car diesel units for regional traffic, and twenty-five diesel express trains comparable to Westrail's "Prospector." In early 1978, the Australian Commonwealth Engineering Company (Comeng) put an interesting alternative on the table. Comeng proposed a diesel multiple-unit train, based on British Railways "Intercity 125 High Speed Train" (HST). Since Comeng was also a licensee of Bombardier (Canada), a version of VIA Rail's LRC was also under discussion. Fairly quickly, the government opted for the British HST, and already in February 1979, the Prime Minister grandly announced that 100 trains (twenty-six diesel-electric power units, sixty-six intermediate, and eight control cars) would be ordered for long-distance and regional service from Sydney to Wollongong, Nowra, Kempsey Grafton, Armidale, Orange, Wagga Wagga, and Canberra. These rail cars were to form eight Intercity

XPT SERVICE IN 2011				
Route	Distance	Trips/Day and direction	Fastest travel time	Average speed
Sydney-Melbourne	596 mi [960 km]	2	10 h 55 min	54.7 mph [88.1 km/h]
Sydney-Dubbo	288 mi [463 km]	1	6 h 29 min	44.2 mph [71.2 km/h]
Sydney-Grafton	432 mi [696 km]	1	10 h 8 min	42.8 mph [68.9 km/h]
Sydney-Casino	519 mi [836 km]	1	11 h 13 min	46.3 mph [74.6 km/h]
Sydney-Brisbane	613 mi [987 km]	1	13 h 36 min	45.1 mph [72.6 km/h]

units of two power cars and five intermediate cars, as well as six units for regional services, in the configuration of power car + three intermediate cars + control car. As it happened, only one contract worth $39 million was signed in March 1980, for the supply of thirty vehicles, to create four seven-car units with two spare power cars.

The powered trucks correspond to the British Type BP10 truck, which was used in the HST, but were given greater vertical mobility by the primary suspension and a smoother secondary suspension. The secondary suspension also has greater lateral mobility to cope with the rougher Australian tracks. By a better arrangement of the units, the power cars' weight was distributed more evenly on the trucks, than in the HST. During the development phase, a number of trucks were tested for suitability for use on the intermediate cars.

The main Melbourne-Sydney route runs over this scenic bridge near Wagga Wagga (NSW); here the "Melbourne XPT" is crossing, underway to Sydney on 11/20/2002.

Paxman Valenta diesel engines, already successfully used in the HST, powered the trains. The original 2,249 hp [1,678 kW] capacity, however, was cut by 10% to 1,980 hp [1,477 kW], so they could function better in the Australian climate. The lower ratio of power to total train weight, in conjunction with a lower transmission, ensured that the train could accelerate better after making intermediate stops or running on stretches with speed restrictions.

The first two vehicles, the XP2000 power car and car XF2200, were delivered on August 23, 1981. After an initial series of trial runs, on September 6, 1981, they set a new Australian speed record of 114 mph [183 km/h], travelling between Table Top and Gerogery (on the Sydney-Albury route). By October 1982, the manufacturer had delivered all the trains in the first order. After the success of the XPT in service to Dubbo, Kempsey, and Albury, it was quickly decided to use the XPT to link the Northern Tablelands and the Australian capital Canberra, to Sydney. For this, the rail operator ordered five additional power cars and fifteen intermediate cars, with seats that could be turned in the direction of travel. The new cars were delivered between November 1983 and September 1984. This made it possible to form six seven-car units (2 + 5). Three power cars and five intermediate cars were kept in reserve. Now passengers could reach Canberra and Tenterfield in the Northern Tablelands on the XPT. In 1992, the operators announced that more trains would be manufactured and the existing units overhauled in succession. This was done especially for the service between Sydney and Melbourne, starting in 1993. ABB Transportation in Dandenong, Victoria, got the contract to manufacture four more power cars, five first class intermediate cars, and eight sleeping cars. The new trains started operation between August 1992 and November 1993. The intermediate and sleeping cars were equipped with new trucks designed by ABB (NMA trucks). Test and express trips were made on the route to Albury, as the new power cars were put into service. During an express run on September 18, 1992, a train was supposed to break through the 124 mph [200 km/h] limit for the first time, but the speedometer only showed a top speed of 120 mph [193 km/h] between Table Top and Yerong Creek. But this was a new record for Australia in any case.

While generally proving to be relatively reliable, the Paxman Valenta engines showed the first signs of aging by the mid-1990s. Various alternatives were tested for replacements, such as newer Valentas, other Paxman engines, or engines from a completely different company. In 1999, the railway administration again

Australia

followed the example of Great Britain and decided to replace them with Paxman Type 12VP185 engines with 2,000 hp [1,492 kW] power output; this had already been successfully carried out on the British HST. Ironically, Paxman itself (then owned by Alstom) did not win the contract to supply and install the new engines, but A. Goninan & Co. of Newcastle, NSW, did, instead. The first XPT power cars, with their new motors, left the factory in mid-2000. By the end of 2002, all the Paxman Valenta engines had been replaced.

Currently, the XPT cars are getting their second general overhaul. They are being outfitted with new seat upholstery, carpets, and curtains. New restrooms will be added and the driver's consoles modernized. With a striking new paint job, the units will wear their third color scheme in their quarter-century-long career.

As Mt. Cooroy reigns aloof in the background, the Tilt Train's tilting electric railcars 301-302 round the bend at Cooroy on 11/26/1998, underway to Rockhampton.

Series designation:	XPT
Road numbers:	XP 2000-2018
Unit configuration:	T+7M+T
Wheel arrangement (power car):	Bo'Bo'
Wheel arrangement (intermediate car):	2'2'
Track gauge (ft [mm]):	4' 8.5" [1,435]
Maximum speed (mph [km/h]):	99 [160]
Output power car (hp [kW]):	2,024 [1,510]
Empty weight power car (t):	76
Service weight power car (t):	85
Empty weight entire train, seven car (t):	76 + 204 + 76
Maximum axle load (t):	19
Length (mm):	17,330 + 5 x 24,100 + 17,350
Distance between truck centers (ft [mm]):	33.7 [10,290]
Distance between truck centers intermediate car (ft [mm]):	52.4 [16,000]
Axle distance powered truck (ft [mm]):	8.5 [2,600]
Axle distance trailer truck (ft [mm]):	8.5 [2,600]
Driver wheel diameter (ft [mm]):	3.3 [1,020]
Trailer wheel diameter (ft [mm]):	3.3 [1,020]
Seats 1st/2nd class (seven car):	257 (77/180)
Commissioning:	1981-1993

Tilting to "zero" altitude in Queensland

On Nov. 6, 1998, the first Australian tilting trains began regular service. Once a day, the two new electric tilting railcars from Queensland Rail (QR) linked the Queensland capital Brisbane, via the 386 mile [622 km] Cape gauge route—narrow gauge track measuring 3' 6" [1,067 mm] wide—to Rockhampton in the north, in less than seven and a half hours.

After the North Coast Line (NCL) between Brisbane and Rockhampton was electrified at 25 kV/50 Hz in 1989, QR introduced a new connection between

two cities, the "Spirit of Capricorn." Along with electrification, there were various other improvements to the tracking, as well as four new long routings: to Eumundi Range, Gympie North, Maryborough West and Benaraby Bank near Gladstone. All this made possible an initially quite attractive travel time of nine hours and forty-five minutes between Brisbane and Rockhampton. But QR wanted more, and therefore decided to try to cut travel time by using tilt technology. On March 6, 1993, QR invited bids from various companies to manufacture two six-car electric tilting trains. After a good year and a half, the Walkers locomotive factory in Maryborough got the contract, worth $62.5 million AU, to assemble two six-car trains with tilting technology from Hitachi.

A six-car operating unit consists of two basic three-car units lined up: railcar, unpowered intermediate car (with buffet), and powered intermediate cars. The basic units cannot be divided up, because, for considerations of weight, the electrical equipment had to be distributed evenly along the three cars. The two powered cars of a basic unit are each equipped with four 255 hp [190 kW] AC motors. The maximum axle load is 12 tons; total weight of a six-car unit is 269 tons. The active tilting system, also used in Japanese Shikoku 8000 type tilting trains, allows a maximum tilt angle of five degrees. The tilting device control is interesting. The tilt mechanism is hydraulically activated, when required, by an on-board computer. The entire route profile between Brisbane and Rockhampton is stored in the on-board computer. At the beginning of the trip, the driver turns on the computer and it is advanced by sections during the trip. This way, the train always knows its current position. The train measures the distance traveled using the speedometer, and compares this with the data in the computer, which then activates the tilting device at the beginning of each curve. As a control, the train position is simultaneously checked by the CTC (Centralized Traffic Control) track magnets.

When the tilt mechanism is activated, the two pantographs of each unit tilt in the opposite direction. Walkers developed and patented a special mechanism to do this. If the active tilt technology fails, the tilt device also functions passively to ensure that the cars are both tilted and righted when rounding curves.

Each six-car unit includes a first class car (one of the two rail cars) and five economy cars. The First Class (Business) offers 30 swivel seats arranged 2 + 1. The 280 seats in Economy, in a 2 + 2 layout, cannot reverse direction. All cars are fully air conditioned and equipped with audio and video equipment. As in an airplane, each seat has controls for audio and video entertainment and folding tables. Headphones are handed out before each trip begins. Card phones and fax machines are also available. There are also outlets for laptops in First Class. Meals and refreshments (included in the ticket price) are here served at the seat, and there is also a selection of newspapers and magazines available. In Economy, passengers are served from a rolling mini bar and can also get their own refreshments in the two buffet cars.

The first three-car basic unit (Set No. 301) finally took its first steps on August 12, 1997, travelling between Maryborough and Gympie North, still pulled by a locomotive and not under its own power. The actual test phase, under its own power, began on October 21, 1997. After slowly powering up, two days later the tilting train toppled the Queensland speed record, reaching 106 mph [170 km/h] while traveling between Curra and Theebine. Only 14 mph [23 km/h] under the Australian speed record held by an XPT from NSW, this represents the highest speed ever reached in Australia on a Cape gauge track. By the autumn of 1998, testing, staff training, and track infrastructure modifications were all completed. On November 6, 1998, both trains started their first regular service. Since then, the tilt trains have been running largely trouble-free, and continue to make the 386 miles [622 kilometers] between Brisbane and Rockhampton in less than seven and a half hours. Including possibly up to eleven intermediate stops, this means a cruising speed of 52.2 mph [84.1 km/h]. Since May 23, 1999, the electric "Tilt Train" has also held the official Australian speed record. On the north coast route near Bundaberg, the Cape gauge Tilt Train, traveling at 130 mph [210 km/h], earned the Australian rail track blue ribbon.

QUEENSLAND'S DIESEL TILTING TRAINS

Along with modernizing, building partial new routes, and electrifying the North Coast section between Brisbane and Rockhampton, the North Coast Line

Waving fields of sugar cane and the Great Dividing Range in the background, this too, is Australia: the north-east coast of Queensland, where this promotional photo of a diesel tilt train (power car 5404 driving) was taken.

(NCL) also modernized the Rockhampton-Cairns connection in the north. It must be understood that this almost 621 mile [1,000 km] long stretch is a conglomerate of many short local tracks, which were once connected to the NCL by a government initiative. But it took great effort by the Queensland Railways QR over the years to adapt the NCL to the general rail network standard.

Even before regular service using the new electric tilting trains started between Brisbane and Rockhampton, the wish developed to establish a faster connection between Brisbane and Cairns, and cut travel time to less than twenty-five hours. As a result, two diesel tilt trains were already ordered from Walkers Ltd. (now EDI Rail) in Maryborough, on September 2, 1998. While the electric tilting train's intermediate cars could, more or less, be taken over as is, the power cars were a novelty on Australian rails, although they had good European models. They created a new Australian record in terms of power to weight ratio, using 3,600 hp [2,700 kW] and weighing no more than sixty tons. This was achieved by installing fast-running MTU diesel engines, combined with a hydraulic Voith gearbox, also known as the "German solution."

Using two power cars ensured that the total nine-car unit would always have enough power to keep the train at the maximum allowable speed and feed the electrical auxiliary systems. The power car bodies are made of stainless steel and are identical in shape to the intermediate cars. The power car "nose" is similar to the front of the electric tilting trains, clearly to project the same image of speed.

Each diesel engine also drives an additional 200 hp [150 kW] generator via a gear system to supply the auxiliary systems. The power units have a synchronization system to control current frequency, thus using the output of more than one generator.

Since one generator is coupled to each of the four diesel engines, there is always sufficient energy to run the train. Each intermediate car has two 33 hp [25 kW] air conditioning systems; the energy for these requires at least three generators on a very hot day at full occupancy. But even with simultaneous use of all four generators, the diesel engines still have 6,400 hp [4,800 kW] for traction. Since EDI Rail is the manufacturer, it is not surprising that the ventilators and cooling systems are modeled on their version of EMD locomotives.

In contrast to the electric Tilt Train, on the diesel-powered Tilt Trains, all cars are called First Class, and therefore have a 2 +1 seating layout. As in electric tilting trains, the car bodies are made of stainless steel with a light wave pattern, so that there is a much longer interval between the ribs, as in commuter and regional train carriages. Each unit consists of three regular passenger cars, two cars that can accommodate disabled people, a luggage/service car, and a Buffet and Club car. All seat backs recline and all the seats can be turned in the travel direction. The two cars designed for disabled people are equipped with restrooms for the disabled and removable seats, giving room for up to three wheelchairs per car, along with appropriate seating for accompanying persons. In the luggage and service car, there is seating for staff, refrigerators for the food, along with the train computer and entertainment system. The Buffet and Club car kitchen, as well as the take-out counter and rolling mini bars, provide "dining at your seat." There is also a small seating and relaxation area. The Hitachi-supplied tilting equipment corresponds to that for the electric tilting trains, allowing a five-degree tilt in each direction, controlled by the train's computer system. The QR company colors of yellow and brown were used for the rail cars, as on the electric tilting trains, while the power cars got a more pleasing design.

In the summer of 2002, the first cars of the two new diesel tilting trains were delivered, costing some $122 million AU. The 99 mph [160 km/h] trains were initially assigned to extensive trial runs. On the first few runs, the track line profile was recorded electronically to provide the basic data for the computer-controlled tilting system. After all

testing was completed and the remaining fifteen cars were available, on June 15, 2003, the first regular Australian diesel tilt train ran on the 1,044 mile [1,681 km] long Cairns-Brisbane route. The tilting trains now make the east coast Cape gauge connection in less than twenty-four hours. The Cairns Tilt Train leaves Brisbane on Mondays and Fridays; the train runs in the opposite direction, from Cairns, on Wednesdays and Sundays.

TILT TRAIN SERVICE IN 2011				
Route	Distance	Trips/ Day and direction	Fastest travel time	Average speed
Brisbane-Cairns	1,044 mi [1,681 km]	2/week	23 h 55 min	43.6 mph [70.3 km/h]
Brisbane-Rockhampton	386 mi [622 km]	1	7 h 25 min	52.2 mph [84.1 km/h]
Brisbane-Bundaberg	209 mi [337 km]	1	4 h 25 min	47.5 mph [76.6 km/h]

SERIES DESIGNATION:	DIESEL TILT TRAIN	ELECTRIC TILT TRAIN
Road numbers:	5401-5404	301-304
Unit configuration:	T+7M+T	T+M+2T+M+T
Wheel arrangement (end car):	B'B'	Bo'Bo'
Wheel arrangement (intermediate car):	2'2'	Bo'Bo' or 2*2
Power system:	-	25 kV/50 Hz
Track gauge [ft [mm]]:	3' 6" [1,067]	3' 6" [1,067]
Maximum speed (mph [km/h]):	99 [160]	106 [170]
Power output powered cars (kW):	2 x 1,350	4 x 190
Empty weight (t):	60 + 7 x 42 + 60	269
Maximum axle load (t):		12
Length (mm):	20,350 + 7 x 22,300 + 20,350	23,000 + 4 x 21,500 + 23,000
Distance between truck centers, power car, rail cars (ft [mm]):	41.3 [12,600]	52.4 [16,000]
Distance between truck centers intermediate car (ft [mm]):	52.4 [16,000]	52.4 [16,000]
Axle distance powered truck (ft [mm]):	8.2 [2,500]	7.3 [2,250]
Axle distance trailer truck (ft [mm]):	7.3 [2,250]	7.3 [2,250]
Driver wheel diameter (ft [mm]):	2.7 [840]	2.6 [810]
Trailer wheel diameter (ft [mm]):	2.6 [810]	2.6 [810]
Seats 1st/2nd class:	183 (only 1st class)	310 (30 + 280)
Commissioning:	2002-2003	1997

THE "PROSPECTOR" IN WESTERN AUSTRALIA

When the first "Prospector" diesel railcar began service in 1971, the new trains were touted in radio and television advertising as a modern railway line from Perth to Kalgoorlie in Western Australia's goldfields. The Prospector was then Australia's fastest train and the first one with full meal service at the passenger's seat, as in an airplane. This new service finally ended the fourteen-hour-long night trip on the old Cape gauge Kalgoorlie Express, a locomotive-hauled train with sleeping and passenger day coaches, since the Prospector covered the distance in less than eight hours.

The new trains (five power cars and three control cars) were developed and built by Commonwealth Engineering (Comeng) in Sydney, but were based on the classic American Budd railcar and the unique Budd "Pioneer III" truck with inner side frame and external disc brakes. The Prospector car bodies were modeled on the Indian Pacific carriages, but were made wider and had roof-mounted air-conditioning systems, with their characteristic bulge. Unlike the North American Budd railcars, in the Prospector, the large seats could be turned in the travel direction and had adjustable seat backs. The fare included a meal prepared in a small galley and then brought to the passenger's seat. There were no passageways, so passengers could not move from car to car. The passage doors could only be used by crew members; the ends of the train were covered with fiberglass panels, which better showed off the streamlined shape of the slanted train ends. The control car had a driver's cab at just one end; instead of a second cab, there was an additional row of seats. In over thirty years in service, the Prospector's method of operation changed little from the original trains, apart from some minor schedule changes. Externally, they got just a few different paint jobs over the years, but there were bigger modifications made in the drive technology. Originally, the railcars each had two 379 hp [283 kW] 12-cylinder boxer engines from MAN. In the 1990s, these were replaced by Cummins engines with an output of 449 hp [335 kW]. The braking system was also modernized at the same time, and the train's auxiliary generators were replaced.

After thirty-two years, carrying some 2.6 million passengers, and covering more than twelve million miles [twenty million kilometers] between Perth and Kalgoorlie, on July 29, 2005, the last first-generation Prospector trains were sent into a well-deserved retirement. These trains set a high standard that their

Seven of the total eight "old" Prospector trains (at the head is control car WCE 922) parked on the sidings in Kewdale, Perth, to await their destiny, on 11/15/2006.

successors had to match. When it began operation, the Prospector represented a greater leap forward than the introduction of the new, second-generation railcars. In any case, it marked the shift from the slow Cape gauge to fast normal gauge, regional passenger transport in Western Australia.

SERIES DESIGNATION:	PROSPECTOR (OLD) (VT)	PROSPECTOR (OLD) (VS)
Road numbers:	WCA 901-905	WCE 921-923
Wheel arrangement:	(1A)(A1)	2'2'
Track gauge (ft [mm]):	4' 8.5" [1,435]	4' 8.5" [1,435]
Maximum speed (mph [km/h]):	99 [160]	99 [160]
Engine power (kW):	2 x 283	-
Transmission:	hydraulic	-
Service weight (t):	68.22	50.37
Maximum axle load (t):	18	13
Coupling length (ft [mm]):	90 [27,432]	90 [27,432]
Axle distance (ft [mm]):	60 [18,288]	60 [18,288]
Axle distance powered truck (ft [mm]):	8.5 [2,591]	8.5 [2,591]
Axle distance trailer truck (ft [mm]):	8.5 [2,591]	8.5 [2,591]
Driver wheel diameter (ft [mm]):	2.8 [860]	2.8 [860]
Trailer wheel diameter (ft [mm]):	2.8 [860]	2.8 [860]
Seats:	60	64
Commissioning:	1971	1971

Australia

New railcars

Much public attention was given to the bid for the new Prospector diesel railcar, set in motion by the government of Western Australia in 1998. It was widely assumed that tilting trains would make the running. The first advertising images, however, showed pictures of the Oslo airport railcars; but these electric trains were of little use on the Perth-Kalgoorlie route. Finally, United Goninan won the bid for its factory at Broadmeadow, NSW. The new trains, after being transferred by rail across the entire continent in mid-2003 and then undergoing extensive test runs, were delivered to their destination on June 27, 2004, by then-Prime Minister of Western Australia Dr. Geoff Gallop, on a special trip from Kalgoorlie to Perth. Scheduled service began the following day, although for some time, various technical problems caused cuts in service, so that the old trains repeatedly had to be brought back as replacements. Since then, the trains have been running satisfactorily; on the fastest trips, they need six hours and thirty-five minutes to make the 407 mile [655 km] long Perth-Kalgoorlie connection. The selected design, while actually reflecting that of the old railcars in many ways, remains at the cutting edge of technology. Again, a 517 hp [386 kW] Cummins diesel engine, via a hydraulic Voith transmission, drives the inner axle of each truck. This was a departure from previous versions of the drive system on Australian diesel railcars, which usually had

Well ahead of schedule on 11/17/2006, the AvonLink (unit WEB041-WEA031) from Northam reaches its terminus, Midland (near Perth).

a larger engine that powered both axles on a truck. The Siemens type Sf 5000 trucks generally match those Siemens manufactured for Melbourne's suburban railcars, although they were modified in various ways to achieve the speed required for the Prospector.

One of the two big innovations was to change configuration to two- and three-car units, which also decreased the number of driver's cabs. In the old single car Prospector trains, the railcars still had two driver's cabs and the control car had one. Another innovation was a refreshment and dining counter, instead of "at-seat service" for all passengers. Only the first class passengers are served meals and other amenities at their seat, if they so choose. Many travelers appreciate the flexibility of a refreshment counter. Installing the counter meant reducing the number of seats from 60 to 38 in those areas.

New safety standards required installing crumple zones at the ends of the cars to provide better protection in case of a crash. Combined with the train design, the result was a rounded end with a driver's cab and a large single window. There are no passageways between the two or three car units, and so, in multiple unit operation, the crew has to staff the refreshment counter in each unit. Other changes included significantly improved facilities for disabled persons, especially for wheelchairs. The stainless steel car bodies have relatively widely spaced ribs, and the windows are set flush to the side wall. The blue-colored panels between the windows give a very sleek appearance. With the

Almost on time, at 7:42 (scheduled at 7:35), the Prospector two-car unit WDA002-WDB012 leaves the Midland train station for Kalgoorlie.

exception of the trucks, all the under-floor equipment is hidden beneath a panel, with numerous flaps to allow access to machines, gears, and other components. The train ends, made of molded/welded components, are painted bright yellow and, in the current Transwa color scheme, the railcar sides are decorated with colored, crescent-like stripes. The swiveling, adjustable, black leather-covered seats have a comfortable and modern look and feel.

The under-floor mounted Cummins diesel engines generate a similar level of performance as the old trains' engines, but are smaller. Unlike the old cars, with their independently operating generators, in the new trains, each diesel engine has a so-called "trans-technology" generator to produce electricity for the auxiliary systems, which requires an appropriately dimensioned converter to maintain constant power for lighting, air-conditioners, and refreshment counter facilities. This method to generate electricity for the auxiliary systems was one of the main problems that caused delays in the new railcars taking over regular service.

Tests revealed a problem in regulating power by the converter. Due to the engines' differing speeds, the generator and converter produced no "clean" power supply, which can cause problems with computer systems. On the Prospector railcars, this problem can lead to other computer-controlled systems failing. This is not a new problem; but it does not occur in diesel railcars with separate converters to generate electricity for the auxiliary systems.

The new AvonLink railcars are generally similar to the Prospector trains. The main difference is a closer seating layout, because they are for shorter distances and are used primarily in commuter traffic. The seats, which have high backrests, are arranged 2 + 3, and cannot be folded down. Although the backs are adjustable and provide reasonable comfort, these seats are not as comfortable as the swivel seats in the old Prospector railcars, which the AvonLink has since also used. Again, each train half has a restroom for the disabled, and space for wheelchairs. These trains do not serve food and drink. These railcars can be easily distinguished from outside, because the AvonLink units' end cars are painted a bright olive-green color instead of "Prospector yellow." Otherwise, everything is the same, including both the blue window frames and the colored "Transwa half-moons."

SERIES DESIGNATION:	WDA/WDB (WEA/WEB), NEW PROSPECTOR TWO CAR, AVONLINK	WDA/WDC/WDB (NEW PROSPECTOR THREE CAR)
Road numbers:	WDA001+WDB011, WDA002+WDB012, WEA031+WEB041	WDA003+ WDC021+ WDB013
Wheel arrangement:	(1A)(A1)+(1A)(A1)	(1A)(A1)+(1A)(A1)+(1A)(A1)
Track gauge (ft [mm]):	4' 8.5" [1,435]	4' 8.5" [1,435]
Maximum speed (mph [km/h]):	124 [200]	124 [200]
Engine power (kW):	4 x 386	6 x 386
Transmission:	hydraulic	hydraulic
Service weight (t):	136	204
Maximum axle load (t):	18	18
Coupling length (mm):	27,400 + 27,400	27,400 + 25,200 + 27,400
Axle distance (mm):	2 x 18,300	3 X 18,300
Axle distance powered truck (ft [mm]):	8.5 [2,600]	8.5 [2,600]
Axle distance trailer truck (ft [mm]):	-	-
Driver wheel diameter (ft [mm]):	2.7 [850]	2.7 [850]
Trailer wheel diameter (ft [mm]):	2.7 [850]	2.7 [850]
Seats:	98 (Prospector), 135 (AvonLink)	158
Commissioning:	2003-2005	2003-2004

VLOCITY IN VICTORIA

When the state of Victoria's rail transport system was divided up, in anticipation of privatization, the franchise agreement for the regional railway service required the new operators to procure twenty-nine two-car diesel rail cars, to improve regional short- and medium-haul transport. In 1999, the Great Britain-based National Express Group (NEG) won this bid and agreed to purchase the new diesel railcars. Bombardier proposed a design based on the Countrylink (NSW) Xplorer, and created the name "VLocity" for the train. Bombardier won the contract with this offer and it was agreed to produce the vehicles at its factory in Dandenong, Victoria. The VLocity contract was initially worth about $410 million AU. On September 5, 2000, the government of Victoria presented its "Regional Fast Rail" project, which provided for the largest-scale expansion of regional rail tracks in 120 years, including modernizing the routes to Ballarat, Bendigo, Geelong, and Traralgon. The extensive improvement work

AUSTRALIA

VLocity unit 44 (sequence 1244-1344-1144), already in the new V/Line colors, could be photographed at the Melbourne suburb of Footscray on January 24, 2011.

led to the acquisition of new trains that have run on a new-and-improved timetable from 2006 onward. One result of the generous improvement plan in train service was that the VLocity contract was increased by a further nine units, to a total of thirty-eight two-car diesel railcars, which was already a large order for Australia. The value of the order rose to some $550 million AU. But things went further: after December 2006, another two double units and fourteen additional motorized intermediate cars, to make three-car trains, went on Bombadier's order books. Eight more intermediate cars were added in October 2007. In late July 2008, the order was again increased to nine more three-car units and another motorized intermediate car.

The VLocity cars are modern, if somewhat conservatively designed, diesel railcars for the fast regional service, similar to the Transwa units of the AvonLink service. After the controversial Victoria Regional Fast Rail project was completed, with its upgraded tracks and modernized signaling system, VLocity was to realize shorter travel times. The VLocity units were originally designed as double trains, of two end railcars with almost identical floor plans. Each

car has an open-plan area, with some seats behind each other and some facing opposite each other. The open-plan cars have automatic sliding doors at each end. Each car has two independent air conditioning systems under hoods on the roof, so that if one unit fails, the second will still provide passengers with cool air. Each carriage has a restroom in the inner end entryway, and a roomier disabled restroom is in an end car. There are two wheelchair spaces in each open seating area. There is also storage space for larger pieces of luggage, bicycles, and surfboards, as well as luggage lockers. A passenger information system in each half car displays the name of the next station. The tinted windows completely fill their frames and give the impression of a continuous ribbon window. Each car has a stainless steel box frame, and the driver's module, made completely of fiberglass, is in the end of the cab. A type of complex steel frame is inserted between the steel body and module, as a front crash-impact absorber, in compliance with the latest safety regulations. Safety is also increased by a front panel that reaches almost to the rails, designed to prevent anything falling under the wheels and derailing the train. Two flat structures on each car roof house the refrigeration and air conditioning equipment. The fiberglass-reinforced plastic roof panels give the impression of a semi-elliptical roof.

A Type OSK 19 R Cummins diesel engine is housed under each car, equipped with a self-diagnostic system to detect and correct problems. Each half car has a 114 hp [85 kW] generator for the auxiliary electrical systems. The rooftop cooling systems include six coolers, for the engine, generator, the hydrodynamic brakes (ventilation and ventilation drive system), and an air cooling mechanism, including a fuel-cooling system and two electric ventilators. The trains are equipped with a Voith three-gear Type T312bre hydrodynamic transmission with integrated hydrodynamic brakes. It has an electronic transmission control, which can also enter and store operating and diagnostic data. Voith also supplied the cardan shafts to connect the transmission to the axles.

The trucks are based on the latest development of Bombadier's M-Series, which feature good road performance, dynamic stability, and low maintenance costs. They can be easily converted to standard gauge as required. Since VLocity requires frequent and quick coupling and uncoupling, it was given the most suitable Scharfenberg coupler. To distinguish the new railcars from the general rolling stock, the V/Line operator gave VLocity a new purple, green, and black color scheme, which harmonizes well with the unpainted stainless steel corrugated side walls. A new VL42 unit wearing the new V/Line company colors made its first appearance in June 2010, featuring crimson instead of purple stripes on the roof, a red rather than green front, and a red stripe along the car side below the windows. The doors now gleam in white instead of green. Other modifications included additional headlights and an improved windshield and wipers.

The first unit was presented to an admiring public in May 2004, and the first test runs began just one month later, since the train had to complete an extensive test program. In the course of these tests, it was found that the noise level in the passenger carriages was much too high, leading to extensive reworking. All twenty-six units had to be refitted with sound-proofing in the floors. Passengers also complained during test runs that there were no refreshments available; they especially emphasized the lack even of drinking water. So Bombardier put drinking fountains in these twenty-six vehicles. The remaining twelve units got these new measures when they were made. The entire trial and

retrofit phase took eighteen months; scheduled service only started after all this. On December 22, 2005, a triple-working two-car unit opened the VLocity service to Ballarat and on to Ararat. By August 2008, the first two three-car units (VL40 and 41) were operating. All the ordered trains should have been delivered by 2012. They are now mainly used on routes to Geelong, Ballarat (and on to Ararat), Bendigo (and on to Eaglehawk and Echuca), Seymour, and Taralgon (and on to Sale).

Ready for a test run, the first VLocity unit (1201-1101) is presented to in-house photographers.

SERIES DESIGNATION:	VLOCITY
Road numbers:	VL0-VL18 (1100/1200-1118/1218), VL19-VL51 (1119/1319/1219-1151/1351/1251)
Wheel arrangement:	B'2'+2'B', B'2'+B'2'+2'B'
Track gauge (ft [mm]):	5' 3" [1,600]
Maximum speed (mph [km/h]):	99 [160]
Engine power (kW):	2 x 559.3 x 559
Transmission:	hydraulic
Service weight two car (t):	116
Maximum axle load (t):	16
Coupling length three car (ft [mm]):	83 + 81+ 83 [25,257 + 24,700 + 25,257]
Axle distance (mm):	2 x 16,800.3 x 16,800
Axle distance powered truck (ft [mm]):	8.5 [2,600]
Axle distance trailer truck (ft [mm]):	8.5 [2,600]
Driver wheel diameter (ft [mm]):	3 [940]
Trailer wheel diameter (ft [mm]):	3 [940]
Seats:	140 (two car), 222 (three car)
Commissioning:	2004-2012

CHINA

In 2000, the Chinese government's new Five Year Plan gave the starting signal for the nation to enter the era of high speed rail. The plan called for constructing an approximately 800 mile-long [1,300 km-long] high-speed line from Beijing to Shanghai, which was calculated to cost almost $17 billion [€13 billion]. A number of existing routes were to be electrified and upgraded, at least in part, so that trains could run at a maximum speed of 124 mph [200 km/h]. The new Beijing-Shanghai project was then put on hold because the alternative, the German Transrapid maglev train, was also under discussion for a time. However, work on upgrading the existing 909 mile [1,463 km] long route from Shanghai via Nanjing, Jinan and Tianjin to Beijing, went even faster. Due to this gung ho action, the route was fully electrified for rail transport by July 2006. Erecting the supports for the overhead wires began in October 2005 and was essentially completed by early November. The track was upgraded in many sections for top speeds of 124 mph [200 km/h] and more. The objective of the sixth acceleration program of October 1, 2005, was to make it possible for trains to make the Beijing-Shanghai trip in a good seven hours, which would mean a 124 mph [200 km/h] cruising speed. Back then, the fastest train took twelve hours. With an investment of nearly $13 billion [€10 billion], the Chinese railways raised the maximum speed on five main lines, some 1,242 miles [2,000 km], to 124 mph [200 km/h]. The upgraded lines included Beijing-Shenyang and Jinan-Qingdao.

In 2004, the Chinese government approved construction of over 1,900 miles [3,200 km] of new high-speed lines. In summer 2005, celebrations for the start of building work on the planned new routes were happening almost on a weekly basis. In June, work was started on the 615 mile [989 km] long north-south Wuchang-Changsha-Guangzhou connection, and the 117 mile [189 km] line from Shijiazhuang to Taiyuan.

A few days later, on July 4, came the starting gun for the new Beijing-Tianjin line, with an investment of some $1.8 billion [€1.4 billion]. Between late September and early October, work began on the Zhengzhou-Xi'an and Xiamen-Fuzhou links. Also in 2005, the ground was broken for the Nanjing-Hefei and Hefei-Wuchang links.

In Shanghai itself, two new stations were built for high speed trains: while the Shanghai Railway Station Nan (= south) was rebuilt as the terminus for trains from Changsha, trains from Beijing, Hefei, and Nanjing used the completely new train station right by the Shanghai Hongqiao Domestic Airport. This train station has a total of thirty tracks.

In August 2008, the 71 mile [115 km] long high-speed Beijing-Tianjin line was opened, as the first "real" high speed line in the People's Republic of China. At peak times, the 186 mph [300 km/h] trains run every three minutes. Soon afterwards came the Zhengzhou-Xi'an high speed line, 286 miles [460 km] long, and, by the end of 2009, the 596 mile [960 km] Wuhan-Guangzhou section of the Beijing-Hong Kong high speed line. In early July 2010, there were already eleven high-speed lines with a total length of 4,300 miles [6,920 km] in operation, with 1,240 miles [1,995 km] designed for a maximum speed even up to 217 mph [350 km/h]. By 2012, the high-speed network was to grow to more than 8,000 miles [13,000 km] long, with 804 new stations planned. Above and beyond this, China is meanwhile also considering the construction of international high speed lines. In April 2011, work began on a link to the Laotian capital of Vientiane. In the long term, a line is planned to run from southern China's Nanning via Hanoi, Bangkok, Penang, and Kuala Lumpur, to Singapore. In addition to this high-speed network, to increase speed on heavily used passenger routes, separate tracks are being laid both for freight and passenger transport.

THE FIRST FAST TRAINS

GRADED AND NEW ROUTES IN THE PRC	LENGTH	MAXIMUM SPEED	OPENING
ghu PDL (= Passenger Dedicated Line)			
Beijing-Tianjin-Jinan-Nanjing	632 mi [1,017 km]	236 mph [380 km/h]	06/30/2011
Nanjing-Shanghai	187 mi [301 km]	236 mph [380 km/h]	07/01/2010
jin Intercity Line			
Beijing-Tianjin (new)	71 mi [115 km]	217 mph [350 km/h]	08/01/2008
ngtai PDL			
Taiyuan-Shijiazhuang	118 mi [190 km]	155 mph [250 km/h]	04/01/2009
Shijiazhuang-Jinan		155 mph [250 km/h]	2012
Jinan-Qingdao	226 mi [364 km]	155 mph [250 km/h]	12/20/2008
hanrong PDL			
Wuchang-Hefei	218 mi [351 km]	155 mph [250 km/h]	04/01/2009
Hefei-Nanjing	103 mi [166 km]	155 mph [250 km/h]	04/18/2008
kun PDL			
Shanghai-Hangzhou	125 mi [202 km]	217 mph [350 km/h]	10/26/2010
Hangzhou-Changsha	575 mi [926 km]	217 mph [350 km/h]	2012
Hangzhou-Kunming		217 mph [350 km/h]	
utheast Coastal			
Hangzhou-Ningbo	94 mi [152 km]	217 mph [350 km/h]	2011
Ningbo-Wenzhou	166 mi [268 km]	155 mph [250 km/h]	09/28/2009
Wenzhou-Fuzhou	185 mi [298 km]	155 mph [250 km/h]	09/28/2009
Fuzhou-Xiamen	161 mi [260 km]	155 mph [250 km/h]	12/31/2009
Xiamen-Shenzen	312 mi [502 km]	155 mph [250 km/h]	2011
an PDL			
Xuzhou-Zhengzhou		217 mph [350 km/h]	
Zhengzhou-Xi'an	301 mi [485 km]	217 mph [350 km/h]	02/06/2010
Xi'an-Baoji		217 mph [350 km/h]	
Baoji-Lanzhou		217 mph [350 km/h]	
gang PDL			
Beijing-Shijiazhuang	135 mi [218 km]	217 mph [350 km/h]	2012
Shijiazhuang-Wuhan	522 mi [840 km]	217 mph [350 km/h]	2012
Wuhan-Changsha-Guangzhou	601 mi [968 km]	217 mph [350 km/h]	12/26/2009
Guangzhou-Shenzhen-Hongkong	88 mi [142 km]	217 mph [350 km/h]	2010
huangdao-Shenyang (Qinshen PDL)	251 mi [404 km]	155 mph [250 km/h]	10/12/2003
nyang-Dandong (Shendan PDL)	139 mi [224 km]		2013
jin-Qinhuangdao (Jinqin PDL)	162 mi [261 km]	217 mph [350 km/h]	2011
nchang-Jiujiang (Changjiu Intercity Line)	84 mi [135 km]	155 mph [250 km/h]	09/20/2010
ei-Bengbu (Hebeng PDL)	81 mi [131 km]	217 mph [350 km/h]	2012
ei-Fuzhou (Hefu PDL)	501 mi [806 km]	217 mph [350 km/h]	2014
jin-Qinhuangdao (Guiguang PDL)	532 mi [857 km]	300 km/h	2014
zhou-Urumqi (Lanxin PDL)	1,103 mi [1,776 km]	217 mph [350 km/h]	2014
ngdu-Chongqing (Chengyu PDL)	189 mi [305 km]	217 mph [350 km/h]	2014
gdao-Rongcheng (Qingyanrong Intercity Line)	186 mi [299 km]	155 mph [250 km/h]	2013
ngdu-Dujiangyan (Chengguan High speed rail)	40 mi [65 km]	137 mph [220 km/h]	05/12/2010
angzhou-Zhuhai (Intercity Mass Rapid Transit)	73 mi [117 km]	124 mph [200 km/h]	01/07/2011
kou-Sanya (Hainan East Ring Intercity Line)	191 mi [308 km]	155 mph [250 km/h]	12/30/2010
ngchun-Jilin (Changji Intercity Line)	69 mi [111 km]	155 mph [250 km/h]	01/10/2011
jing-Anqing (Ningan Intercity Line)	160 mi [257 km]	155 mph [250 km/h]	2012
jing-Hangzhou (Ninghang Intercity Line)	156 mi [251 km]	217 mph [350 km/h]	2012

When upgrade work was finished on the 91 mi [146 km] Guangzhou-Shenzhen railway in the 1990s, trains could run at 124 mph [200 km/h] for the first time in the People's Republic of China. The Chinese part of the former Guangzhou-Kowloon Railway (Guangzhou-Hong Kong) has a rail line speed of 137 mph [220 km/h], but normal traffic only runs at a maximum of 124 mph [200 km/h]. Passenger trains on this route are partly run by the privately owned Guangshen Railway Corporation (GSRC), which put the first high speed train in China into operation in early 1998. This was an X2, built by the train manufacturer ADtranz (now Bombardier), which was allowed to manufacture the train on its own account after it had delivered forty-three multiple unit trains to the Swedish State Railways. This seven-car unit was initially only on loan to the Guangshen Railway Corporation; in January 1998, it was shipped from Gothenburg to China. After a three-month testing and acceptance phase, the Chinese X2 was to run on the Guangzhou-Shenzhen-Hong Kong link for at least two years. In October 2000, the railcars were purchased by China Railways.

CHINA

A Chinese X2 rounds a curve near Hong Kong University in June 2004.

To give China's own trains a chance, however, no more of these trains were ordered. The Chinese X2 ran as the "*Xinshisu*" (= new speed) twice daily until 2007, the fastest train between Hong Kong and Guangzhou; it makes this trip in just ninety-two minutes.

On Oct. 1, 1999 (the 50th anniversary of the founding of the People's Republic of China), the GSRC started regular service using the first Chinese-built high-speed train. The unit's series designation is DDJ1; it has a top speed of 124 mph [200 km/h]. It is not a classic railcar, but a power car with five intermediate cars and a control car. The power car was built by Zhuzhou Electric Locomotive Works; the intermediate and control cars were made by several large Chinese construction companies. The cars had individual features, depending on their builder. The first intermediate car following the power car was designed as a double-decker car, using tried and true drive technology. The power unit has four alternating-current series-wound motors, to generate 5,300 hp [4,000 kW] drive power, regulated by DC control. The nose, which remotely resembles that of an ICE 1, was made of fiberglass. The DDJ1 ran between Guangzhou and Shenzhen until 2005, but is now out of service.

Beginning on November 5, 2000, a new multiple-unit train made its first test runs between Guangzhou and Shenzhen. In contrast to its predecessor, the "*Lanjian*" (= blue arrow), series designation DJJ1, represented something approaching a technological quantum leap. Although the multiple-unit train configuration—power car, five intermediate cars, and a control car—was retained, the drive technology, with four three-phase

asynchronous motors and 6,400 hp [4,800 kW] drive power, was that of a really modern train. The Zhuzhou Electric Locomotive Works again manufactured the power cars; the intermediate and control cars were made by the Changchun Works. The DJJ1's top speed is 130 mph [210 km/h], but on a December 2000 test run the speedometer stayed at 146 mph [235 km/h]. Since December 28, 2000, eight "*Lanjian*" units have been in regular service between Guangzhou and Shenzhen.

SERIES DESIGNATION:	X2000	DDJL	DJJ1 (LANJIAN)
Road numbers:			001-008
Unit configuration:	T+5M+S	T+5M+S	T+5M+S
Wheel arrangement (motor end coach):	Bo'Bo'	Bo'Bo'	Bo'Bo'
Wheel arrangement (intermediate car):	2'2'	2'2'	2'2'
Wheel arrangement (control car):	2'2'	2'2'	2'2'
Power system:	25 kV/ 50 Hz	25 kV/50 Hz	25 kV/50 Hz
Track gauge (ft [mm]):	4' 8.5" [1,435]	4' 8.5" [1,435]	4' 8.5" [1,435]
Maximum speed (mph [km/h]):	130 [210]	124 [200]	130 [210]
Output powered cars (hp [kW]):	4,370 [3,260]	5360 [4,000]	6,400 [4,800]
Empty weight (t):	366 (seven car)	440	
Maximum axle load (t):	18.5	19.5	19.5
Power car length (ft [mm]):	58.2 [17,750]	61.7 [18,816]	67.2 [20,500]
Control car length (ft [mm]):	72.1 [21,980]	83.6 [25,500]	83.6 [25,500]
Intermediate car length (ft [mm]):	80 [24,400]	83.6 [25,500]	83.6 [25,500]
Coupling length (ft [mm]):	541 [165,000] (seven car)	564 [171,816]	569 [173,500]
Distance between truck centers (ft [mm]):	29.4 [8,975]		37 [11,280]
Axle distance powered truck (ft [mm]):	9.5 [2,900]	9.5 [2,900]	9.8 [3,000]
Axle distance trailer truck (ft [mm]):	9.5 [2,900]	8.2 [2,500]	8.2 [2,500]
Driver wheel diameter (ft [mm]):	3.6 [1,100]	3.6 [1,100]	3.4 [1,050]
Trailer wheel diameter (ft [mm]):	2.8 [880]	3 [915]	3 [915]
Seats:	309 (seven car)	438	421
Commissioning:	1998	1999	2000-2001

"CHINA STAR" (SERIES DJJ2)

Initially, the Chinese wanted to get in on the act, using their own designs in the area of "real" high-speed transport. In 2002, the fast "China Star" (series DJJ2)—which runs up to 168 mph [270 km/h]—celebrated its roll-out at the Zhuzhou Electric Locomotive Works.

The Guangshen Railway Company Limited's DJJ1 0005 making itself useful on the rails between Shenzhen and Guangzhou on March 3, 2007.

SERIES DESIGNATION:	DJJ2 "CHINA STAR"
Road numbers:	
Unit configuration:	T+9M+T
Wheel arrangement (motor end coach):	Bo'Bo'
Wheel arrangement (intermediate car):	2'2'
Power system:	25 kV/50 Hz
Track gauge (ft [mm]):	4' 8.5" [1,435]
Maximum speed (mph [km/h]):	168 [270]
Output powered cars (hp [kW]):	12,870 [9,600 (8 x 1,200)]
Service weight power car (t):	78
Service weight entire train (t):	478
Maximum axle load (t):	19.5
Power car length (ft [mm]):	71.1 [21,700]
Intermediate car length (ft [mm]):	83.6 [25,500]
Coupling length (ft [mm]):	895 [272,900]
Distance between truck centers (ft [mm]):	
Axle distance powered truck (ft [mm]):	9.8 [3,000]
Axle distance trailer truck (ft [mm]):	8.2 [2,500]
Driver wheel diameter (ft [mm]):	3.4 [1,050]
Trailer wheel diameter (ft [mm]):	3 [915]
Seats:	772
Commissioning:	2002

These trains featured some borrowings from the ICE 1. The China Star was composed of two power cars, with nine unpowered intermediate cars lined up in between; specifically, six Second Class passenger cars, two First Class passenger cars, and a bar car. Four three-phase asynchronous motors provided 6,400 hp [4,800 kW] drive power per power car, controlled via a water-cooled GTO thyristor chopper.

The car sections were made in super lightweight construction. In 2005, the train began regular passenger service on the Shenyang-Shanhaiguan route, but was limited to a top speed of 99 mph [160 km/h]. As of August 2006, this service was stopped and the China Star has been parked in the Shenyang depot since 2007.

THE CHR 2 SERIES (SHINKANSEN E2 DERIVATIVE)

After China's own inadequate attempts, the Japanese Shinkansen technology first got an opportunity to run on the new Chinese upgraded and high-speed lines. As part of a multi-billion dollar investment package, in early October 2004 a consortium of six Japanese companies, including Kawasaki, Hitachi, and Mitsubishi Electric, won the first bid for high-speed trains.

An unknown CRH2A flying along the Shanghai-Nanjing high-speed line on July 17, 2010.

The consortium, which operated under the name Koki Railway System, was made responsible for supplying sixty eight-car Shinkansen trains. The trains are based on the JR East Series E2-1000, but have a top speed of just 155 mph [250 km/h]. The first three units were built entirely in Japan. Six other trains went to China as an "assembly kit," where they were assembled by the Chinese manufacturer CSR Sifang. As part of

SERIES DESIGNATION:	CRH2A	CRH2B	CHRH2C	CRH2E
Road numbers:	001A-060A, 151A-190A *)	111B-120B	061C-090C *), 091C-110C, 141C-150C	121E-140E
Unit configuration:	S+2T+2M+2T+S	S+2T+2M+2T+2M+2T+2M+2T+S	S+6T+S	S+2T+2M+2T+2M+2T+2M+2T+S
Wheel arrangement (end car):	2'2'	2'2'	2'2'	2'2'
Wheel arrangement (intermediate car):	Bo'Bo' or 2'2'	Bo'Bo' or 2'2'	Bo'Bo' or 2'2'	Bo'Bo' or 2'2'
Power system:	25 kV/50 Hz	25 kV/50 Hz	25 kV/50 Hz	25 kV/50 Hz
Track gauge (ft [mm]):	4' 8.5" [1,435]	4' 8.5" [1,435]	4' 8.5" [1,435]	4' 8.5" [1,435]
Maximum speed (mph [km/h]):	155 [250]	155 [250]	186 [300]*), 217 [350]	155 [250]
Output powered cars (kW):	4 x 300	4 x 300	4 x 300*), 4 x 365	4 x 300
Empty weight entire train (t):	345			
Maximum axle load (t):	14	14	14*), 15	14
End car length (ft [mm]):	84.3 [25,700]	84.3 [25,700]	84.3 [25,700]	84.3 [25,700]
Intermediate car length (ft [mm]):	82 [25,000]	82 [25,000]	82 [25,000]	82 [25,000]
Entire train length (ft [mm]):	1,317 [401,400]	1,317 [401,400]	661 [201,400]	1,317 [401,400]
Distance between truck centers (ft [mm]):	57.4 [17,500]	57.4 [17,500]	57.4 [17,500]	57.4 [17,500]
Axle distance powered truck (ft [mm]):	8.2 [2,500]	8.2 [2,500]	8.2 [2,500]	8.2 [2,500]
Axle distance trailer truck (ft [mm]):	8.2 [2,500]	8.2 [2,500]	8.2 [2,500]	8.2 [2,500]
Driver wheel diameter (ft [mm]):	2.8 [860]	2.8 [860]	2.8 [860]	2.8 [860]
Trailer wheel diameter (ft [mm]):	2.8 [860]	2.8 [860]	2.8 [860]	2.8 [860]
Seats (1st/2nd class):	610 (51/559), *) 600 (67/533)	1,230 (155/1,075)	610 (51/559)	2nd class: 110, sleeper: 520
Commissioning:	2004-2012	2008-2009	2007-2012	2008-2010

the technology transfer agreement, CSR Sifang then finished the remaining fifty-one multiple-unit trains itself. The first unit from the Kobe factory of Kawasaki Heavy Industries was shipped to Qingdao in northern China on March 3, 2006, as Series CRH2A (CRH = China Railway High speed)—without much media attention, so as to avoid fueling any anti-Japanese sentiment in China.

After the first sixty CRH2A trains were delivered, the Japanese work was done and the Chinese built all of the following CHR 2 derivatives on their own from 2007 forward. In fact, the Japanese had not imagined that this technological catch-up and copying process would proceed so fast. So much for technology transfer.

On September 14, 2010, the Chinese Ministry of Railways ordered another forty CRH2A units (CRH2 151A-190A) from CSR Sifang, to be delivered by 2012. Already in November 2007, the Ministry of Railways ordered ten sixteen-car CRH2 trainsets with the designation CRH2B, and six sixteen-car sleeping car trains, called CRH2E. A month later came an increased order for fourteen more CRH2E units. Their eight powered cars give the trainsets a total 12,800 hp [9,600 kW] capacity and a top speed of 155 mph [250 km/h]. The CRH2B can seat passengers in three First Class carriages and twelve Second Class, and also has a dining car. The CRH2E has thirteen First Class

sleeping cars, two Second Class passenger cars, and a dining car. The first CRH2B was delivered on June 29, 2008, and was already in scheduled service on the Hefei-Nanjing high speed line by August 1, 2008. The first six CRH2E started service on December 21, 2008, between Beijing and Shanghai. Between June and September 2005, the Ministry of Railways announced that trains would be manufactured that could run at a maximum speed of 186 mph [300 km/h]. CSR Sifang offered to supply, together with the Siemens Velaro derivative CRH3C, sixty multiple-unit type CRH2C trains, divided between thirty "CRH2C Version 1" (186 mph [300 km/h]) and thirty "CRH2C Version 2" (217 mph [350 km/h]) trainsets. The Ministry then ordered both versions of the CRH2C, in the quantities offered.

The "CRH2C Version 1" is a modified version of the CRH2, in which the two non-motorized intermediate cars were replaced by motorized cars, to enable the train to reach 186 mph [300 km/h]. The vehicle is state-of-the-art (Chinese) technology, with reduced-weight car bodies made of an aluminum alloy, high-speed trucks and pantographs, and a fiber optics-based integrated control system. On December 22, 2007, the first CRH2-061C rolled out of the factory. During test runs on April 22, 2008, the train reached a top speed of 230 mph [370 km/h] on the high speed Beijing-Tianjin line, and on December 11, 2009, even

CRH2-028A awaiting departure for its continued trip, at the Jinan station on September 21, 2008.

hit 245 mph [394.2 km/h] on the Zhengzhou-Xi'an high speed line. Currently, mostly CRH2C Version 1 railcars are travelling between Shanghai and Nanjing. CRH2C Version 2 is the name of the "redesigned" version of the CRH2. Some details were taken from the CRH3C (Velaro CN), such as the torsion-resistant aluminum car bodies and noise abatement accessories. In addition, China's newest and (especially) foreign technologies were used to increase the maximum speed to 217 mph [350 km/h]. The truck axle load was increased from fourteen to fifteen tons, to prevent the train from vibrating at higher speeds. The gear ratio was improved from 3.036 to 2.379, and the critical speed is now reportedly 342 mph [550 km/h]. To generate the necessary total 11,742 hp [8,760 kW] drive power, the train has twenty-four 489 hp [365 kW] three-phase asynchronous motors. The first CRH2-091C unit was introduced in January 2010 and began operation in February 2010 on the Zhangzhou-Xi'an high speed line.

THE CHR5 ("NEW PENDOLINO" WITHOUT TILTING TECHNOLOGY)

Shortly after Shinkansen got its order in October 2004, Alstom also got a piece of the pie. The Chinese Ministry of Railways concluded an agreement with Alstom, similar to that with the Japanese: the Alstom contract, valued at some $800 million [€620 million], was for sixty eight-car railcars with a top speed of 124 mph [200 km/h], which were used for fast regional transit from 2007. They were based on the "New Pendolino," but without tilting technology. Three trains were manufactured entirely in Europe; another six were sent to China in parts. The remaining fifty-one units were built under a technology transfer agreement by

the Chinese partner company, Changchun Railway Vehicles Company Ltd. (CNR), with Alstom contributing necessary pieces of equipment from its plants in Savigliano, Italy, and La Rochelle, France. The first train (CRH5-001A) left the port of Savigliano on December 11, 2006, and reached the Chinese port of Dalian on January 28, 2007. As the first completely self-manufactured CNR unit, CRH5-010A rolled out of the factory in April 2007. Initially, the trains had a lot of problems, attributable to the new technologies as well as the relatively short delivery time. After a period, the CRH5 trains ran largely without problems, and

The CRH5-058A, before departure from the Beijing central Railway Station, on July 14, 2010.

SERIES DESIGNATION:	CRH5A
Road numbers:	001A-110A
Wheel arrangement (eight car):	(1A)(A1)+(1A)(A1)+2'2'+(1A)(A1)+2'2'+2'2'+(1A)(A1)(A1)+(1A)(A1)
Power system:	25 kV/50 Hz
Track gauge (ft [mm]):	4' 8.5" [1,435]
Maximum speed (mph [km/h]):	155 [250]
Hourly output (kW):	
Nominal power (continuous power) (hp [kW]):	7,400 [5,500 (10 x 550)]
Empty weight (t), eight car:	451
Service weight (t), eight car:	
Maximum axle load (t):	17
Coupling length (ft [mm]), eight car:	693.8 [211,500]
End car length (ft [mm]):	90.5 [27,600]
Intermediate car length (ft [mm]):	82 [25,000]
Distance between truck centers (mm):	8 x 19,000
Axle distance powered truck (ft [mm]):	8.8 [2,700]
Axle distance trailer truck (ft [mm]):	8.8 [2,700]
Driver wheel diameter (ft [mm]):	2.9 [890]
Trailer wheel diameter (ft [mm]):	2.9 [890]
Seats (eight car):	586 (112 + 474)
Commissioning:	2006-2012

CH NA

therefore China ordered thirty additional trainsets in 2009, and twenty more units followed 2010. CNR was the exclusive supplier. The CRH5A runs mainly on the northern and eastern China high speed lines—the Jingha, the Jingguang, and Shitai railways.

Just a few minutes ago, the CRH1-001A departed on its trip from Guangzhou to Shenzhen on March 3, 2007.

SERIES DESIGNATION:	CRH1A	CRH1B
Road numbers:	001A-040A, 081A-120A*)	061B-080B
Unit configuration:	T+M+2T+M+T+M+T	T+M+2T+M+T+M+2T+M+T+M+2T+M+T
Wheel arrangement (end car):	Bo'Bo'	Bo'Bo'
Wheel arrangement (intermediate car):	Bo'Bo' or 2'2'	Bo'Bo' or 2'2'
Power system:	25 kV/50 Hz	25 kV/50 Hz
Track gauge (ft [mm]):	4' 8.5" [1,435]	4' 8.5" [1,435]
Maximum speed (mph [km/h]):	137 [220], 155 [250]*)	155 [250]
Output powered cars (kW):	4 x 265	4 x 275
Empty weight entire train (t):	435	850
Maximum axle load (t):	18.5	18.5
End car length (ft [mm]):	88.4 [26,950]	88.4 [26,950]
Intermediate car length (ft [mm]):	87.2 [26,600]	87.2 [26,600]
Entire train length (ft [mm]):	700.4 [213,500]	1,398.6 [426,300]
Distance between truck centers (mm):	16 x 19,000	16 x 19,000
Axle distance powered truck (ft [mm]):	8.8 [2,700]	8.8 [2,700]
Axle distance trailer truck (ft [mm]):	8.8 [2,700]	8.8 [2,700]
Driver wheel diameter (ft [mm]):	2.7 [840]	2.7 [840]
Trailer wheel diameter (ft [mm]):	2.7 [840]	2.7 [840]
Seats (1st/2nd class):	611 – 668	1,299 (208/1,091)
Commissioning:	2004-2011	2008-2009

THE CRH1 REGINA DERIVATIVES

The Bombardier Sifang Power Corporation (BSP) consortium, including Bombardier and its joint venture partners, Power Corporation of Canada and China South Locomotive and Rolling Stock Industry Corporation, got a contract in October 2004 to manufacture twenty eight-car high-speed trains. Their top speed was to be 137 mph [220 km/h]. This order was increased for twenty more trains, in spring 2005. The total order was worth around $720 [€560] million, with Bombardier's share amounting to some $395 [€306] million. Bombadier developed the trains in Vasteras, Sweden. Parts of the drive system rolled off the line there, while the trucks were produced at Bombardier's German plant in Siegen. The car bodies were built in China, however, where final assembly was done under the responsibility of BSP. The CRH1-001A was the first of the forty units delivered, starting on August 30, 2006; all the units were finished by December 2007. The trains began scheduled service on February 1, 2007, on the Guangzhou-Shenzhen route.

Under the motto, "Eight cars are not enough," on October 31, 2007, the Ministry of Railways ordered sixteen-car multiple unit trains from BSP 20. This train, the CRH1B, was basically a double CRH1A. The trains are designed for a speed of 155 mph [250 km/h], and include three First Class cars, twelve Second Class cars, and a dining car. In April 2009, the first CRH1B began regular service on the Shanghai-Nanjing and Shanghai-Hangzhou routes. The Ministry of Railways ordered another forty type CRH1A trainsets in July 2010, but now wanted them to have an operating speed of 155 mph [250 km/h]. During its test runs in September 2010, the CRH1-081A reached a maximum speed of 173 mph [278 km/h] on the Qinhuangdao-Shenyang high speed line.

The sixteen-car CRH1E sleeper car train, photographed in the Beijing trainyard on June 4, 2010.

Series designation:	CRH1E	CRH380D	CRH380DL
Road numbers:	061E-080E	6601-6620	6621L-6680L
Unit configuration:	T+M+2T+M+ T+M+2T+M+ T+M+2T+M+T	T+M+T+2M +T+M+T	T+M+T+2M+T+ M+2T+M+T+ 2M+T+M+T
Wheel arrangement (end car):	Bo'Bo'	Bo'Bo'	Bo'Bo'
Wheel arrangement (intermediate car):	Bo'Bo' or 2'2'	Bo'Bo' or 2'2'	Bo'Bo' or 2'2'
Power system:	25 kV/50 Hz	25 kV/50 Hz	25 kV/50 Hz
Track gauge (ft [mm]):	4' 8.5" [1,435]	4' 8.5" [1,435]	4' 8.5" [1,435]
Maximum speed (mph [km/h]):	155 [250]	236 [380]	236 [380]
Power output powered cars (kW):	4 x 275	4 x 625	4 x 625
Empty weight entire train (t):	859	462	934
Maximum axle load (t):	16.5	17	17
End car length (ft [mm]):	92.6 [28,250]	91.3 [27,850]	91.3 [27,850]
Intermediate car length (ft [mm]):	87.2 [26,600]	87.2 [26,600]	87.2 [26,600]
Entire train length (ft [mm]):	1,407 [428,900]	706.3 [215,300]	1,404.5 [428,100]
Distance between truck centers (mm):	16 x 19,000	8 x 19,000	16 x 19,000
Axle distance powered truck (ft [mm]):	8.8 [2,700]	8.8 [2,700]	8.8 [2,700]
Axle distance trailer truck (ft [mm]):	8.8 [2,700]	8.8 [2,700]	8.8 [2,700]
Driver wheel diameter (ft [mm]):	2.7 [840]	2.7 [840]	2.7 [840]
Trailer wheel diameter (ft [mm]):	2.7 [840]	2.7 [840]	2.7 [840]
Seats (VIP/1st /2nd class):	2nd class: 122, Sleeper: 480 + 16 VIP	495 (14/90/391)	1,013 (52/126/835)
Commissioning:	2009-2010	2012-2014	2012-2014

THE ZEFIRO VERSIONS (CRHIE, CRH380D/DL)

On October 31, 2007, the Chinese Ministry of Railways ordered twenty sixteen-sleeping-car trains based on BSP's so-called Zefiro 250. These trainsets, series designation CRH1E, are largely revamped sixteen-car Regina railcars, with a modified "Zagato design" nose. Each unit includes a luxury sleeper, twelve normal sleepers, two 2nd Class day coaches, and a dining car. The train's interior design and furnishings set new standards in China for high-speed night trains, since their sleeping compartments meet the highest demands for comfort. The first CRH1E trainset was delivered in October 2009 and began regular service between Beijing and Shanghai on November 4, 2009.

In July 2010, the Ministry of Railways ordered forty more trains based on the ZEFIRO 250. They were supplied in an eight-car version for normal passenger travel and have VIP, 1st, and 2nd Class seating. At the

end of September 2009, Bombardier let it be known that it had received an order from the Ministry of Railways to manufacture eighty ZEFIRO 380 high speed trains. They were to be built by the joint venture Bombardier Sifang (BSP). The order included twenty eight-car (CRH380D) and sixty sixteen-car (CRH380DL) trains, costing an estimated $3.4 [€2.7] billion, with Bombardier's share amounting to some $1.6 [€1.3] billion. The trains are based on the latest generation of ZEFIRO high-speed technology, and have a maximum operating speed of 236 mph [380 km/h]. They are equipped with energy-efficient MITRAC drive and control technology and energy-saving EC04 technology. Delivery of new trains is expected between 2012 to 2014.

THE CRH3 VERSIONS

After emerging empty-handed from long negotiations in the "great bidding" in 2004, the German locomotive manufacturer Siemens got its opportunity anyway, on November 10, 2005. It was allowed to supply sixty of the ICE 3-based high-speed trains ("Velaro CN"). With the designation CRH3C, this eight-car, 186 mph [300 km/h] fast streak of lightning, was to go into service between Beijing and Tianjinin in 2008, in time for the Olympic Games.

A lucky shot for the photographer: two double-unit CRH3Cs running by each other on the high-speed Beijing-Tianjin line, on February 16, 2010.

The Chinese vehicle clearance profile would allow the trains to be built twelve inches [30 cm] wider than the German or Spanish models. This allows a 2 + 3 seat layout in 2nd Class and 2 + 2 in 1st Class, providing seating for some 600 passengers. The first three units were built completely in Uerdingen, Germany. The remaining trains were assembled by the Chinese

Series designation:	CRH3C "Velaro CN"			CRH380B	CRH380BL, CL
Road numbers:	001C to 080C			6231 to 6270	6201L to 6230L, 6271L to 6285L, 6301L to 6325L, 6401L to 6470L
Wheel arrangement (configuration):	Bo'Bo'+2'2'+Bo'Bo'+2'2'+2'2'+Bo'Bo'+2'2'+Bo'Bo'				T+M+T+2M+T+M+2T+M+T+2M+T+M+T
Power system:	25 kV/50 Hz			25 kV/50 Hz	25 kV/50 Hz
Track gauge (ft [mm]):	4' 8.5" [1,435]			4' 8.5" [1,435]	4' 8.5" [1,435]
Maximum speed (mph [km/h]):	217 [350]			236 [380]	236 [380]
Nominal power (continuous power) (hp [kW]):	11,800 [8,800 (16 x 550)]			12,330 [9,200 (16 x 575)]	24,660 [18,400 (32 x 575)]
Empty weight (t):	425				
Service weight (t):	462				
Maximum axle load (t):	17			17	17
End car length (ft [mm]):	83.7 [25,535]			83.7 [25,535]	84.8 [25,850]
Intermediate car length (ft [mm]):	79.3 [24,175]			79.3 [24,175]	81.4 [24,825]
Coupling length (ft [mm]):	657.2 [200,320]			657.2 [200,320]	1,309.9 [399,270]
Distance between truck centers (mm):	8 x 17,375			8 x 17,375	16 x 17,375
Axle distance powered truck (ft [mm]):	8.2 [2,500]			8.2 [2,500]	8.2 [2,500]
Axle distance trailer truck (ft [mm]):	8.2 [2,500]			8.2 [2,500]	8.2 [2,500]
Driver wheel diameter (ft [mm]):	3 [920]			3 [920]	3 [920]
Trailer wheel diameter (ft [mm]):	3 [920]			3 [920]	3 [920]
Seats (VIP/1st/2nd Class):	556 (16 + 50 + 490)				1,004 (13/77/914)
Commissioning:	2008-2010			2011-	2010-

partner, Tangshan Locomotive & Rolling Stock Works, with the proportion of European supplies declining steadily as technology transfer increased accordingly. As time was rather pressing because of the Olympics and EXPO 2010, the contract had to be fulfilled quite quickly. At the peak of production, four trains would run off the production line in Tangshan per month, and the last unit left the factory in December 2009. During a test run between Beijing and Tianjin, the CRH3 001C reached a top speed of 245 mph [394.3 km/h] on June 24, 2008. The units 013C and 017C CRH3 set a new world record for a double-unit on December 9, 2009; they hit a maximum speed of 244.9 mph [394.2 km/h] on the high speed line from Zhengzhou to Xi'an. As early as September 28, 2009, the Ministry of Railways ordered twenty more CRH3C, which have since been delivered.

In March 2009, the Ministry signed another contract with CNR to manufacture 100 sixteen-car multiple-unit trains based on the Velaro (CRH380BL) for delivery in October 2010. This order, for a total of 1,600 individual cars, is larger than the total production of all Velaro and ICE trains to date. These trains were built by the CNR subsidiaries Tangshan Railway Vehicles and Changchun Railway Vehicles, with the help of Siemens technology transfers; they are designed to run at 236 mph [380 km/h]. However, under this contract, Siemens still supplied eighteen percent of the components. Another contract to manufacture forty additional sixteen-car CRH380BL trainsets and forty

eight-car CRH380B units was signed on September 28, 2009. Changchun Railway Vehicle presented a revised front design for the CRH380B at the "Modern Railways 2010" in Beijing on December 6. This new design is currently called CRH380CL, and has electrical equipment from Hitachi. The Ministry has decided to have twenty-five of these sixteen-car trains made, instead of the twenty-five CRH380BL ordered.

Unit CRH380B-6401LA was the first sixteen-car train to roll off the production line in Tangshan, and was presented to the public in September 2010. Beginning in November 2010, the railcar underwent test runs on the Beijing-Shanghai high speed line, where it hit a top speed of 284 mph [457 km/h] on December 5, 2010. One month later, on January 10, 2011, a CRH380BL trainset broke even the Chinese speed record, traveling at 302.7 mph [487.3 km/h]; a CRH380A running at 302 mph [486.1 km/h] had held the previous record. Since January 13, 2011, the first CRH380BL have been in scheduled service on the high speed Shanghai-Hangzhou and Shanghai-Nanjing lines.

THE CRH380A

Since China's own nationally developed technology had yet to be proven, China at first reverted to the tried and tested means of technology transfer. After having bought various high-speed trains from the major European locomotive manufacturers, Alstom, Bombardier, and

Siemens—including the fundamental technologies—they finally had enough know-how to put a functioning "self developed" technology on the rails. The result was the CRH380A, a combination of the Regina, Velaro, Zefiro, and especially of the Shinkansen. In September 2009, the Chinese Ministry of Railways eventually ordered 100 sixteen-car (CRH380AL) and forty eight-car (CRH380A) trainsets from CSR Sifang.

Of course, a new design had to be created for the CRH380 "nose." Any similarities with the latest Shinkansen are entirely coincidental. The car bodies are made of a lightweight aluminum alloy and use a variety of new materials providing sufficient vibration absorption. The undercarriage uses advanced Shinkansen trucks, which should reduce structural vibration at high speeds and improve ride comfort.

SERIES DESIGNATION:	CRH380A	CRH380AL
Road numbers:	6001-6040	6041L-6140L
Unit configuration:	S+6T+S	S+14T+S
Wheel arrangement (end car):	2'2'	2'2'
Wheel arrangement (intermediate car):	Bo'Bo'	Bo'Bo'
Power system:	25 kV/50 Hz	25 kV/50 Hz
Track gauge (ft [mm]):	4' 8.5" [1,435]	4' 8.5" [1,435]
Maximum speed (mph [km/h]):	380	380
Power output powered cars (kW):	4 x 365	4 x 365
Empty weight entire train (t):		
Maximum axle load (t):	15	15
End car length (ft [mm]):	84.3 [25,700]	84.3 [25,700]
Intermediate car length (ft [mm]):	82 [25,000]	82 [25,000]
Entire train length (ft [mm]):	666 [203,000]	1,322 [403,000]
Distance between truck centers (mm):	8 x 17,500	16 x 17,500
Axle distance powered truck (ft [mm]):	8.2 [2,500]	8.2 [2,500]
Axle distance trailer truck (ft [mm]):	8.2 [2,500]	8.2 [2,500]
Driver wheel diameter (ft [mm]):	2.8 [860]	2.8 [860]
Trailer wheel diameter (ft [mm]):	2.8 [860]	2.8 [860]
Seats (1st/2nd Class):	494 (107/387)	1,027
Commissioning:	2010-2011	2010-2012

The new CRH380A power unit just had to be at the Expo in Shanghai on August 16, 2010.

The pressure-tight car bodies reduce noise levels at top speed to an acceptable level, due to usage of new sound-absorbing and insulating materials. So-called high-performance engines (three-phase asynchronous 489 hp [365 kW] motors) provide the drive power. By comparison: the latest DB generation of the Velaro (BR 407) has engines with an output of 670 hp [500 kW]. The regenerative brakes make it possible to feed a corresponding amount of energy back into the power supply.

An eight-car prototype left the factory in April 2010, underwent its first tests at the Beijing test ring beginning on April 26, 2010, and eventually graduated from its extensive trial runs to the high speed Zhengzhou-Xi'an railway on June 7, 2010. The first serial-production CRH380A unit was delivered in August 2010. During test runs on the Shanghai-Hangzhou high speed line on September 28, 2010, it attained the respectable top speed of 258.8 mph [416.6 km/h]. From September 30, 2010, it was in temporary regular service on the Shanghai-Nanjing high speed railway. More CRH380A trainsets went into service on this route beginning on

October 26, 2010, as well as between Shanghai and Hangzhou. The travel time between Shanghai and Hangzhou is now cut from 1 hour 18 minutes to 45 minutes, and between Nanjing and Hangzhou, from 3 hours 19 minutes to 2 hours 48 minutes. The CRH380A took over another field of operation—on the high speed Wuhan-Guangzhou rail link—on December 3, 2010.

The first sixteen-car CRH380A-6041L celebrated its roll out in October 2010. Beginning on November 8, 2010, tests on Beijing's test ring followed. High-speed travel between Beijing and Shanghai began on November 20, 2010. There it set a short-lived Chinese speed record of 302 mph [486.1 km/h] on December 3, 2010.

THE "SLOW DOWN"

Amazingly, even China's railways now began to think about energy costs. Beginning on July 1, 2011, a reduced maximum speed of 186 mph [300 km/h] instead of the previous 217 mph [350 km/h] was enacted, so as to significantly reduce energy and maintenance costs. This "speed limit" brings China's high speed trains back into European speed ranges. Indeed, the European railways recognized some time ago that speeds above 205 mph [330 km/h] require dramatically more energy and produce much more wear and tear. So we can keep wondering about the further development of China's "speed mania."

JAPAN

Japan's first efforts to build a standard gauge high speed rail line started as early as the 1930s. The increase in traffic on the Tokaido and Sanyo lines (Tokyo-Osaka-Hakata) was so great by 1935, that the Japanese began to build a new standard gauge track for high speed trains in September 1940. The trains' speed was to be fast enough so they would need only four and a half hours to travel from Tokyo to Osaka, and nine hours from Tokyo to Shimonoseki, the southwestern-most city on Japan's main island of Honshu. Due to the course of the war, however, work had to be stopped in 1944, without a single section being completed.

Japan's economy only reached prewar levels in the late 1950s, a good ten years after the disastrous Second World War. Then, many years of remarkable economic growth began. Sustaining that economic growth required much higher capacity in both passenger and freight transport, which was being limited by the large proportion of mainly Cape gauge railways (3' 6" [1,067 mm]) in Japan's internal transport market. The Japanese National Railways, JNR, made large-scale investment during the 1960s to advance modernization of the major routes. By the end of the war, the Japanese National Railways (JNR from 1949) had run exclusively on steam power, while private railways in urban areas were already electrified, and the small and minor private local railways increasingly relied on diesel railcars. The state railways were only electrified in the metropolitan areas of Tokyo and Osaka, and on rail lines with long tunnels. Many of the private railway companies, however, had been nationalized during the war, and these already had electrified lines. As a result, by 1950, JNR had an electrified rail network of 1,031 miles [1,659 kilometers], eight percent of a total network of 12,294 miles [19,786 kilometers]. The trains ran electrically on 1,500-volt direct current.

As already noted, at that time the JNR was suffering from a serious problem: the volume of transport on the 345 mile [556 km] long Tokaido route from Tokyo to Osaka, the industrial and commercial center of western Japan, was rising sharply due to the rapid post-war growth of the Japanese economy. The rail line's capacity was largely exhausted, even as they were being fully electrified during the fall of 1956. Some twenty-four percent of the total passenger ridership and twenty-three percent of total cargo volume that was handled on the state railways travelled on this rail line. Transport volume rose by 7.6% annually, although the route length was only 3% of the total JNR railroad network. It was clear to everybody that the capacity of the existing Tokaido Line had to be doubled to meet demand, but, as to the "how," there were three completely different opinions:

- construction of a new Cape gauge route parallel to the existing one;
- construction of a new Cape gauge route with a completely new routing plan;
- and construction of a standard gauge track based on the model of European main rail lines.

Those responsible were soon convinced that only a normal gauge Tokaido route could ensure a decisive level of improvement, which would enable the railways to compete with the American and European railroads. In addition, Japan had excellent experience with railcars to date, and these could be used on the new route. In terms of design, they had proven that distributing the tractive power was a great advantage. With all axles powered, it would be possible to generate the propulsion needed for the required speed, without exceeding axle load limits. In addition, there was the risk of heat damage to the wheels and axles from quickly braking a train from high speed with block or disc brakes. Motorized axles solved this problem, because they now could be braked electrically. Improving the electrical braking to regenerative braking (which feeds back the electric energy) would yield energy saving economic effects.

BUILDING THE SHINKANSEN

After all questions were clarified, the government decided in December 1958 to build a new standard gauge railway (*Shin-Kan-Sen* = new main line) along the Tokaido line. The government estimated that a construction time of five years and investment of some $2.03 [¥194.8] billion would be required to connect Tokyo with Osaka in a travel time of about three hours.

To secure the necessary funding and remain independent of political developments, Japan obtained a large portion of the required financing a loan of $80 million from the World Bank. To get such a loan, the government had to guarantee completion of the project in good time, and that no newly elected government could change this. At the beginning of 1960, the World Bank was convinced that the "Shinkansen" would not involve any experimental technologies, but exclusively use proven new technologies, under the motto "safety first."

The top priority now was to have the Shinkansen operating before October 1964, when the Tokyo Olympic Games would begin. Since a large part of the required land had been acquired before the war, construction proceeded fairly rapidly. However, the government-approved budget was kept to a minimum from the outset, for political considerations; the lack of financial resources became increasingly evident as

construction continued. This developed into a serious political problem. By the end, costs had risen to $3.96 [¥380] billion, almost twice as high as estimated. The JNR leadership assumed responsibility, and as a result, the "inventor" of the Shinkansen, JNR President Sogo, and his vice president Shima, resigned shortly before completion of the new line.

Based on the standards defined for the new line, the smallest curve radius was kept to 8200 ft [2,500 m], the maximum slope to 1:50, and the top speed to 130 mph [210 km/h] (168 mph [now 270 km/h]). The rail line was electrified with AC 25 kV/60 Hz; there were no street-level crossings along the entire route. The most advanced safety systems, including cab signaling and automatic speed control (ATC—automatic train speed control), were applied. On October 1, 1964, the Tokaido Shinkansen was finally opened, in time for the Olympics. For the first time in the world, there was a train that regularly reached the 124 mph [200 km/h] mark and demonstrated its high safety standards at the same time. Previously, Japanese railway technology had not enjoyed any great international reputation, partially based on the restrictions due to the Cape gauge. But with the success of the Shinkansen, Japan's railways began attracting global attention.

From 1965 on, the "*Hikari*" (= light), could travel the 320 miles [515 km] between Tokyo and Osaka, with only a few stops, in three hours and ten minutes. More exactly, the Tokaido Shinkansen ends at the Shin-Osaka train station—meaning nothing more than "newer" or "Shinkansen" station—which has no link to the normal Cape gauge network. Initially, only two trains—including the "*Kodama*" (= echo), which stops at all stations—ran on the new route every hour in each direction, but frequency has kept increasing year by year. The Tokaido Shinkansen became a world model for high-speed transport, such as the French TGV or the German ICE. Although construction was financed largely by loans, the strong demand quickly ensured its commercial success.

CONNECTING THE FOUR MAIN ISLANDS

After the success of the Tokaido Shinkansen, construction started on the Sanyo Shinkansen to extend the Shinkansen westwards. In 1975, the new line reached Hakata in Fukuoka, on the island of Kyushu. The planned maximum speed was 162 mph [260 km/h], so that the train route parameters were set for a minimum curve radius of 13,124 ft [4,000 m] and a maximum gradient of 1:67. The route includes many tunnels, including the remarkable 11.6 mile [18.7 km] long Kanmon tunnel under the strait between the islands of Honshu and Kyushu.

Public opinion now strongly demanded that Shinkansen lines be built throughout the country. The Japanese government decided to promote construction of more extensions. In 1970, it passed the "Law on the National Development of the Shinkansen." Both the Tohoku Shinkansen to Morioka and the Joetsu Shinkansen to Niigata were built, based on this Act. Both lines were almost fully operational by 1982; only the connection to Tokyo itself could not be completed until 1991, due to various problems. Since the Joetsu Shinkansen crosses the island of Honshu from south to north, it has many long tunnels, including the 13.7 mile [22.2 km] long Daishimizu tunnel. Since 1990, some trains have run on this route at a top speed of 170 mph [275 km/h].

Construction costs for Shinkansen lines keep rising to dizzying heights, not least due to the increasingly challenging topography. Japan began looking for less costly alternatives. Planners came up with the idea to simply modify the Cape gauge routes to standard gauge, and this is how the mini-Shinkansen was developed. Top speed had to be limited, however, on these modified Cape gauge stretches. They also required special trains, since the vehicle clearance profile was not increased.

The Shinkansen boom continued unbroken, but naturally the number of new routes opening declined over the years. Today (as of June 2013) the Shinkansen network has a total length of 1,484 mi [2,388 km]. The newest addition (opened on March 12, 2011) is the section between Yatsushiro and Fukuoka on Kyushu. Three other short sections, with a total length of 262 mi [422 km] and planned opening between 2014 and 2018, are currently under construction and another 217 mi [350 km] are planned.

THE SHINKANSEN RAIL LINES:				
Name	Route	Length	Opening	Operator
Tokaido-Shinkansen	Tokyo-Nagoya-Osaka	320.2 mi [515.4 km]	10/01/1964	JR Central
Sanyo-Shinkansen	Osaka-Okayama-Hiroshima-Kokura-Hakata	344 mi [553.7 km]		JR West
	Osaka-Okayama	99.9 mi [160.9 km]	03/15/1972	
	Okayama-Hiroshima-Kokura-Hakata	244 mi [392.8 km]	10/03/1975	
Hakata-Minami Line	Hakata-Hakata-Minami	5.2 mi [8.5 km]	04/01/1990	JR West
Kyushu Shinkansen	Hakata-Yatsushiro-Kagoshima-Chuo	159.5 mi [256.8 km]		JR Kyushu
	Hakata-Minami-Kumamoto-Yatsushiro	80.7 mi [130.0 km]	03/12/2011	
	Yatsushiro-Kagoshima-Chuo	78.7 mi [126.8 km]	03/13/2004	
Kyushu Shinkansen	Hakata-Nagasaki			JR Kyushu
	Hakata-) Tosu-Takeo-Onsen	route planning still open		
	Takeo-Onsen-Isahaya	28.3 mi [45.7 km]	still open	
	Isahaya-Nagasaki	12.6 mi [20.3 km]	still open	
Tohoku Shinkansen	Tokyo-Ueno-Omiya-Fukushima-Sendai-Morioka-Hachinohe-Aomori	419.3 mi [674.9 km]		JR East
	Omiya-Morioka	289 mi [465.2 km]	06/23/1982	
	Ueno-Omiya	17.2 mi [27.7 km]	03/14/1985	
	Tokyo-Ueno	2.2 mi [3.6 km]	06/20/1991	
	Morioka-Hachinohe	60 mi [96.6 km]	01/12/2002	
	Hachinohe-Aomori	50.8 mi [81.8 km]	04/12/2010	
Hokkaido Shinkansen	Aomori-Hakodate-Sapporo	223.8 mi [360.2 km]		JR Hokkaido
	Aomori-Hakodate	92.5 mi [148.9 km]	planned for 2015	
	Hakodate-Sapporo	131.2 mi [211.3 km]	still open	
Joetsu-Shinkansen	Omiya-Takasaki-Niigata	167.4 mi [269.5 km]	11/15/1982	JR East/JR West
Hokuriku or Nagano Shinkansen	Takasaki-Nagano	72.9 mi [117.4 km]	01/10/1997	JR East
	Nagano-Toyama	100.7 mi [162.1 km]	planned for 2012	JR East/JR West
	Toyama-Isurugi-Kanazawa	36.3 mi [58.5 km]	planned for 2014	JR West
	Kanazawa-Tsuruga	74.8 mi [120.5 km]	still open	JR West
	Tsuruga-Osaka	route planning still open		JR West
Yamagata Shinkansen (mini-Shinkansen)	Fukushima-Yamagata-Shinjo	92.3 mi [148.6 km]		JR East
	Fukushima-Yamagata	54.1 mi [87.1 km]	03/14/1992	
	Yamagata-Shinjo	38.2 mi [61.5 km]	12/04/1999	
Akita Shinkansen (mini-Shinkansen)	Morioka-Akita	79.1 mi [127.3 km]	03/22/1997	JR East

THE SUPER-ON-TIME SHINKANSEN

During the past year, the Shinkansen have reportedly never been delayed by more than twelve seconds (the year before, it was no more than eighteen seconds). This is not good enough for the railway companies; they want to cut this delay to zero at most! In comparison: on the DB, trains arriving less than five minutes late are considered on time. Since in Japan, trains running, for example, between Tokyo and Osaka, the second largest city, depart just a few minutes apart, any greater delay would cause chaos—160,000 Shinkansen run every year just between these two cities.

TECHNICAL DATA OF THE SHINKANSEN 0-500:

SERIES DESIGNATION	0	100	200	300	400	500
Road numbers:	R61-68	K51-K60, P1-12	F8, F19, K21-31, K41-51	F1-9, J1-61	L1-12	W1-9
Unit configuration:	4T, 6T, 12T, 16T	4T, 6T, S + 10T + S, S+6T+2M+6T+S, 6T+4M+6T	10T, 12T, 6T + M + 6T, 8T + 2M + 6T	S+T+M+2T+M+2T +M+2T+M+2T +M+T	6T, 4T + M +2T	16T
Wheel arrangement (end car):	Bo'Bo'	Bo'Bo' or 2'2'	Bo'Bo'	Bo'Bo' or 2'2'	Bo'Bo'	Bo'Bo'
Wheel arrangement (intermediate car):	Bo'Bo'	Bo'Bo' or 2'2'	Bo'Bo' or 2'2'	Bo'Bo' or 2'2'	Bo'Bo' or 2'2'	Bo'Bo'
Power system:	25 kV/60 Hz	25 kV/60 Hz	25 kV/60 Hz	25 kV/60 Hz	20/25 kV/50 Hz	25 kV/60 Hz
Track gauge (ft [mm]):	4' 8.5" [1,435]	4' 8.5" [1,435]	4' 8.5" [1,435]	4' 8.5" [1,435]	4' 8.5" [1,435]	4' 8.5" [1,435]
Maximum speed (mph [km/h]):	137 [220]	168 [270]	171 [275]	168 [270]	149 [240]	199 [320]
Power output powered cars (kW):	4 x 185	4 x 230	4 x 230	4 x 300	4 x 210	4 x 285
Empty weight car (t):	53-57.5	46-56	57-62	38-41.8	39.6-49.0	39.5
Empty weight entire train (t)						
Maximum axle load (t):	16		17			
End car length (ft [mm]):	82.5 [25,150]	85.4 [26,050]	82.5 [25,150]	85.4 [26,050]	75.7 [23,075]	88.5 [27,000]
Intermediate car length (ft [mm]):	82 [25,000]	82 [25,000]	82 [25,000]	82 [25,000]	67.2 [20,500]	82 [25,000]
Entire train length (ft [mm])						
Distance between truck centers (ft [mm]):	57.4 [17,500]	57.4 [17,500]	57.4 [17,500]	57.4 [17,500]	46.4 [14,150]	57.4 [17,500]
Axle distance powered truck (ft [mm]):	8.2 [2,500]	8.2 [2,500]	8.2 [2,500]	8.2 [2,500]	7.3 [2,250]	8.2 [2,500]
Axle distance trailer truck (ft [mm]):	-	8.2 [2,500]	8.2 [2,500]	8.2 [2,500]	7.3 [2,250]	8.2 [2,500]
Driver wheel diameter (ft [mm]):	2.9 [910]	2.9 [910]	2.9 [910]	2.8 [860]	2.8 [860]	2.8 [860]
Trailer wheel diameter (ft [mm]):	-	2.9 [910]	2.9 [910]	2.8 [860]	2.8 [860]	2.8 [860]
Seats:						
Commissioning:	1964-1986	1984-1991	1980-1986	1989-1998	1990-1992	1995-1998

EARTHQUAKES

Seismic activity is nothing unusual on the Japanese islands, and earthquakes are relatively common. This meant that special measures had to be taken on the Shinkansen routes, to avoid accidents caused by earthquakes. As a result, for example, there are sensors along the tracks to record seismic activity and, in case of increasing earthquake waves, to immediately turn off the power supply in the substations. The power cut will immediately activate an emergency brake on the trains. After several earthquakes, the operators reviewed their infrastructure as to earthquake safety and initiated various measures to strengthen bridges and elevated sections, further reducing any future damage from earthquakes. A Shinkansen derailment was thoroughly investigated. As a further measure, the early warning systems have been improved, so that a train can stop even one second before the onset of an earthquake. Up to the present, the Shinkansen can boast that no passenger has been injured on any of the trains. Let us hope this continues.

THE SHINKANSEN TRAINS

During the time of the national railway, until 1987, they often acquired several hundred—even at times more than 3,000—railcars of a single series in a unified design. Today, however, there is no longer any real national railway in Japan; in 1987, the JNR was split into six regional JR passenger transport companies and a national freight company. Japan's geography played an important role in this division. Passenger traffic and the route network on the three smaller main islands of Hokkaido, Shikoku, and Kyushu were each taken over by a company of the same name; transport and the routes on Honshu was shared among three companies: JR East took over metropolitan Tokyo and the rural areas of northeastern Japan, JR Central, the Nagoya metropolitan area and central Japan, and JR West, the Osaka metropolitan area and rural western Japan. These six completely independent companies form the JR Group, which is represented to the outside world by a common logo. In Japan, there was no separation of railway infrastructure and operation, and service

121

TECHNICAL DATA OF THE SHINKANSEN: 700 – E6:

700	N700	800	E1	E2	E3	E4	E5	E6
B1-15, C1-60, E1-16	Z0, Z1-80, N1-16, S1-19, R1-10	U001-U006	M1-6	N1-13, N21, J2-15, J51-75	R1-26, L51-53, L61-72	P1-22, P51-52, P81-82	S11, U2-60	S12
S+6T+2M+6T+S, S+6T+S	S+14T+S.8T	6T	S+2T+2M+2T +2M+2T+S	S+6T+S, S+8T+S	2T+2M+2T, 2T+M+T+M+2T	S+2T+2M+2T+S	S+8T+S	T+M+3T+M+T
2'2'	2'2'	Bo'Bo'	2'2'	2'2'	Bo'Bo'	2'2'	2'2'	Bo'Bo'
Bo'Bo' or 2'2'	Bo'Bo'	Bo'Bo'	Bo'Bo' or 2'2'	Bo'Bo'	Bo'Bo' or 2'2'	Bo'Bo' or 2'2'	Bo'Bo'	Bo'Bo' or 2'2'
25 kV/60 Hz	25 kV/60 Hz	25 kV/60 Hz	25 kV/60 Hz	25 kV/50/60 Hz	20/25 kV/50 Hz	25 kV/60 Hz	25 kV/50 Hz	20/25 kV/50 Hz
4' 8.5" [1,435]	4' 8.5" [1,435]	4' 8.5" [1,435]	4' 8.5" [1,435]	4' 8.5" [1,435]	4' 8.5" [1,435]	4' 8.5" [1,435]	4' 8.5" [1,435]	4' 8.5" [1,435]
177 [285]	186 [300]	161 [260]	149 [240]	171 [275]	171 [275]	149 [240]	199 [320]	199 [320]
4 x 275	4 x 305	4 x 275	4 x 410	4 x 300	4 x 300	4 x 420	4 x 311	4 x 311
40.0			53.6-62.0	39.0-46.0	40.6-46.6	50.3-56.9	41.9-46.8	42.5-45.7
	715 (16 car)						453.5	
			17.0	13.0	12.0	16.0		
89.7 [27,350]	89.7 [27,350]	89.7 [27,350]	85.4 [26,050]	84.3 [25,700]	75.7 [23,075]	82.2 [25,070]	86.9 [26,500]	75.7 [23,075]
82 [25,000]	82 [25,000]	82 [25,000]	82 [25,000]	82 [25,000]	67.2 [20,500]	82 [25,000]	82 [25,000]	67.2 [20,500]
							830 [253,000]	487.6 [148,650]
57.4 [17,500]	57.4 [17,500]	57.4 [17,500]	57.4 [17,500]	57.4 [17,500]	46.4 [14,150]	57.4 [17,500]	57.4 [17,500]	46.4 [14,150]
8.2 [2,500]	8.2 [2,500]	8.2 [2,500]	8.2 [2,500]	8.2 [2,500]	7.3 [2,250]	8.2 [2,500]	8.2 [2,500]	7.3 [2,250]
8.2 [2,500]	8.2 [2,500]	8.2 [2,500]	8.2 [2,500]	8.2 [2,500]	7.3 [2,250]	8.2 [2,500]	8.2 [2,500]	7.3 [2,250]
2.8 [860]	2.8 [860]	2.8 [860]	2.9 [910]	2.8 [860]	2.8 [860]	2.9 [910]	2.8 [860]	2.8 [860]
2.8 [860]	2.8 [860]	2.8 [860]	2.9 [910]	2.8 [860]	2.8 [860]	2.9 [910]	2.8 [860]	2.8 [860]
							731 (18 + 55 + 658)	338 (23 + 315)
1997-2005	2005-2011	2003-2005	1994-1995	1995-2010	1995-2010	1997-2003	2009-	2010-

and quality of rail transport improved, rather than becoming worse. Passengers really do not get the impression that rail service is distributed among several companies, since tickets are issued for the entire network and there is a common railroad timetable. In the train sector, the 1987 railway reform has led to many new series, as, by now, practically every single rail line has gotten a specially-fitted train. Individual finishes, seating, and panoramic windows also make it easier to market a relationship.

THE PROTOTYPES

In the years 1961 and 1962, various manufacturers delivered six prototype vehicles, which were used to form two trial multiple-unit trains as follows:
- Unit A of cars 1001 + 1002,
- Unit B of the cars 1003 + 1004 +1005 +1006.

All cars have a welded steel construction. The end car front windows were rounded, with the exception of end car 1006. Ultimately, the 1006 rectangular driver's cab window was used for the series trains. Car 1004, which was designed with a different structure, had unusually long hexagonal side windows. Seven different seating arrangements were tried inside the trains, including fixed, back-to-back seating groups, or seats with folding backrests. The latter were eventually used in the series. Such features as outward-opening doors and the "luminous nose," lit from the inside by fifteen 20-W fluorescent tubes, were not included in the series production. Cars 1002, 1004, and 1006 had additional auxiliary pantographs, along with the actual pantographs.

The 23 mile [37 km] new track between Kamonomiya and Ayase was made available for test runs. In October 1962, unit B first reached the 124 mph [200-km/h] mark and, on March 30, 1963, this unit set a new Japanese record of 159 mph [256 km/h]. When regular service began on the Tokaido Shinkansen in July 1964, unit A was converted to a relief train for emergencies (Series 941) and unit B to a test train of Series 922/0. Both prototypes were taken out of service and scrapped in August 1976.

THE SERIES 0

The Series 0 (originally 000) is the classic Shinkansen, which celebrated its brilliant trial period in 1964 with the opening of the Tokaido Shinkansen between Tokyo and Osaka. The distinctive feature of this revolutionary-looking train was its "nose," which allegedly was modeled on the front tip of a DC 8, then the most advanced passenger aircraft in international aviation. The standard gauge line profile allowed cars to be 82 feet [25 m] long, and they also could be 1.3 ft [400 mm] wider than those on the Cape gauge trains. Initially, a Shinkansen was made up of twelve cars, with all axles equipped with a 248 hp [185-kW] motor. For the electrical equipment, they relied on a rather simple technology, which functioned from the beginning. Two cars always made up a solid unit, with a common pantograph. Initially, top speed was set at 130 mph [210 km/h]; beginning in 1986, after infrastructure improvements, 137 mph [220 km/h] was allowed. Some 3,216 cars were built between 1963 and 1986. Of these, 2,288 cars were sub-series 0; 619 sub-series 1000, with small windows, and 309 sub-series 2000, with more space between the seats. Initially, the 0 Series trains ran only as twelve-car units; from 1971 on, they were generally increased to sixteen-car units. Due to problems with pressure tightness, corrosion, and high maintenance costs, the original Shinkansen was already taken out of service by 1976. The last sixteen-car trains ran until December 1999; the last twelve-car units until April 2000.

The four-car series 0 trains only had a short run. They ran from 1997 in shuttle service on the Hakata-Kokura/Hiroshima and Hakata-Hakata-Minami connections. The last four-unit was already mustered out by September 2001.

The four-car trains were given a brief interlude between 1997 and 2001, running as commuter service between Hakata and Kokura/Hiroshima, and on the short Hakata-Hakata-Minami route. Up to fall 2008, JR West only had six-car units still operating, mainly for the Hakata-Osaka commuter service and on the short-haul Hakata-Minami route. The trains made their last regular run on November 30, 2008, and the final trip was on December 14, 2008. By August 2008, a train had already been sent to the Saitama Railway Museum.

Several Series 0 cars found their way into museums after they were taken out of service. The power car 22-75 has been in the Ome Railway Park (near Tokyo) since 10/19/1997.

THE SERIES 100

The Series 100 trains represent the second generation Shinkansen, for use on the Tokaido and Sanyo lines. A total of 1,056 vehicles (= sixty-six sixteen-car units) were manufactured between 1984 and 1991. Externally they resembled the Series 0, but the front was designed as a more pointed "shark's nose." The problematic level of noise from the Series 0 pantographs was minimized by reducing the number of pantographs. Although the trains had four unpowered cars, the more powerful engines (308 hp [230 kW]), the first-time thyristor control, and reduced weight were to ensure a "theoretical" maximum speed of 168 mph [270 km/h]. Because of the continued noise problem for the passengers, the trains were initially limited to 137 mph [220 km/h]; in 1989, the speed was first raised to 243 mph [230 km/h] for the Sanyo Shinkansen "Grand Hikari." The trains also got improved seats with larger seat pitch (3.4 ft [1,040 mm] in 2nd Class and 3.8 ft [1,160 mm] in 1st Class). The basic configuration is a sixteen-car train, with a control car at each end and two double-decker, unpowered

A Series 200 unit passing the Omiya Station on January 6, 1998, on its way north.

A meeting of two Series 100 units on July 7, 1995, in Kyoto Station: Left, a "Kodama" is ready to depart for Tokyo, while on the right, a "Hikari," underway to Osaka, is arriving.

intermediate cars in the middle of the train. These units ran for the last time in 2003. Between 1989 and 2002, JR West operated nine sixteen-car units with powered end cars and four unpowered double-decker intermediate cars in the middle. For a brief time in 1986, there were some twelve-car units operating. In the meantime, a large number of these trains have been scrapped. Only the six-car units (all powered cars) were still in operation at the time of this writing; these run on the Sanyo Line between the Okayama and Hakata train stations. They were taken out of service in March 2012.

THE 200 SERIES

Some 700 Series 200 trains ran on the Tohoku and Joetsu Shinkansen between 1980 and 1986. Their design relied heavily on the Series 0, but to reduce weight, the car bodies were now made of an aluminum alloy. All of the first twelve-car units were powered, making it possible to attain high speeds on steep mountain rail tracks. To protect against snow, there were special panels on the trucks and over the underfloor equipment, mini-snowplows at each end, as well as modified air vents for the air conditioning system. The fronts of the sub-series 200-2000 trains were made with the "shark-nose look" from the Series 100.

By inserting additional intermediate cars (sometimes unpowered and double-decker), some thirteen- and sixteen-car trains were created over the years. Starting in 1987, there were also ten-car trains, and from 1988, eight-car units. The trains were retired over time, and today

the very few eight- and ten-car units in the train pool stopped running in 2011.

THE SERIES 300

JR Central and JR West acquired the sixteen-car trains of this series starting in 1992; the trains were inaugurated as the so-called "Super Hikari" trains running at a speed of 168 mph [270 km/h] on the Tokaido and Sanyo rail links. Some 1,120 trains (70 units) had been manufactured by 1998. A unit consists of ten powered and six non-powered cars. On the outside, they can be distinguished from earlier multiple unit trains by the entirely new train front design and the lower aluminum car bodies. For the first time, 400

A Series 300 "Kodama" 44 train, just arriving on January 2, 2005, at the Odawara train station. The "Kodama" stopped at (almost) all stations, but, because of the only double-tracked line, had to be as fast as a "Nozomi."

hp [300 kW] three-phase asynchronous motors were installed for the required drive power. The trains had newly designed trucks and only three (later reduced to two) pantographs. Starting in October 2004, JR Central began to improve the sixty-one units' running properties. Seven cars per multiple-unit train got a semi-active vibration control. All cars were equipped with non-linear air suspension and a new secondary suspension to better balance lateral movement. The first trains were already taken out of service in 2007, after delivery of the new N700 series. The last of JR Central's original sixty-one units were gone by March 2012.

THE SERIES 400

This series includes the first "mini-Shinkansen," to run on the converted Cape gauge lines, as well as on normal Shinkansen routes. JR East put twelve six-car, all-powered axle units on the rails between 1990 and 1992 for the "Tsubasa" service between Tokyo and Yamagata. The trains can reach the top speed of 149 mph [240 km/h] on the Shinkansen lines; on the modified gauge, curvy route from Fukushima to Yamagata, 80 mph [130 km/h] is the maximum. There, the overhead line voltage is as low as 20 kV. Because of the limited Cape gauge vehicle clearance profile, the car bodies were made both narrower and shorter.

To compensate, an extendable ramp was installed on normal Shinkansen station platforms, to bridge the gap. For the last time in a Shinkansen train, the drive power was provided by DC motors (281 hp [210 kW])

with thyristor control. There are retractable couplers on the Tokyo end of the trains, so that they can operate coupled to Series 200 and E2 units between Tokyo and Fukushima. Due to the huge success of the "Tsubasa," the trains were expanded in late 1995, with a non-powered intermediate car. Between December 2008 and the summer of 2009, most of the trainsets were retired and replaced with the new E3-2000 trains. Only unit L3 remained in service until April 18, 2010, to be able to celebrate a full eighteen years on the rails.

THE SERIES 500

The first sixteen-car unit of what was then the fastest scheduled Shinkansen was delivered in December 1995. Starting on March 22, 1997, the Series 500 ran as the "Nozomi" (= hope) between Shin-Osaka and Hakata, at a top speed of 186 mph [300 km/h], which made it the fastest scheduled train in Japan. Each axle is powered by an AC motor with 382 hp [285 kW] output, yielding a total 24,450 hp [18,240 kW] to reach a maximum speed of 199 mph [320 km/h]. An active damping system improves the train's running properties, while more stabilizers between the cars provides improved stability. The current is supplied via two aerodynamically designed pantographs. Due to the extremely elongated "nose," the end cars are 88.5 ft [27 m] long, but the intermediate cars are the usual 82 ft [25 m], giving an overall unit length of 1,326 ft [404 m]. The Munich star designer Alexander Neumeister, by the way, is responsible for the extremely sleek design.

A mini-Shinkansen Series 400 (front) and a Series E4 unit (rear) underway to Fukushima coupled together on March 11, 2008; then they go their separate ways.

A Shinkansen Series 500 "Nozomi" races through the Odawara train station on January 2, 2005, making the Tokyo-Hakata connection in just five hours and five minutes.

The Series 500 trains cut travel time between Tokyo and Hakata from 5 hours 4 minutes to 4 hours 49 minutes, although they can only travel at a full 186 mph [300 km/h] on the Sanyo Shinkansen between Nishi-Akashi and Hakata. Only nine units were put in operation. Between 2008 and 2010, six of the original nine-car trainsets were shortened to eight-car units (Series 500-7000). These then took over the "Kodama" service (the slowest Shinkansen between Osaka and Hakata) from the retired Series 0 trains on December 1, 2008.

THE SERIES 700

This series was developed by JR Central and JR West to offer new trains with improved ride comfort and better interior design on the Tokaido and Sanyo Shinkansen; at the same time, it meant the operators would not have to use the indeed powerful, but also very expensive, Series 500 units any longer. With procurement costs at some $41 million [four billion yen], a sixteen-car unit ultimately cost about twenty percent less than a Series 500 train. The first series-production trains began regular service in March 1999. Up to 2005, the rail operators obtained seventy-five sixteen-car and sixteen eight-car units. On the sixteen-car trains, the two control cars and the middle two intermediate cars are made unpowered; on the eight-car units, only the two control cars are unpowered. To ensure the same appropriate running properties as in the Series 500, yaw dampers were installed between the cars and all cars were equipped with a semi-active damper. Three-

phase motors with 369 hp [275 kW] output provide the necessary thrust for the powered axles and allow a maximum speed of 177 mph [285 km/h].

Only JR West bought the eight-car units (sub-series 700-7000), for use as "Hikari Rail Star" trains between Osaka and Hakata. These trains were given the required couplings to allow double heading operation in peak periods. So far, however, this capability has never been used.

THE SERIES N700

This series includes the eight- and sixteen-car trains on the Tokaido and Sanyo systems, which were developed jointly by JR Central and JR West, based on the design of the Series 700. A first pre-series (unit Z0) was delivered to JR Central in February 2005 for comprehensive tests before mass production began. The first sub-series N700-0 series trains began service in summer 2007 at JR Central. JR West started using the first units of the identical sub-series N700 3000 at almost the same time, so that this sub-series is only characteristic of that owner. The trains could run on the Tokaido Shinkansen at up to 168 mph [270 km/h] and reached 186 mph [300 km/h] on the Sanyo Shinkansen. Apart from the two control cars, all cars are powered. A three-phase motor with 409 hp [305 kW] output powers each axle, controlled by IGBT converters. The streamlined train end design was developed further, into a sort of wedge shape. The inter-carriage passages are fully paneled. The cars are equipped with

A series 700 Shinkansen, running as Hikari 268, passes through Odawara station underway to Tokyo on January 2, 2005.

The N700 Series (JR Central) pre-series Z0 pauses in the Gifu Hashima train station on January 30, 2011.

a tilting system over air suspension, which allows a more limited car tilt of one degree. This system lets the train round even 8,200 ft [2,500 m] radius curves at 168 mph [270 km/h]. Using a new digital, automatic train control system (ATC = Automatic Train Control) and its high acceleration capability allowed the train to cut travel time between Tokyo and Osaka by at least five minutes, and between Tokyo and Hakata by about thirteen minutes. The prototype reached the 168 mph [270 km/h] mark some forty percent faster than the Series 700 trains. JR Central now operates eighty units, and JR West sixteen units. The sixteen-car N700 had completely replaced the Series 300, 500, and 700 trains on the fast "Nozomi" service on the Tokaido and Sanyo Shinkansen by 2011.

In 2007, JR West and JR Kyushu developed the eight-car sub-series N700-7000, which was to start running after the Kyushu Shinkansen was completed, and also on the Sanyo Shinkansen. A first prototype was delivered in October 2008. These railcars differ markedly from the sixteen-car N700. First of all, the axles are powered to provide enough power for the steeply graded sections of the Kyushu railways. The aluminum car bodies correspond to the basic design, except that the power cables are no longer installed inside the cars. To give a smoother ride, the Series 500 and 700 have yaw dampers mounted between the truck and car body, and the whole trainset is equipped with semi-active damping. But there is no tilting technology. The Standard Class has a 2 + 2 seat division, while the sixteen-car sets have a seat division of 2 + 3. Here again, there is a sub-series difference between the railway operators: in spring 2010, nineteen units went as the N700-7000 to JR West; ten trainsets as N700-8000 to JR Kyushu. The eight-car units have travelled mainly as the slower "*Sakura*" (= cherry blossom) and faster "*Mizuho*" between Kagoshima and Osaka from March 12, 2011, onward.

Unit U007 of sub-series 800-100 rolls into the Kurume train station on April 17, 2011.

"duck bill" was eliminated. Their maximum speed is currently set at 162 mph [260 km/h], although they are designed for a speed of 177 mph [285 km/h]. The interior was also improved: the fittings were generally made of traditional materials, such as wood for the seats.

In December 2008, JR Kyushu let it be known that it would acquire three additional Series 800 units, which were delivered between August 2009 and autumn 2010. This order should be seen in relation to the completion of the entire Kyushu Shinkansen (Hakata-Yatsushiro-Kagoshima-Chuo) railway in the spring of 2011. Outside, the new units have a modified version of the red trim stripe; inside, each train has different colored seat upholstery. Units U007 and U009 also got track-monitoring equipment and are assigned to the sub-series 800-1000, while unit U008 is equipped for an overhead catenary line and signal monitoring, and operates as sub-series 800-2000.

THE SERIES 800

These six-car, all-powered-axles trains first operated in spring 2004 as the "*Tsubame*" (= swallow) on the first section of the Kyushu Shinkansen between Yatsushiro and Kagoshima; since March 12, 2011, they have been running on the northern Yatsushiro-Hakate section. Although the "Tsubame" could now be transferred to the Sanyo Shinkansen, they generally remain true to their home track. The six-unit series is technically based on the design of the 700. Their attractive head shape is similar to a sharply pointed nose, and the rather unattractive Series 700

THE SERIES E1 "MAX"

These are the first Shinkansen made completely as double-decker trains. Originally, these trains were to be given series designation 600, but JR East's new designation came into use instead, so the trains are classified as Series E1. The marketing name "Max" is used more commonly; this stands for "Multi Amenity Express." At first, the trains were marketed with the rather trivial name "DDS" (Double-Decker Shinkansen).

A modernized JR East E1 unit approaching the Omiya station on May 21, 2008, in service on the Joetsu line.

Between March 1994 and the end of 1995, six twelve-car units were delivered for service on the Tohoku and Joetsu Shinkansen lines. Six of the twelve cars are powered by a 550 hp [410 kW] three-phase motor with regenerative braking on each axle. The top speed is 149 mph [240 km/h]. The "Max" trains should particularly contribute to relieving the consistent over-crowding on long-distance commuter trains to Tokyo. Four cars have a 3 + 3 seat division on the upper deck. These seats cannot be reserved. Overall, the double-decker trains provide forty percent more space than a Series 200 twelve-car unit. Beginning in 2003, the trains got a complete overhaul, when new seats were installed. The El trains were elminated in September 2012, and the plan is to eliminate the E4 Series by 2016.

THE E2 SERIES

The first two pre-series trains (S6, later N1, and S7, later J1 and then N21) were delivered in April and June 1995 as eight-car units. All cars, except for the two control cars, are driven with a 402 hp [300 kW] three-phase motor on each axle. The trains are designed for a maximum speed of 196 mph [315 km/h], but go no faster than 171 mph [275 km/h] in regular service. This is the maximum speed on the Tohoku Shinkansen from Tokyo to Hachinohe, while north of Morioka only 162 mph [260 km/h] is allowed. On the Nagano Shinkansen, 162 mph [260 km/h] is the maximum speed. The trains can run both using 50 Hz (normal frequency of JR East) and 60 Hz (on the Nagano Shinkansen west of Karuizawa).

As the first series, six sub-series E2 eight-car trains started running between December 1996 to March 1997; these were needed to expand service on the Tohoku Shinkansen, because the Akita mini-Shinkansen was taken out of service. They were given retractable couplers on the Morioka direction ends, so they could be coupled with the Series E3 mini-Shinkansen between Tokyo and Morioka. There, the E3 units were uncoupled and continued on their own to Akita. Another four Series E2 units were delivered in October and November 1998; another five sets followed a year later, to accommodate the increased demand on the JR East Shinkansen lines. Beginning in September 2002, the E2 was expanded to ten cars, to meet the demand for the "Hayate" service on the Tohoku Shinkansen link to Hachinohe, which opened in December 2002.

For the "Asama" service on the Hokuriku Shinkansen link to Nagano, which opened on October 1, 1997, JR East put twelve eight-car Series E2 units in service between March and September 1997. Their top speed is limited to 162 mph [260 km/h].

At the end of December 2000, the prototype of the improved sub-series E2-1000, was delivered to JR East. These units, at first made up of eight cars, began operation, after extensive testing, in November 2001. The first series trains were available beginning in July 2002, now made as ten-car units. These trains replaced, above all, the aging Series 200 trains in the new "Hayate" service on the Tohoku Shinkansen. The Series E2-1000 features a number of improvements, of which the most obvious are the new large side windows (similar to those in the Series E4). The trains received new single-arm pantographs on a streamlined platform; this eliminated the need for a pantograph cover panel.

An E2 unit en route to Hachinohe (Tohoku Shinkansen) arrives at Omiya station on December 30, 2004.

Since the units are only designed for a current lower than 50 Hz, they can only travel on the Tohoku and Joetsu Shinkansen.

THE E3 SERIES

Like the Series 400, the Series E3 was conceptualized as a mini-Shinkansen, which was to take over the "Komachi" service on the modified gauge section from Morioka to Akita, beginning in March 1997. The first sixteen five-car units could travel at the normal Shinkansen 171 mph [275 km/h], but on the modified gauge lines, only 81 mph [130 km/h] was allowed. Four cars per unit are powered; the middle intermediate car was unpowered. The cars work using 20 kV on the Morioka-Akita line, and 25 kV on the Tohoku Shinkansen. Like the E3, the cars are designed for a mini-Shinkansen and are shorter and narrower. The end cars are 75.4 ft [23 m] long; the intermediate cars 74.8 ft [22.8 m]. In October to November 1998, JR East expanded the trains with another unpowered middle car. An additional six-car unit was delivered in the same year. Two more multiple-unit trains followed in late 2002, and by 2005, another seven units were manufactured with minor modifications (improved seats and IGBT VVVF inverters). All trains have a retractable coupling on the Tokyo end, so they can run coupled with Series E2 trains between Tokyo and Morioka.

To extend the Yamagata mini-Shinkansen service to Shinjo in December 1999, the rail operator acquired two seven-car sub-series E3-1000 units in August and September 1999. They were to augment the 400 fleet used on that rail line, for the new expanded "Tsubasa"

service. This configuration has five powered cars—cars 2 and 5 remained unpowered. A third seven-car unit became available from July 2005.

The first seven-car Shinkansen, of a total of twelve units of the new E3-2000 sub-series, began operating as the Tsubasa service on the Yamagata line on December 20, 2008. By summer 2009, these trainsets had completely replaced the Series 400 trains. The E3 2000 was equipped with small improvements such as an active suspension system, colored LED destination displays, and outlets in all cars.

THE E4 SERIES "MAX"

These eight-car double-decker trains are based largely on the E1 Series. They are fitted at each end with an automatic, retractable coupling to run in double heading. The sixteen-car units provide 1,600 seats to reduce the bottlenecks in capacity on the Tohoku Shinkansen during peak times for commuter travel to Tokyo. As with the Series E1, there are unreserved seats in part of the upper deck; these seats, arranged in a 3 + 3 division, have fixed backrests. Four cars of a unit are powered, with a 563 hp [420 kW] three-phase motor on each axle. As usual, the car bodies are made of aluminum, keeping the axle load to sixteen tons. The top speed is 149 mph [240 km/h].

Mini-Shinkansen E3 R17 is in the lead, followed by a Series E2 unit on March 5, 2009. Both are travelling coupled to Morioka; then they go their separate ways.

A double-decker Shinkansen Series E4 "Max" arrives at Omiya station from Niigata on December 30, 2004.

JR East got the first three units in October 1997. They stared operating in December of that year on the Tohoku Shinkansen. More trains expanded the fleet in early 1999, so that the E4 was running together with Series 400 trains between Tokyo and Fukushima, beginning in April 1999. The E4 started some service on the Joetsu Shinkansen beginning in May 2001. In 2003, JR East acquired two units that can run under both frequencies, for service using 50 Hz and 60 Hz on the Nagano Shinkansen. For all other E4s, Karuizawa is the end station, because they are only equipped to operate using 50 Hz frequency.

MODERN TEST TRAINS

FASTECH 360S (SERIES E954) AND FASTECH 360Z (E955 SERIES)

In March 2004, JR East ordered two test trains from the railroad industry. The rail operator received the eight-car "Fastech 360S" in June 2005. It has a top speed of 252 mph [405 km/h], and was designed as the prototype of the next generation of trains intended to run at up to 224 mph [360 km/h] on the Tohoku Shinkansen, beginning in 2013. A number of measures were taken to reduce the noise created at high speed, both outside and inside the train; these include using low, single-arm pantographs, since in normal operation, only one of these has to connect to the overhead contact wire. The prototype's active suspension and tilt capacity of up to two degrees will improve ride comfort. The train has two end cars of different design, to test how to best reduce the "tunnel boom" generated when it enters and

JR East's E954 Series (Fastech 360S) test train, photographed on May 19, 2008, still in the Omiya train station on May 19, 2008. Just 17 months later, it was taken out of operation and scrapped.

leaves a tunnel at high speed. One end car has a more streamlined form, while the second is more arrow-shaped. For the first time in a Shinkansen, a type of pneumatically actuated "brake ears" were mounted on the roof, to make it possible to brake and slow the train down more quickly at high speed, in case of an emergency.

The high-speed test runs were carried out at night on the Tohoku Shinkansen between Sendai and Kitakami train stations. The prototype hit a top speed of 247 mph [398 km/h] on a trial run in August 2005. Regular daytime tests were started in April 2006, with the train reaching speeds of up to 199 mph [320 km/h] travelling between Sendai and Morioka.

The six-car "Fastech 360Z" was first delivered to the Sendai Depot in March 2006. This unit has a narrow carriage body profile; it was intended as the prototype next generation mini-Shinkansen, to run on the Yamagata and Akita Shinkansen in the future. Like its big brother "Fastech 360S," this train has a top speed of 252 mph [405 km/h]. Both end cars have the same arrow-shaped tip, but of different lengths (43 and 52 ft [13 and 16 m]). This train was tested extensively together with the "Fastech 360S" on the Tohoku Shinkansen, including encountering other trains at high speeds. High-speed test runs with coupled trains began in late 2006.

THE E5 SERIES

In spring 2011, the first new Series E5 Shinkansen started scheduled service on the Tohoku Shinkansen from Tokyo to Aomori. The Shinkansen E5 Series shines in all the latest developments for ride comfort and safety. The test Fastech 360S train was the model for the E5's futuristic appearance. The generous interior layout allows for comfortable travel, including for disabled people. Each unit has three classes: In Standard Class, seat division is 3.4 ft [1,040 mm] (2.3" [60 mm] more than the E2 series). In the Green Class, spacing increases to 3.8 ft [1,160 mm], and in the super comfortable Grand Class seats, to 4.2 ft [1,300 mm]. The train's most striking feature is its elegant and smooth long nose, specially designed to reduce the so-called "tunnel boom" phenomenon. When trains enter a tunnel at speeds of over 124 mph [200 km/h], the sudden increase in air pressure can generate a loud boom at the other end of the tunnel. The E5 Series' 49.2 ft [15 m] "long nose" design (29.5 ft [9 m] longer than on the E2) is the result of numerous experiments to limit the boom. Another E5 feature is its newly designed, extremely quiet pantograph. The streamlined aluminum

JR East's Series E5 is also called the "Peregrine Falcon" (Hayabusa); here, "Hayabusa 4" is arriving on March 6, 2011, at Omiya train station.

car bodies now fully enclose the trucks and wheels, to reduce the noise from their rail contact. There are also noise absorbing panels under the seats. The trainsets are equipped with an active suspension system, which detects and balances tilting and lateral movement. A special pneumatic tilting system, with a maximum tilt angle of 1.5 degrees, reduces centrifugal force when rounding curves. The braking system was improved and strengthened using German technology (Knorr brakes), to make braking even safer and more controlled at the train's maximum speed. Previous braking systems could only do this up to 171 mph [275 km/h]. In addition to the pre-series S11, fifty-nine more trainsets are on order, and are currently being manufactured.

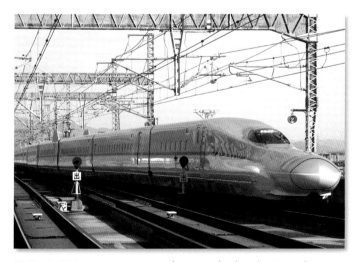

JR East's E5's pre-series train, photographed at the Morioka train station on June 3, 2010.

THE E6 SERIES

JR East had the new Series E6 railcar developed to run as a "mini-Shinkansen" on the Tohoku and Akita lines, with the Fastech 360Z test train as its godfather. The trainsets are designed with seven narrow profile cars, to provide the same capacity as the six-car E3 trains; the 42.6 ft [13 m] long noses reduced space for passengers in the end cars. The car bodies are completely covered, including the trucks, and have an active tilt system up to 1.5 degrees. The improved passenger comfort on the E6 matches the E5 Series; these include power outlets at every seat and video surveillance of the boarding areas. The seat layout in both Standard and Green Class is 2 + 2. The first pre-series S12 was delivered in June 2010, and trials began on the Tohoku Shinkansen a month later. The first production trains were planned to start regular service in 2012. As of March 2013, two or three train pairs will run with the new E6; to and from Morioka in combination with the new Series E5 railcars. Within another year, all the "old" E3 trainsets shall have been replaced by the new trains on the Akita Shinkansen.

JR East's Series E6 pre-series unit S12 makes a short stop at Morioka station during a July 25, 2010, test run.

SOUTH KOREA

The initiative to build high-speed railways in South Korea dates back to the 1980s, when the country first began to suffer from severe congestion on its roads. This was caused by a disproportionate rise in car registrations—an average annual increase of seventeen percent at the time. The ever-growing congestion on the roads, especially in the important Seoul-Busan corridor, meant higher logistics costs, which weaken industrial competitiveness. This corridor is where some three-quarters of the South Korean population lives. As a result, in May 1989, the government decided to build a high-speed rail line between the two main economic centers of Seoul and Busan (the Gyeongbu line). A high-speed railway, when compared to a four-lane highway or a conventional double-tracked line, seemed the best way to fulfill the need for long distance "mass transportation."

The project began to take concrete shape in 1992, when construction started on a test track between Cheonan and Daejeon. Then came the selection of future rolling stock. The choice was among the German ICE, the French TGV, and the Japanese Shinkansen.

Although the Japanese super train was actually the first choice, both geographically and technically, there were historical reasons against this train, since Korea had suffered under the burden of being a Japanese colony in the first half of the twentieth century. Siemens, with the ICE, and Alstom, with the TGV, fought bitter battles through several rounds of bidding, until finally, in the summer of 1993, Alstom was in the lead. The rumor mill had it that there was considerable (including financial) support from the French government.

The Asian economic crisis of 1997 forced a radical change of plan. In the summer of 1998, the government announced that the new Daegu-Gyeongju-Busan rail link would be set aside, in favor of electrifying and modernizing the existing line from Daegu to Busan. The Honam line, which branches off at Daejeon to Mokpo in southwestern Korea, would also be electrified and modernized, to be able to serve the country's main railway axes—which converge in Daejeon—and would in future be significantly improved by use of the new trains. By 2010, in a second phase, the new Daegu, Gyeongju, and Busan connection would follow, as well as construction of the new tunnels needed for the Daejeon and Daegu stretches.

As transportation, the KTX starts at Seoul's main train station; in terms of operation, the actual new line begins in Gwangmyeong, at 11 miles [18 km] southeast of the Seoul station, with a nearly 8.6 mile [14 km] long tunnel. Some 2 miles [3.5 km] into this tunnel comes an impressive KTX station on the outskirts of Seoul. Short tunnels and bridges alternate on the way up to mile 39 [km 63], while the final stretch to Cheonan (at mile 57 [km 92]) runs mainly over bridges, viaducts, and elevated track. The Cheonan-Asan Station, situated among green fields, provides the KTX connection for the city of Cheonan, population 450,000. As far as the end of the first new rail lines, just before mile 96 [km 155], the long, mainly elevated section is again interrupted by two series of bridges and tunnels. The Osong depot is located between miles 76 and 77 [kms 123 and 125]; this was used during the test phase and today serves as the construction and maintenance center for the entire new line. After Daejeon, at mile 108 [km 175], the second stretch of the new line begins; here, many bridges and short tunnels alternate, up to mile 124 [km 200]. Then follow in quick succession two long tunnels, 3.7 miles [6 km] and 6.2 miles [10 km]. Two more series of bridges and viaducts, coupled with short tunnels, complete the new line section, which ends at Sindong (mile 165 [km 266]), where the KTX switches back to the old Gyeongbu line, to run via Daegu to Busan. While the Seoul and Busan train stations are only a few meters above sea level, the highest point of the new line, at mile 126 [km 203], is some 227 miles [365 km] above sea level. The train route has a maximum twenty-five percent gradient and a minimum curve radius of 4.3 miles [7 km]. Almost forty percent of the line runs over bridges, viaducts, or on an elevated track, and a good thirty-two percent through tunnels.

Construction work started on the deferred Daegu-Gyeongju-Busan connection in June 2002. The 79.5 mile [128.1 km] long new section constitutes a long arc via Gyeongju northeast of the existing Gyeongbu route. It includes fifty-four viaducts, with a total length of 14.5 miles [23.4 km], and thirty-eight tunnels, with a total length of 46.1 miles [74.2 km]. The builders drilled the longest and second longest tunnels in Korea: the 66,676 ft [20,323 m] Geomjeung tunnel near Busan, and the 43,537 ft [13,270 m] Wonhyo tunnel southwest of Ulsan. Controversy over the environmental impact of the Wonhyo tunnel delayed the entire project, so that work had to be suspended for a time. Finally, on November 1, 2010, high-speed traffic could finally be launched between Daegu and Busan. Two sections—a total of 25.4 miles [40.9 km] through the cities of

Daejeon and Daegu—still must be built. They should be completed by 2014.

Other plans include constructing a high-speed line from Osong (on the high-speed Seoul-Daejeon line) to Mokpo, which will be built in two parts. The first, 115.42 mile [185.75 km] long, section will run from Osong to the new Gwangju-Songjeong train station, and should be completed by 2014. Construction began on December 4, 2009. A further 37.9 mile [61.1 km] branch line will run from Suseo (southeast of Seoul) to the Seoul-Daejeon high speed line. Detailed planning has been in the works since September 2010, and opening is set for late 2014. Longer-term plans provide for more high speed lines from Seoul to Sokcho on the east coast, and a branch line from the high speed Daejeon-Daegu line southwards via Jinju to the coast.

THE KTX-I

The KTX (Korea Train eXpress) super trains can hardly deny their descent from the TGV Reseau. The most striking difference is the much greater length: unlike the ten-car TGV, the KTX includes twenty. Accordingly, a KTX needs more power and therefore, next to the all powered axles power cars on each end, the adjacent truck on the next intermediate car is also motorized.

A full five KTX-I trains (from left to right, units 15, 17, 20, 19, and 16) present themselves for the photographers at the opening of the new line on April 1, 2004.

There are two 1,475 hp [1,100 kW] motors in each of the six powered trucks to provide the necessary thrust. The trains have a total of 17,694 hp [13,200 kW], so they can accelerate to 186 mph [300 km/h] in three minutes. Each 1,273 ft [388 meter] long train offers 935 seats. Of these, 127 are in First Class (three seats per row = 2 + 1) and 808 in Second Class (four seats per row = 2 + 2). All First Class seats can be turned in the direction of travel using a handle. Since the trip only takes less than three hours, a dining car was omitted. A mini bar, snack and beverage vending machines, near the passageways between carriages, provide sustenance for the passengers.

The KTX head car shape resembles that of the Spanish AVE, with the exception of the headlights. The regenerative braking system is new to the KTX; this ensures a 20,997 ft [6,400 m] braking distance at 186 mph [300 km/h]. The pressure tightness also broke new ground: to reduce pressure differences to zero, before the train enters a tunnel, all its openings are closed with flaps that are controlled by balises (electronic beacons or transponders) mounted on the tracks. Safe operation is ensured by the on-board computer system (OBCS), a smoke detection system, and numerous automatic sensors to detect any possible malfunction. The first twelve KTX trains were manufactured entirely in France.

Series designation:	Korean Train eXpress 1 (KTX-I)
Road numbers:	01 - 46
Wheel arrangement (20 car):	Bo'Bo'+Bo'(2)'(2)'(2)'(2)'(2)'(2)'(2)'(2)' (2)'(2)'(2)'(2)'(2)'(2)'(2)'BO'+Bo'Bo'
Power system:	25 kV/60 Hz
Track gauge (ft [mm]):	4' 8.5" [1,435]
Maximum speed (mph [km/h]):	190 [305]
Power output (hp [kW]):	18,177 [13,560 (12 x 1,130)]
Empty weight twenty car (t):	701
Service weight twenty car (t):	773.8
Maximum axle load (t):	17
End car length (ft [mm]):	74.1 [22,607]
Intermediate car length (mm):	21,845 + 16 x 18,700 + 21,845
Length twenty car (ft [mm]):	1,273 [388,104]
Distance between truck centers (mm):	14,000 + 18 x 18,700 + 14,000
Axle interval powered truck (ft [mm]):	9.8 [3,000]
Axle interval trailer truck (ft [mm]):	9.8 [3,000]
Driver wheel diameter (ft [mm]):	3 [920]
Trailer wheel diameter (ft [mm]):	3 [920]
Seats (twenty car):	935 + 30 folding seats
Commissioning:	1997-2004

The first unit KTX 01 was introduced in La Rochelle, at the end of May 1997. On December 16, it graduated from its extensive test runs on the French TGV network. KTX 02 was shipped in April 1998, bringing the first super train to South Korea. It only made its maiden voyage on the new high speed line on November 4, 1999, and then just at a maximum speed of 124 mph [200 km/h]. A KTX reached the 186 mph [300 km/h] mark for the first time on Korean soil, on June 20, 2000. The KTX 01, which remained in France

for some time, hit 186 mph [300 km/h] for the first time on May 18, 1998, after further testing. The last train manufactured in France arrived in South Korea on December 21, 2000. Under a technology transfer agreement with Alstom, the last thirty-four units were built in South Korea. As a result, the number of locally produced components could be continually increased over time. This rose to a proud ninety-four percent for the last train. KTX 13 was the first unit built in South Korea; it was delivered on June 14, 2002, and was accepted as a success after reaching a speed of 205 mph [330 km/h] on September 6, 2002. KTX 21 first ran on the high-speed Seoul Daejeon connection on August 29, 2003, while KTX 12 was the first to reach Daegu on the new line, on October 21.

The KTX opened up a new era of transportation history in South Korea, as it started regular service on April 1, 2004, with a top speed of 186 mph [300 km/h]. There have not been any actual train failures since the trains began operating, and punctuality (with a tolerance limit of ten minutes) reached a record high of ninety-seven percent for the KTS's 126 daily round trips, as early as April 2004. Despite these successes, the mass media in Korea have fixated on the many small problems and disturbances. Particularly noteworthy are the supposedly narrow and nonreversible 2nd Class seats. One of the most remarkable effects resulting from the start-up of KTX transport has been the large-scale reduction of travel time. Approximately seventy percent of the population now lives within a three hour travel distance, which has led to significant time savings for them. The travel time from Seoul to Busan was shortened by two hours, to a mere 160 minutes, while the Seoul to Mokpo connection can be made in just 2 hours 58 minutes, instead of 4 hours 32 minutes. The KTX also extended the commuter radius of Seoul from 93 to 124 miles [150 to 200 km]. It takes no more than 34 or 49 minutes to get to Seoul from Cheonan-Asan or Daejeon.

Korea's self development of HSR-350X

South Korea began to develop its own high-speed train, the so-called HSR-350X, in 1996. It was designed in collaboration with Rotem, South Korea's largest rolling stock manufacturer, and should provide more flexibility and capacity for railway operation. The train successfully reached 186 mph [300 km/h] on a trial run in September 2003, and the planned maximum speed is 217 mph [350 km/h]. The seven-car, 310-ton prototype travels in the configuration of power car, powered intermediate car, three unpowered intermediate cars, powered intermediate car, and power car. The aim was to create a twenty-car train with two power cars, and four powered and fourteen unpowered intermediate cars. After an extensive, multi-year test phase, the X-HSR350 is to be tried out in regular service. Its new design includes seats that can be rotated in the travel direction in all classes, to satisfy the substantial demand from Korean passengers.

So far, developing the HSR-350X has cost some $215 [€165] million. Opinion about the train among Korean experts, ranges from "of little use/barely acceptable," to "we will conquer the world with it."

KTX-II

Although the KTX-II is based entirely on Korea's self-developed HSR-350X, the TGV was again the inspiration for various features. The KTX-II consists of a unit with two power cars and eight unpowered intermediate cars. Using a Scharfenberg type automatic coupling, two trainsets can operate as a dual unit. Supplied by Voith, the nose cone with the couplings and the impact protection elements form a unit. The French studio MBD Design created the train's exterior aerodynamic form, inspired by the cherry salmon, a salmon found in the western Pacific.

The intermediate car bodies are made of aluminum, and the trucks, in contrast to the HSR-350X, are not covered. Window thickness was increased with a fourth layer by 0.3" [9 mm], compared to the KTX-I, to improve sound and pressure isolation. In addition, the cars—based on the KTX-I—were made 2.5" [66 mm] wider.

The KTX-II train's traction motors, transformers, traction control, and braking system have all been developed in South Korea, and were already tested in the HSR-350X. Three-phase asynchronous induction motors propel this train, instead of the synchronous motors in the KTX-I. The final drive comes from Voith. The power electronics in the converters use new type IGBTs, which come from an American semiconductor manufacturer. Each traction converter consists of two parallel, connected four-quadrant converters, which convert the single-phase alternating current from the overhead contact wires into three-phase current for the motors. The pantographs came from an Austrian company. They are a standard type, certified for 217 miles [350 km], and were also used in the Siemens Velaro family trains.

The third KTX-II intermediate car provides special comfort with its 1st Class seats. There are both a snack bar and special family compartments in the fourth intermediate car. All other cars are only 2nd

Still showing something from the TGV: the new KTX-II, on a trial run, here still without markings.

Class. All seats are designed to swivel and can always be rotated to the travel direction. To provide more legroom than the KTX-I, space between seats was increased from 3 to 3.2 ft [930 to 980 mm]. Other comfort features include wireless Internet access, digital multimedia broadcasting, and business compartments with small tables. In addition to the ATC signaling for high speed lines and the normal ATS signaling for conventional routes, the KTX-II also has the new ATP (= automatic train protection) system, developed in South Korea. This system, compatible with the ERTMS, is a significant improvement over the ATS commonly used on conventional lines.

SERIES DESIGNATION:	KOREAN TRAIN EXPRESS II (KTX-II)
Road numbers:	01 - 24
Wheel arrangement (ten car):	Bo'Bo'+2'(2)'(2)'(2)'(2)'(2)'(2)'2'+ Bo'Bo'
Power system:	25 kV/60 Hz
Track gauge (ft [mm]):	4' 8.5" [1,435]
Maximum speed (mph [km/h]):	190 [305]
Power output (hp [kW]):	11,796 [8,800 (8 x 1,100)]
Empty weight (t), ten car:	403
Service weight (t), ten car:	434
Maximum axle load (t):	17
End car length (ft [mm]):	74.4 [22,690]
Intermediate car length (mm):	21,845 + 6 x 18,700 + 21,845
Length, ten car (ft [mm]):	659 [200,870]
Distance between truck centers (mm):	14,000 + 8 x 18,700 + 14,000
Axle interval powered truck (ft [mm]):	9.8 [3,000]
Axle interval trailer truck (ft [mm]):	9.8 [3,000]
Driver wheel diameter (ft [mm]):	3 [920]
Trailer wheel diameter (ft [mm]):	3 [920]
Seats 1st/2nd Class (ten car):	363 (30/328 + 5)
Commissioning:	2008-2011

TAIWAN

The island of Taiwan lies some 99 miles [160 km] east of mainland China. The main island is 22,357 square miles [35,980 square km], and is seventy percent covered by forested mountains, especially on its east side. In contrast, about ninety-five percent of Taiwan's twenty-two million inhabitants are concentrated on the island's western plains. Taiwan's strong economic growth during the last decades has made it into a very highly developed and densely populated region of Southeast Asia. The majority of Taiwan's economy is based on high tech industries. Although Taiwan was also hit by both the global economic and Asian financial crises, the island state has not been discouraged from looking into the future and making timely preparation for its next economic miracle. This foresight included a huge infrastructure program, with an ambitious railway-building project as its centerpiece: the so-called "Taiwan North-South High Speed Rail Project" (THSRP), a high-speed rail link between Taiwan's two major cities, the capital city of Taipei in the north and the huge container port Kaohsiung in the south. Formally, the project really began in November 1996, with the founding of the "Taiwan High Speed Rail Consortium" (THSRC, from May 1998, the "Taiwan High Speed Rail Corporation"), which initially led the negotiations with the prospective competitors to provide the rolling stock.

The narrowed-down field of choices included the Japanese Shinkansen Group, led by Mitsui, and the Eurotrain consortium, led by the European railroad giants Siemens and GEC Alsthom, which looked at first to be a sure winner. The unexpected end came for the Europeans at the end of 1999, when, in a complete surprise, the THSRC gave its support to the Shinkansen, on December 28. The THSRC based its decision on the results of years of comparisons, which led them to consider the Shinkansen the better system, in terms of price, technology, and maintenance. Observers cited three factors as the reasons for the sudden change of heart: Taiwan's sensitive political relations with Japan and Europe, the competitors' financing commitments, as well as safety concerns.

After intense negotiations, THSRC and Shinkansen Consortium signed a contract for supply of basic equipment for the first high speed line on the island, worth $2.87 billion, in December 2000. The contract included the multiple-unit trains, the signaling system, electrical power supply, and overhead contact wires, the communication system, other electrical and mechanical equipment, and a vehicle simulator for training the train drivers.

The standard gauge high speed line between Taipei and Kaohsiung was built with a total investment of $16 billion. The similarities to Japan emerge immediately: Taiwan's "normal" rail network is also in Cape gauge (3' 6" [1,067 mm]); for the high speed line, standard gauge tracks were built on the island for the first time. The new route extends 214.3 miles [345 km] along the west coast, covering a large part of the 244.8 mile [394 km] long island.

Due to intense land use and difficult topography, about 155.9 miles [251 km] (approx. seventy-seven percent) of the track runs over bridges and viaducts. Another 29.2 miles [47 km] of tracks passes through tunnels, and only about 24.8 miles [40 km] of the route lies at ground level. The high level of seismic activity in Taiwan created complications. The most recent big earthquake was in 1999, magnitude 7.6 on the Richter scale, which killed 2,400 people. As in Japan, special emphasis had to be put on earthquake-resistant design when constructing bridges and viaducts. The following requirements had to be taken in consideration: in areas with less pronounced seismic activity, the so-called "simple earthquake design" could be used.

Unit TR 19 is ready for its return trip to Taipei in Kaohsiung's Zuoying Railway Station on July 22, 2009.

SERIES DESIGNATION:	THSR 700 T
Road numbers:	TR 01-TR 30
Unit configuration	S+3T+M+6T+S
Wheel arrangement (end car):	2'2'
Wheel arrangement (intermediate car):	Bo'Bo' or 2'2'
Power system:	25 kV/60 Hz
Track gauge (ft [mm]):	4' 8.5" [1,435]
Maximum speed (mph [km/h]):	186 [300]
Power output powered cars (kW):	4 x 285
Empty weight of entire train (t):	41.9
Maximum axle load (t):	14
End car length (ft [mm]):	88.5 [27,000]
Intermediate car length (ft [mm]):	82 [25,000]
Distance between truck centers (ft [mm]):	57.4 [17,500]
Axle distance powered truck (ft [mm]):	0.2 [2,500]
Axle distance trailer truck (ft [mm]):	8.2 [2,500]
Driver wheel diameter (ft [mm]):	2.8 [860]
Trailer wheel diameter (ft [mm]):	2.8 [860]
Seats (1st/2nd class):	989 (923 + 66)
Commissioning:	2004-2005

This meant that a bridge structure might indeed have repairable damage after an earthquake, but would not collapse. In regions with higher seismic activity, the bridge structure, in contrast, must be constructed to be so "elastic" that it remains undamaged. Furthermore, the trains must be able to keep operating, and to brake without being derailed.

The trains in service are Type 700T twelve-car railcars, which are based externally on the Shinkansen 700 Series, while the technical part is modeled on the 500 Series. They offer 923 Second Class seats, thanks to its 3 + 2 seat layout. There are 66 seats for First Class passengers. The vehicles were developed by the Taiwan Shinkansen Corporation, a consortium of seven Japanese manufacturers, including Kawasaki and Mitsubishi. This is the first time that Japanese super trains could be sold abroad.

The ceremonial rollout of the first unit took place in Japan on January 30, 2004. On May 18, 2004, the train was shipped from Kobe to Taiwan. The test runs in Taiwan began in late January 2005. After a slow powering up into a higher speed range, a multiple-unit train cracked the 124 mph [200 km/h] mark for the first time in August 2005. Two months later, it set a new speed record for Taiwan of 196 mph [315 km/h] during a trial run. In November 2005, the last unit reached the island, so that, by the time operations started, there were a full thirty new trains available.

On January 7, 2007, the white-orange, arrow-shaped Shinkansen, for the first time carrying passengers, swept along the high-speed line. After twenty years of bad luck, mishaps, and political wrangling, the Japanese high speed train was running at up to 186 mph [300 km/h] on the island. The first section in operation was that between Banciao and Zuoying, and, until January 31, passengers only had to pay half price. As of February, regular fares went into effect.

The complete railway from Taipei in the north to the Zuoying (Kaohsiung) train station in the south, opened for travel starting on March 2, 2007. The fastest express trains from Taipei to Kaohsiung, with a stop in Taichung, now take just ninety minutes, while the Cape gauge trains would take about four and half hours. Even with stops at all intermediate stations, the trip takes exactly two hours. Initially, the plan was to run nineteen round trips on the new section. Today, normally twenty-three pairs of the super trains make the trip, with two stops, in Banciao and Taichung, in a travel time of ninety-six minutes. There are also thirty-two train pairs which make the trip in 120 minutes, stopping at all stations. A few extra trains make special trips on the weekends. Since the start of operations, the high-speed trains have been racing along at 186 mph [300 km/h] for some eighteen hours a day on the railway. Theoretically, the new route is designed for speeds even up to 217 mph [350 km/h].

The 214.3 mile [345 km] long new track runs over 156 miles [251 km] of viaducts and bridges and through 29.2 miles [47 km] of tunnels. So it is not really that hard to catch a THSR 700 T above the earth.

On December 11, 2000, Amtrak's Acela Express began the first scheduled high-speed rail transport in the United States. The fast trains have been running ever since, between Washington D.C., New York, and Boston. But Amtrak is not employing any new idea. Since the nineteenth century, transportation planners and railway companies had been seeking to significantly increase the speed of passenger transport in the most densely populated region of the country. In the late nineteenth and early twentieth centuries, the U.S. government took a leadership role in the construction and operation of railways. For a while, the U.S. rail industry was the largest industrial division in the country, with the fastest rate of economic growth in the world. In its heyday, it employed more than one million people and included 248,548 miles [400,000 km] of tracks. It is no exaggeration to say that the U.S. railways played a critical role in building the new nation and defining its culture. Indeed, the government gave the railroads both land and tax breaks to encourage them to build new lines, but, in general, that was the full extent of government influence. The railway companies remained private businesses, with no government funding.

THE ROAD TO HIGHER SPEED

The Pennsylvania Railroad was one of the largest and most powerful companies formed during the American railway boom. For a period, it proclaimed itself, in an advertising slogan, to be the "Standard Railroad of the World," meaning then that it was the best railroad in the world and all others should emulate it. Whether it was the best or not, the nicknamed "Pennsy" railroad company was definitely blessed with innovative and entrepreneurial vision. In the 1930s, they began one of the most ambitious projects at that time, electrifying its main line between New York and the nation's capital, Washington. This can be considered the first foundation stone for the Acela Express service sixty years later.

By the mid-1960s, the major advances in rail transport, particularly in Japan and France, made U.S. politicians and businesses sit up and take notice. Above all, the sleek Shinkansen, with its time-devouring speed of 124 mph [200 km/h] between Tokyo and Osaka, made for big headlines.

Trains travelled on the only electrified U.S. main track at no more than a maximum 89 mph [144 km/h], were pulled by thirty-year-old locomotives, and had to endure more and more travel delays due to deteriorating infrastructure caused by decreasing maintenance levels. In response to the international developments, in 1965, the U.S. Congress passed the High Speed Ground Transportation Act, which included such provisions as establishing the Office of High-Speed Ground Transportation, and allocated $490 million for research and development in the field of rapid ground transportation. A number of experiments followed: in 1966, researchers installed an aircraft twin turbine engine on the roof of an old Budd Type RDC3 diesel railcar. The project was already stopped before it barely got started. It was more of a stunt experiment than a test program. However, this vehicle, called the M-497, attained the remarkable speed of 182 mph [293 km/h] on one of its test runs on the New York Central line in northern Ohio. Although the M-497 never ran again and was soon scrapped, for many years it held the North American speed record for rail vehicles.

A Metroliner end car that has survived in the "Railroad Museum of Pennsylvania" in Strasburg; it was number 860 on the Pennsylvania Railroad (photo from 8/27/2009).

THE METROLINER

Meanwhile, the U.S. Department of Transportation was working on a more practical application—a train that was to be known as the "Metroliner." A consortium of Westinghouse, General Electric, the Budd Company, and the Pennsylvania Railroad joined forces to create a fleet of fifty stainless steel railcar units. A slightly modified railcar unit reached a speed of 166 mph [267 km/h] during test runs on a specially prepared section of track in New Jersey. During their regular service as Metroliners, beginning in January 1969, these trains ran at speeds of up to 109 mph [176 km/h]. From 1983 on, Metroliner trains broke through the 124 mph [200-km/h] limit, as they were converted to locomotive-hauled trains with more conventional cars.

In the 1960s, rail passenger travel in the U.S. was in free fall. The U.S. private rail companies, which were generally in a desperate financial situation, wanted, above all, to be relieved of their unprofitable passenger service. Therefore, the Congress passed the Rail Passenger Service Act of 1970, which brought the National Railroad Passenger Corporation to life. The new national rail company was given the name Amtrak, a contraction of "American travel on track." It began operation on May 1, 1971.

The Metroliner was among the trains that were part of the fledgling Amtrak operation, from day one. They were considered the most successful U.S. passenger trains, because they were relatively fast underway, ran frequently enough, and occupied a market niche between its final destinations in New York and Washington, D.C. Even then, the North-East Corridor (NEC) between Washington D.C., New York, and Boston—the most densely populated region in the U.S.—suffered from rapidly increasing transport problems, both on land and in the air. Obviously, there was a need for more and better transportation possibilities in this bottleneck. To achieve significant improvement, the so-called "Northeast High Speed Rail Improvement Project" (NEHRIP) was launched. The greatest density of long distance passenger trains in America was in the NEC. While the southern Washington-New York section, which had been electrified since the 1930s with alternating current, belonged to the PRR, the New York, New Haven & Hartford Railroad (short: New Haven) had started electrical traction on its own northern New York-Boston section some twenty years before. Its catenary wire, however, ended in New Haven, Connecticut, where the trains had to change from electric to steam power, and later to diesel locomotives. This left more than two-thirds of the rather inconveniently laid out stretch between New York and Boston, which dated back to the nineteenth century, without overhead catenary wires. To increase speed, shorten travel time, and allow efficient operation, electrification had to be extended beyond New Haven. This was eventually done by implementing the NEHRIP.

EUROPEAN GUESTS

After a series of meetings with representatives of the Swedish State Railways, Amtrak arranged for a test run of Sweden's popular new X2000 tilting train on the NEC in 1992. This was to kill two birds with one stone:

it would be a publicity stunt to draw attention to modern foreign passenger train technology, and also an opportunity to collect technical data to help Amtrak determine the specifications for its own high-speed train. To demonstrate the high level of acceptance of such new technology, the manufacturer ABB arranged, together with Amtrak, for the train to tour the entire U.S.A., where, outside the electrified NEC area, it was pulled and pushed by Amtrak diesel locomotives. The tour was a huge success, attracting thousands of viewers everywhere. For more than a year, the X2000 ran in regular service between Washington D.C., New York and New Haven. During the X2000's visit, Siemens and Amtrak agreed to also test the new German ICE. In test runs on the NEC, both trains reached the speed limit for that track. The X2000 kept its speedometer at 154 mph [248 km/h] and the ICE kept its at 165 mph [265 km/h]. In 1993, the ICE took its promotional tour, and then ran for several months in regular service between Washington D.C. and New York. These tests with the Swedish and German trains were extremely useful for getting a response from the potential users of modern trains.

NEW SPECIFICATIONS

As Amtrak called for proposals to manufacture the new, yet-unnamed high-speed train in 1993, the three qualified bidders quickly became clear: ABB, Siemens, and a consortium of Bombardier and Alstom. Although the bids included similarities with pre-existing trains, there were also specifications that had never been called for anywhere else in the world. The trains were to be designed as two-way vehicles, have outstanding acceleration and braking systems, as well as the capacity to round the many curves on the NEC route at higher speeds than conventional trains could. This made tilting technology mandatory. However, there was an unprecedented demand for the new trains: they had to have a level of impact protection much higher than the worldwide norm. The driver's cab of the new train would require an axial thrust of 600 tons [544,310 kilograms], more than twice the prescribed international standard.

On March 15, 1996, Amtrak announced the winner of the bid: the consortium of Alstom and Bombardier won the contract to build eighteen units (later increased to twenty) for high-speed multiple-unit trains and fifteen extremely powerful conventional electric locomotives. The new trains were to be supplied beginning in early 1999. The package also included building three new maintenance and service centers for the new trains,

one each in Washington D.C., New York, and Boston. The new trains had to be able to use a track built in the nineteenth century, not a new line, as the French TGV or the Japanese Shinkansen did. Tracks, signaling systems, and power supply had to be modernized and maintenance upgraded to a good level, to meet the train's new performance capabilities. Concrete ties and welded tracks had been installed as early as the 1980s in some sections of the NEC, but many gaps still remained to be filled. The NEHRIP project to electrify and modernize the New Haven-Boston stretch made rapid progress, while the consortium began to manufacture the structural parts of the high-speed cars in La Pocatiere, Canada. Final assembly of the trains was done in Barre, Vermont, while the new locomotives took shape in Plattsburgh, New York. It was a race against the clock, to modernize the rail route and deliver enough multiple unit trains to maintain the start up of the Acela Express in 1999.

In early 1999, there was a small controversy over the design of the car structure, which was allegedly 4" [10 cm] wider than it should have been made. In some sections of the NEC, because of the vehicle clearance profile, the maximum allowable tilt had to be reduced to 4.2 degrees from 6.5. Bombardier and Amtrak argued that this would have no appreciable impact on the design of the timetable. The first completed unit took its first steps in mid-1999, on the Transportation Test Center in Pueblo, Colorado. A second unit performed test runs on the NEC. The first trains were actually to start scheduled service in late 1999. Various technical problems, such as excessive wheel tire wear, defective screws and bolts, and many other "little things," delayed the start of service, time after time

On March 9, 1999, Amtrak announced that the new trains would be called "Acela." This made-up word is based on a combination of the words "acceleration" and "excellence." The Acela finally became big news in November 2000, when it made its maiden trip from Washington D.C. to Boston. The United States now had a high speed train of which they could be proud, and many hopes were set on Amtrak having a "secret weapon" in one of the busiest and most highly competitive travel markets in the world.

THE ACELA

From December 11, 2000 on, despite everything, the limited, irregular Acela service between Washington D.C., New York, and Boston proved fascinating for large numbers of people. With its two sleek, 5997 hp [4,474 kW] power cars, and six day coaches in

The drawbridge over Shaw's Cove is probably the most famous photo location in New London, Connecticut. Here Acela Express 2251 with power car 2030, runs over it on 09/04/2010.

between, the trains were something never before seen in the U.S.—even if people had seen the performances of the X2000 and the ICE a few years earlier. Four Business Class (Second Class) carriages, a First Class carriage, and a cafeteria car provided a total of 304 seats. The large windows, excellent interior lighting, spacious, attractive restrooms, electrical outlets at every seat, seat service in the First Class, and the quiet, almost floating ride at speeds of up to 149 mph [240 km/h], immediately created a profound impression on passengers.

The power cars are based on third-generation TGV technology. The main transformer is mounted beneath the floor. In each powered truck, there is an inverter with water-cooled GTO technology. The inverter provides the alternating current for the asynchronously operating induction motors. Using regenerative braking, each power unit can develop 4,000 hp [3,000 kW] braking power. The six intermediate cars are equipped with an active tilting system, based on the proven system of Bombardier's LRC trains. The tilting system becomes fully functional at speeds over 62 mph [100 km/h]. The trucks are rather similar to the TGV standard design, with a welded H-shaped steel frame. Unlike the TGV, each axle has only three disc brakes (TGV: four). As is usual with the TGV, the primary suspension is coil springs and there is a pneumatic secondary suspension. The hydraulic tilting device is activated on each intermediate car by an under-floor-mounted control unit that operates independently of the other cars. The tilting

system itself is controlled by the main tilt regulator in the power units. The power cars have no tilting device. The car body structure is of stainless steel and designed to survive even an extremely forceful impact. In addition to the TGV's usual crumple zones, the Acela Express also meets the latest American stability requirements, which are regarded as the world's toughest. The equipment under the car floor is protected by reinforced panels, to minimize the danger, especially in urban areas, of any impact with objects lying on the tracks, such as shopping carts, car tires, or similar things. The disadvantage of this extremely passive safety standard, is the train's significantly greater weight, compared to the usual norm in global high-speed transport. The Acela is about forty-five percent heavier than a normal TGV.

The Acela Express has to manage three power systems, just on a trip from Washington to Boston:

- 12 kV/25 Hz from Washington to New York
- 12 kV/60 Hz from New York to New Haven
- 25 kV/60 Hz from New Haven to Boston.

The power system change is done automatically, without slowing the train down and without interruptions of the secondary power circuits that supply the lighting, air conditioning, etc. A power system switch is signaled to the train in good time, via transponders installed on the tracks, so the main transformer can be adjusted to the new system.

SERIES DESIGNATION:	ACELA EXPRESS
Road numbers:	2001-2040
Wheel arrangement (eight car):	Bo'Bo' + 6 x 2'2' + Bo'Bo'
Power systems:	11.5 kV/25 Hz, 12.5 kV/60 Hz, 25 kV/60 Hz
Track gauge (ft [mm]):	4' 8.5" [1,435]
Maximum speed (mph [km/h]):	165 [264]
Output (kW):	8 x 1,150
Empty weight eight car (t):	566.0
Service weight eight car (t):	624.0
Maximum axle load (t):	22
Coupling length (ft [mm]), eight car:	657 [200,308]
End car length (ft [mm]):	69.6 [21,219]
Intermediate car length (ft [mm]):	87.4 [26,645]
Distance between truck centers (mm):	10,744 + 6 x 18,135 + 10,744
Axle distance powered truck (ft [mm]):	9.3 [2,845]
Axle distance trailer truck (ft [mm]):	9.8 [3,000]
Driver wheel diameter (ft [mm]):	3.3 [1,016]
Trailer wheel diameter (ft [mm]):	2.9 [914]
Seats 1st/2nd class (eight car):	304 (44 + 260)
Commissioning:	1998-2002

USA

Amtrak's Acela Express 2159 with power unit 2031 at the end of the train, arriving at Philadelphia's 30th Street Station on 09/10/2009. To the right in the background is the de-electrified High Line, which bypasses the station.

OPERATION

The Acela Express reduced travel time between Boston and New York from some four or five hours, to 3 hours and 23 minutes. This included saving a quarter of an hour between New York and Washington, from three hours to 2 hours and 45 minutes. The Acela Express reaches its highest speed of 150 mph [241 km/h] on two stretches, a total of 18 miles [29 km] long, in Massachusetts and Rhode Island. On the many modernized sections north of New Haven, speeds of 109 mph [177 km/h] or 125 mph [201 km/h] are possible. South of New York, the Acela Express can go up to 135 mph [217 km/h], although many sections are limited to 125 mph [201 km/h]. Although the tracks in some areas are good enough for the train to run at 150 mph [241 km/h], the overhead wires, built during the Great Depression, would not allow any speed over 135 mph [217 km/h]. Those wires are not as evenly taut as the new catenary east of New Haven. The slowest stretch on the electrified NEC is the section between New Haven and New Rochelle, which is owned by Metro-North Railroad and the Connecticut Department of Transportation. There trains can travel at just 90 mph [145 km/h] on the 3.7 mile [6 km] stretch, and have to brake down to 68 mph [109 km/h] at the state border between New York and Connecticut.

Like many other new multiple-unit trains, the Acela Express was plagued in its early phases by many problems, large and small. In August 2002, all units had to be temporarily taken out of operation, since cracks were found on the suspensions between the truck and car bodies on the power units. After intensive checking and repair work, the units gradually started running

again. At the same time, the interval between checks on the trains was drastically shortened. Subsequently, the suspensions were redesigned and the older parts, prone to cracking, were replaced. With improved frequency and shorter travel times, Amtrak was able to successively increase the number of Acela units in regular service. In 2004, the fifteen scheduled weekday Acelas made forty-six departures from Washington D.C., New York, and Boston. The remaining five trains were kept in reserve, in case of failure or maintenance work. Thanks to its new popular features, Amtrak's transport market share between Washington D.C. and New York rose from thirty-six percent to fifty-three percent, while the airlines' share fell from sixty-four percent to forty-seven percent. Amtrak showed an even more dramatic increase, from eighteen percent to forty percent, on the New York-Boston connection. In the first quarter of 2004, of the approximately 4,767,000 rail and air travelers in the NEC region, approximately 2,928,000 (sixty-one percent) used Amtrak trains.

Thus, the national Amtrak service, with its new super trains, was able to bring more than half of the combined air and rail transport market between Washington D.C. and New York under its wings. If you add in the intermediate cities, such as Baltimore and Philadelphia, Amtrak's share of the air and rail transport market rises to about seventy-five percent. The popular trains carry more than two million passengers a year, or more than ten percent of Amtrak's total of twenty-four million passengers. A major setback occurred in spring 2005, when Amtrak had to take its entire fleet of Acela Express trains out of service on April 15, after hairline cracks were observed in the disc brakes of some cars. The hairline cracks were caused by vibration and material fatigue. Slower Metroliners and other regional trains ran as replacements. With new brake discs, the first two Acela trains started operating again on July 11. The other units followed in succession. On September 21, 2005, Amtrak finally announced that all twenty units were back in service. After this incident, experts speculated on whether the combination of the TGV-style high speed trains and American tracks was a particularly happy one.

For fiscal 2014, Amtrak has planned to acquire forty additional Acela intermediate cars, to expand the seating capacity in all high-speed trains for the increased ridership. But that purchase is dependent on approval by Congress.

THE HHP-8

The HHP-8 is a normal electric locomotive with two driver's cabs; the Alstom-Bombardier consortium built twenty-one of these units at the turn of the millennium.

Amtrak's HHP-8 engines then shared the hauling of the Northeast Regional trains on the NEC with Series AEM-7 electric locomotives, while the MARC HHP-8 engines pulled regional trains between Perryville, Maryland and Washington D.C. Railway workers often jokingly refer to the HHP-8 as "hippos," "rhinos," or "bananas."

SERIES DESIGNATION:	HHP-8
Road numbers:	Amtrak: 650-664, MARC: 4910-4915
Wheel arrangement:	Bo'Bo'
Power systems:	11.5 kV/25 Hz, 12.5 kV/60 Hz, 25 kV/60 Hz
Track gauge (ft [mm]):	4' 8.5" [1,435]
Maximum speed (mph [km/h]):	135 [217]
Hourly output (kW):	
Nominal power (continuous power) (hp [kW]):	8000 [5,970 (4 x 1,493)]
Service weight (t):	99.79
Maximum axle load (t):	25
Length over buffers (ft [mm]):	67 20,447
Distance between truck centers (ft [mm]):	35.2 [10,744]
Axle distance powered truck (ft [mm]):	9.3 [2,845]
Driver wheel diameter (ft [mm]):	3.3 [1,016]
Commissioning:	1999-2000

FURTHER PLANS

Despite all the problems, the success of the Acela inevitably raised the question of when similar trains would start operating in other regions of North America. Projects were soon being planned in California, Florida, the Midwest, and the Pacific Northwest. As always, cost became a crucial issue, and developed rapidly into an obstacle.

The most advanced planning at the turn of the millennium was for the so-called Florida High Speed Rail project, a high-speed network in Florida. A first section from Tampa to Orlando was to start operation by 2009. An extension from Tampa to St. Petersburg was also planned, as well as successive extensions of the network to Miami, Fort Myers, Jacksonville, Tallahassee, and Pensacola. But this project has been on hold since November 2004. Only after Barack Obama was elected President of the United States, did the projects for new high speed or upgraded railways get new life. In response to the 2009 financial crisis, on January 28, 2010, Obama named those rail projects that would receive funds from the approximately $7.3 [€5.7] billion government budget. Funding for the construction of high-speed lines would go to California and Florida as follows:

HHP-8 651 has just brought the Vermonter No. 56 (Washington, D.C.-St. Albans, Vermont) to New Haven on 09/03/2010. It will immediately de-couple and leave the train to a diesel locomotive for the rest of the trip.

Amtrak obtained fifteen of the engines, while the MARC operating company (Maryland Area Rail Commuter) got six locomotives. The abbreviation HHP-8 stands for "High Horsepower 8000". In principle, the engines are based on the French electric locomotive BB36000 Series. They have the same drive technology as the Acelas and also have approximately the same head shape as the high-speed trains. Their "noses" are just a bit shorter and flatter. On the HHP-8, the automatic couplers are not hidden behind hoods, as on the Acela. The control lines for push-pull operation are attached on both fronts. With its 8,000 hp [6,000 kW] capacity, the engine can travel at up to 135 mph [217 km/h]. This is ensured by a gear transmission ratio of 71:23. Test runs made between 1999 and 2000 revealed several problems: the locomotives had been equipped with automatic current-voltage switches, to deal with the changes to the different supply voltages on the NEC, but these malfunctioned continuously during the testing phase. Cracks in the trucks were identified as another potential problem during testing. But the view was, with appropriately frequent checks of the engines, measures could be taken in time to deal with such problems. The HHP-8 engines had to be temporarily taken out of operation in August 2002, because the fasteners for the lateral dampers tended to break. At first, the rail operators attempted to use more frequent inspections to find any damaged fasteners in time. Eventually, these problems were satisfactorily dealt with by installing newly dimensioned fasteners.

USA

- $1.25 billion to Florida, first to build an 84 mile high-speed line between Tampa and Orlando. In a second step, Orlando would be connected to Miami via a 240 mile link.
- $2.344 billion to California, to construct an 800 mile high-speed Sacramento-San Francisco-Los Angeles-San Diego railway, for over 300 trains per day. The Los Angeles-San Francisco link should be realized by 2020, the extensions to Sacramento and San Diego by 2026. The trains, running at a speed of 217 mph [350 km/h], will cut travel time between Los Angeles and San Francisco to under 2 hours 40 minutes, compared to six hours by automobile.

While the Florida high-speed plans died again after the last gubernatorial elections, there seems to be progress in California: the California High-Speed Rail Authority (CHSRA) has specified the section where the first part of the newly planned $43 [€32.44] billion high-speed network will be built. Engineers have recommended to CHSRA a 66 mile [106 km] stretch in the Central Valley between Madera and Corcoran, where construction should start. The environmental impact study for the project was to be completed by September 2010. The new route could be completed by 2017. CHSRA also plans to buy railroad property for the HST in the Los Angeles area. The Authority intends to spend around $30 million to acquire property, such as for Union Station in Los Angeles.

Nothing doing: at least for Bombadier's Jet Train, here making its rounds, with power unit 2200 in front, on the Pueblo, Colorado test track.

magnetic flywheel energy storage system, was to follow. In the early years of the new millennium, Bombardier tried to market its Jet Train as an affordable alternative for high-speed rail in North America. But Bombardier had no luck. Neither the Florida high-speed project nor a plan by Bombardier and VIA Rail to use the Jet Train on the eastern Canadian corridor between Quebec and Windsor, went anywhere. Once again, state funding was not approved. So Bombardier indeed has the fastest fossil fueled high-speed train in the world, but cannot find any commercial application for it.

THE JET TRAIN

The Jet Train is an experimental high-speed train built by Bombardier, at its own expense, to run on the usually non-electrified rail lines in North America, at speeds similar to those in Europe. This train, which was introduced in 2002, can run at a speed of 150 mph [241 km/h]. On the power units, a modified gas turbine from Pratt & Whitney, a derivative from the aerospace sector, with 5,000 hp [3,730 kW] output, will provide the required drive power for the electric motors. The Acela Express is the model for the power unit's mechanical parts. The train's advantages include a good ratio between power and weight (only 91t) and its low center of gravity. The tilt technology already in use on the Acela was installed in the intermediate cars. In test runs, the train, which reached a speed of 205 mph [330 km/h], set a new American record, and impressively demonstrated its capacity as a high-speed train on non-electrified routes. An improved drive technology, with a projected high-rpm generator and

SERIES DESIGNATION:	JET TRAIN
Road numbers:	
Unit configuration	T+6M+T
Wheel arrangement power unit:	Bo'Bo'
Wheel arrangement intermediate car:	2'2'
Track gauge (ft [mm]):	4' 8.5" [1,435]
Maximum speed (mph [km/h]):	149 [240 km/h]
Turbine output (kW):	5,000 [3,750]
Power unit output (kW):	4 x 825
Empty weight power unit (t):	90.7
Empty weight intermediate car (t):	576 to 59.9
Maximum axle load (t):	25
Power unit length (ft [mm]):	69.6 [21,219]
Intermediate car length (ft [mm]):	87.4 [26,645]
Length of entire train, eight car (ft [mm]):	663.6 [202,280]
Distance between truck centers (mm):	10,744 + 6 x 18,135 + 10,744
Axle distance powered truck (ft [mm]):	9.3 [2,845]
Axle distance trailer truck (ft [mm])	9.8 [3,000]
Driver wheel diameter (ft [mm]):	3.3 [1,016]
Trailer wheel diameter (ft [mm]):	2.9 [914]
Seats:	304
Commissioning:	2002